The
Buffet
Book

The
Buffet
Book

Inspired Ideas for
New-Style Entertaining,
with 175 Recipes

Carole Peck
with Carolyn Hart Bryant

Photographs by Alex McLean

VIKING

VIKING
Published by the Penguin Group
Penguin Books USA Inc., 375 Hudson Street, New York, New York 10014, U.S.A.
Penguin Books Ltd, 27 Wrights Lane, London W8 5TZ, England
Penguin Books Australia Ltd, Ringwood, Victoria, Australia
Penguin Books Canada Ltd, 10 Alcorn Avenue, Toronto, Ontario, Canada M4V 3B2
Penguin Books (N.Z.) Ltd, 182-190 Wairau Road,
Auckland 10, New Zealand

Penguin Books Ltd, Registered Offices:
Harmondsworth, Middlesex, England

First published in 1997 by Viking Penguin,
a division of Penguin Books USA Inc.

1 3 5 7 9 10 8 6 4 2

LIBRARY OF CONGRESS CATALOGING-IN-PUBLICATION DATA
Peck, Carole.
The buffet book / by Carole Peck, Carolyn Hart Bryant.
p.   cm.
Includes index.
ISBN 0-670-86516-8 (alk. paper)
1. Buffets (Cookery) I. Bryant, Carolyn Hart. II. Title.
TX738.5.P43   1997
642′.4—dc20   96-38747

This book is printed on acid-free paper.

Printed in the United States of America
Set in Perpetua and Baskerville MT
Designed by Kathryn Parise

To Bernard,
my loving Frenchman

C.P.

To Lanning
for ten years of "shared happiness"
and to our children, Jamey and Allison,
with love

C. H. B.

Acknowledgments

With special thanks to my crew at the Good News Café for always pitching in to help, especially Gonzolo and Julio Fajardo, Becky Shea, and Ricardo. Thanks to my other colleagues—Ken Eden, Jeff Unkel, Mary Perna, and Terry Karpen—for listening and understanding. And to Jeanne and Chris DiGiacomo from "Affairs of the Heart."

To Dawn Drzal, our editor, for coming to us with the idea for a book on buffets, and to her many supportive colleagues at Viking.

To Angela Miller, for her persistence and calls.

To Carolyn Bryant, for seeing the book through to the end, and for understanding my handwriting.

To Alex McLean, for his beautiful photographs.

To all my clients, who have become friends and graciously opened their homes to make these parties happen: Peggy and Keith Anderson; Susan Buckley and Lance Sherman; Leonard, Ruth, and the double Diamonds; Ruth Henderson at the Silo; the Jacobys; Darla and John Karlton; Joan Lerned; John Mauer; the Rosenthals; Susan and Jim Scott; Monique Shay (my friend of many years); Diana and Bob Slodowitz; and, last but not least, Julia and Carter Walker.

And, last, to all the friends and customers who kept asking and encouraging me to do this book.
                                                                            Carole Peck

Thanks to Angela Miller, my publishing friend of many years, for encouraging me to make the leap from editor to writer, and for suggesting a collaboration with Carole Peck. To Carole, for her creativity and great ideas, which inspired the text in so many ways. To Dawn Drzal, our superb editor at Viking, for her vision, good taste, and professionalism—and for believing that a new book on buffets needed to be written. To her editorial assistant, Paul Morris, thanks for the hard work and good humor on a tight book schedule.

Heartfelt thanks to all my family, but particularly my mother and father, Eunice and Winston Hart, for their encouragement and unwavering support. And to my mother-in-law, Irma Bryant, for her continuing interest in this project. To my children, Jamey and Allison, who kept me on track and brightened every day with their smiles. And to my husband, Lanning, for his love and support always.
                                                                   Carolyn Hart Bryant

Contents

Introduction

I have always thought that buffets are one of the best ways to bring good food and good people together. Over the years I have created so many buffet parties—for myself, my catering clients, restaurants, and clubs—that it seemed only natural for me to do a book about them. I am delighted to have the opportunity here to share the menus, recipes, and ideas that have proven successful for me.

Lifestyles have changed dramatically in the last two decades, and so have styles of entertaining. When I was a student at the Culinary Institute, I was trained to do classical grand-style buffets. We often worked through the night decorating and glazing food to make it look like something it was not, adding sculptures in butter, sugar confectionery, even taxidermy pheasants to buffet tables that were often 40 feet long. Granted these buffets were miraculous to look at, but who would really want to do them, especially at home?

Now, when I do "new-style" buffets, I concentrate first on taste, offering foods that are seasonal, fresh, and appealing. The menus include a variety of dishes, with interesting combinations of flavors. The tables have a lot of color and texture, but the design is simple and natural, in keeping with the menu. Most important, the buffets I do today are flexible and fun, with an emphasis on personal style.

Buffets are not the only way to entertain, of course, but I find them advantageous for the following reasons:

—Most buffet dishes can be prepared ahead, either partially or completely. In fact, the flavor of many hot buffet dishes improves when they are made ahead and briefly reheated at serving time.

—Once the buffet is set out, you can enjoy being with your guests, leaving the cleanup until later. At a seated dinner, on the other hand, the host can wind up ricocheting back and forth between the kitchen and the table for every course. Even if you have hired servers, you still have to check on things, and who would want to be your dinner partner?

—Foods can be kept at the proper temperatures more easily: hot foods held over warming devices, cold foods cold, other foods at room temperature. At a seated dinner it is almost impossible to get everyone's plate to the table at the same time.

—You can offer a more varied menu and accommodate individual food preferences, such as vegetarian, or dietary restrictions.

—Buffet parties are invariably lively because guests can mingle more easily than at a seated meal.

—A beautifully designed, visually striking buffet table can be the focal point of a party and contribute to the ambience or theme.

—Buffets give you a chance to showcase different rooms of your home—for example, a lovely porch, an expansive kitchen, a cozy library or study.

Although buffets have an air of casualness, they do require planning, organization, and attention to details. Here are some basic guidelines I use.

The First Stage

Ask yourself the following questions:

—What is the occasion?
—What is the date and time?
—Where will the party be held? Indoors or outdoors?
—How many guests? Will there be children?
—What will the ambience or theme be?
—What is the budget?
—How many buffet areas or stations will there be?
—Will guests sit or stand? How much seating is needed?
—What types of beverages? Full bar, limited bar, nonalcoholic?
—Will you need to hire help? A bartender, servers, or kitchen help?

Menu Planning

Your menu will depend on whether guests will be standing, eating on their laps, or seated at a table. If they will be standing or lap-eating, you need to offer foods that are easy to pick up and eat with your fingers or foods that require a fork only. If serving pasta, for example, use chunky shapes like raviolis or penne; avoid long pastas such as fettuccine. If serving meat, make sure it is tender, boneless, skinless, and cut into bite-size pieces. If guests will be seated, and knives offered, you can choose foods that require cutting.

Next, consider the tastes, colors, and textures of the dishes on your menu. Visualize what the food will look like on a buffet plate, and choose foods with complementary colors. Balance mild and strong-flavor foods, crispy and creamy-textured. Consider your guests' food preferences, and always include at least one vegetarian dish. If you know there will be children, make sure some of the foods will appeal to them. Plan your menu around produce and foods in season, do not skimp on quality, and avoid repeating similar-flavor dishes. To keep plates from looking messy, offer only one sauced dish. Avoid mayonnaises, especially in warm weather; serve vinaigrettes and fresh salsas instead. Choose foods that are either good at room temperature or that won't overcook if kept continuously hot over a warming device. Hot foods should be kept 140 degrees or warmer, cold foods 40 degrees or colder. Room temperature foods should not sit on the buffet table for more than 2 hours.

THE BUFFET TABLE

Many types of tables or other surfaces can be used to present a buffet, from kitchen counters, sideboards, and formal dining tables to coffee tables and garden benches. Throughout the book you will see examples of different buffet tables I have set up. Any surface that is flat and accessible is worth considering, even an old farm flatbed or large flat rock formation.

Survey the area in which you plan to set up the buffet, and consider the traffic flow. Plan for enough room at the beginning of the buffet to form a line, and at the end of the buffet for an easy exit or turnaround.

Double-line buffets, serving the same food, are essential for over one hundred people. Long rectangular tables can be arranged in an L or U shape, visually separated by a round table on which a flower arrangement or decoration has been placed. In my experience most people quickly figure out that the food is the same on both buffet tables, but if this is a concern, you can have someone direct your guests.

Think of your buffet as a three-dimensional canvas, and try to create an interesting mix of colors, textures, and heights. I frequently use pedestals and tiered platters to create vertical height and maximize the table space. For a really big or important buffet, it's not a bad idea to have a "platter rehearsal" and lay out all the serving pieces, dishes, warming devices, and so on that you will need. Check your equipment to see if you will need electrical outlets nearby.

Arrange the buffet dishes on the table in roughly the same order as your menu. Unless your guests will be seated at pre-set tables, place the flatware on the buffet either at the beginning or the end. I usually put the flatware with handles upright in a basket or other container, which adds a little height to the table, or else I wrap individual sets of flatware in a large napkin. Wherever you put the flatware, make sure it is clearly visible and easy to reach.

SEATING

Seating depends on the type of party, the location, space, and ambience. A cocktail and hors d'oeuvres party, for example, may not require seating at all or very limited seating. At an informal barbecue or pool party, where guests may be eating from plates on their laps, casually arranged chairs and benches work fine. For a more formal party, I like to provide seating at tables for all guests. Another factor to consider: When people are walking around, from indoor to outdoors or from room to room, you will need less seating than when people stay in one place for the entire party.

TABLE COVERINGS AND NAPKINS

Linens or fabrics in a variety of colors and patterns can be used as table coverings, depending on the style of the party. For a casual party I might cut a swath of interesting fabric with pinking shears and use it unhemmed to cover a buffet table; for a more formal party I usually swag the fabric with ribbons or flowers and layer it with linen tablecloths for a gracefully draped table.

As for napkins, feel free to use paper for cocktail parties, but my personal preference for dinners is large (about 12 to 14 inches square) cloth napkins for a number of reasons: Cloth napkins are sturdy and can hold wrapped flatware; they don't tear or blow away at breezy outdoor events; they are more absorbent; oversized napkins can function as "personal tablecloths" for guests eating from their laps.

I collect cloth napkins and have many different ones, from vintage to new, which I mix together in table settings. An advantage to old cotton napkins is that they have a wonderful soft feel from years of repeated washings and require very little, if any, ironing. I have also used oversized cotton dishtowels and bandanas as napkins for casual buffets.

Another option is to make your own napkins from a bolt of 54-inch-wide fabric. Cut them out with pinking shears or hem with four quick seams. I can generally get six napkins from one yard of fabric.

TABLEWARE

Remember that there are a lot of opportunities to buy inexpensive tableware, at flea markets, tag sales, and discount stores. I'm a hopeless collector (some might call me a pack rat), but it is great fun to use my wonderful finds for parties.

Plates: For smaller parties I mix plates if I don't have enough of one pattern. For larger parties I usually rent china. I prefer to use bigger, 12-inch "chop plates" whenever possible rather than standard-size (9 to 10 inches in diameter) dinner plates, because they hold more food and are easier to balance.

When determining how many plates you will need, figure one plate per person, plus an extra 10 percent to allow for second helpings.

Glasses: For pool parties I use plastic or paper cups. Otherwise, I like to use an all-purpose 12 ounce stemmed glass for all drinks, from juices and sodas to wines, beers, and mixed drinks. I find this is much simpler than trying to figure out how many tumblers, how many rocks glasses, and so on.

If guests will be sitting at assigned, pre-set tables, allow two to two and a half glasses per person for the cocktail hour, in addition to a water, wine, and possibly champagne glass at each place setting. If seating is open, allow a total of three all-purpose glasses per person for cocktails and a full buffet.

Flatware: For me, plastic is taboo except for packed picnics. For smaller parties at home, I like the look of an eclectic mix of flatware. For large parties I simply rent flatware.

Count on approximately 10 percent more flatware than the number of guests to avoid running out.

Serving platters: I like assorted platters, choosing them by size, shape, color, and design. Keep in mind that the border design of a platter is more important than the center design, because the platter is covered with food. I use platters made of many different materials, including porcelain, glass, wood, metal, plastic, and even coated papier-mâché.

When choosing platters, don't be limited by their intended use. For example, I use a long fish platter to serve vegetable antipasto, and a wooden bread board to serve roast pork. Both give the table character and style.

If possible, place at least one or two serving platters on pedestals to make the table visually interesting and to give you more space for other platters underneath.

WARMING DEVICES

Warming candles, canned liquid fuel, alcohol lamps, electric trays, and chafing dishes are the most common equipment used to keep food warm on a buffet table. With them I use copper, stainless, or enamel cookware, which can stand the heat and is good-looking, too. I sometimes build my own heaters, using clay or glass bricks around canned liquid fuel. Another alternative is to use a butane canister fuel stove, which has regulated heat from low to high and can be used for cooking as well as warming.

BEVERAGES AND BARS

Throughout this book I offer fresh juices, flavored teas, hot chocolates, and other mostly nonalcoholic drinks. However, since wines, beers, and liquors are an important part of many gatherings, you need to know how to set them up. Whatever kind of bar you choose, remember that it is your choice, and don't feel you have to offer a full bar unless you want to. For many parties, wine, beer, and perhaps champagne are sufficient.

For more than thirty guests you should consider hiring a bartender. For fewer than thirty, guests can serve themselves if the bar is organized and everything is in plain sight.

You will need plenty of ice for chilling beers, white wine, and champagne, and for serving in drinks. Have lemons and limes on hand, cocktail olives perhaps, and coarse salt if you are serving margaritas. Other necessary items include a small ice scoop, corkscrews, bottle openers, pitchers for waters and juices, cocktail napkins, a bar towel to wipe up spills, a trash can, and boxes to hold bottles and cans for recycling.

As for liquors, don't feel you need to offer an extensive range of choices. I find the preferred alcohols these days are vodka, scotch, gin, tequila, rum, and sometimes bourbon. A good liquor store can help you decide and also figure out the amounts you will need for your number of guests. Here are some general guidelines:

Wine
One 750-ml bottle = 5 (7-ounce) glasses
Twelve 750-ml bottles per case = 60 (7-ounce) glasses
One 1½-liter bottle = 10 (7-ounce) glasses

Champagne
One bottle = 6–7 flute (4–5 ounce) glasses
Twelve bottles per case = approximately 75 flute glasses

Liquor
Twenty-one 1½-ounce drinks per 1-quart bottle

Beer
Beers usually come in 12-ounce bottles or cans, and you will need to offer a variety of types, imported and domestic. For a large beer-loving crowd consider having a keg of beer and drafting it. And don't forget the tap to dispense it.

Mixers and Sodas
I usually offer club soda, tonic water, diet and regular colas, gingerale, mineral waters, and, if needed, orange juice, cranberry juice, and Bloody Mary mixes.

THE BUFFET KITCHEN

Although I am a trained chef, I have created recipes for this book that really work at home. Don't be intimidated by some of the longer recipes; they can all be prepared ahead in a series of steps that are not difficult to master. In addition, I have given you a lot of advance preparation advice throughout the book. Look for these tips at the end of each recipe in a special section called Planning Ahead.

These recipes don't require a lot of special cooking equipment, because I truly believe that all you need in the kitchen are good-quality, heavy-duty pots and pans, bowls, sharp knives, a food processor, a standing electric mixer, a juicer, a hand-held immersion or regular blender, a large cutting board, and a good heat source. I am very partial to Asian woks, ladles, and spatulas, but they are not essential.

I don't think a huge pantry is necessary either. Mine includes best-quality vinegars, oils, mustards, chili paste, anchovies, sun-dried tomatoes, honey, sugar, flour, rices, beans, dried pastas, and Asian soy, fish, and oyster sauces. I use mostly fresh herbs and some dried spices. I prefer coarse salt (kosher or sea salt) in cooking and baking because it has a better flavor and does not contain preservatives.

I have used a minimum of butter and cream in these recipes, because that is my style of cooking. I rarely make rich sauces, but will often make different-flavored chutneys and salsas to accompany entrées.

Many of the recipes in this book are cross-cultural, combining the flavors of different world cuisines. I like this global approach to food, and encourage you to start experimenting on your own if you haven't already.

I have given lots of options with each menu, realizing that you probably won't make every dish. Feel free to add your "tried-and-true" favorites or to substitute or combine dishes from different menus in the book. If you use great-quality ingredients and fresh seasonal foods, you are practically guaranteed success.

I hope these menus will inspire you to think creatively about buffets, to incorporate your own personal touches, and to enjoy giving buffet parties as much as I do.

A NOTE ABOUT PORTIONS: Buffet portions are generally smaller than portions for a sit-down meal, because guests are being offered more choices. For most of the dishes in this book (except desserts, which are usually not part of the main buffet), you will note that I say at the end of each recipe, for example, "Serves 10, as part of buffet." This is to remind you that if you choose to make this dish by itself or as part of a plated meal where there will be just a couple of other menu items, then you will need to figure on the dish serving fewer people than indicated.

SPRING

SUMMER

Spring Ahead Dinner

This is a perfect buffet for family and friends during the Passover and Easter season. We photographed the menu at a friend's picturesque early Colonial house down by the Shepang River, with sweeping views of a springtime landscape alive with budding trees, forsythia bushes, azaleas, and daffodils. The table was set in front of French doors that opened out onto a lovely porch; if the weather had been a bit warmer we could have moved the table outside.

Because the weather can be capricious in spring—warm and sunny one day, rainy and cold the next—this menu included both light and robust dishes. The menu was also designed to take advantage of favorite foods that begin to appear in markets in the spring: asparagus, Vidalia onions, fiddlehead ferns, creamer potatoes, and rhubarb.

Spring is the season for halibut, a mild white fish that just about everyone likes, even children. But for those who preferred a heartier meat dish, veal shanks were also offered on this menu. Veal (or lamb) shanks are ideal for buffets because their flavor improves when they are cooked a day ahead, stored in their braising sauce, and reheated at serving time.

The asparagus, fiddleheads, and potatoes were prepared in the simplest way possible to allow their fresh, pure flavors to be appreciated. Fiddleheads—the coiled shoots of the edible ostrich fern—are synonymous with spring here in the Northeast. They are available in markets, of course, but every year I look forward to foraging for them in the Litchfield hills. They are so tender I can just snap them off with my fingers.

An incredibly light and fluffy coconut cake, chocolate-dipped almond macaroons, and a strawberry-rhubarb torte provided a sweet finish for this springtime buffet. We also set out a heaping dish of red ripe strawberries with whipped cream.

The dinner buffet. COUNTERCLOCKWISE FROM LOWER LEFT: *Asparagus with herb dressing; halibut topped with olive tapenade; braised veal shanks; roasted creamer potatoes; arugula, Vidalia onion, and blueberry salad; assorted breads and muffins.*

Lemon verbena iced tea (page 36) was a light and refreshing accompaniment. Had wine been desired, a dry rosé would have been a fine choice.

Spring is such a happy, lighthearted time of year that it is appropriate to be a bit whimsical with your table decorations. We used apple blossoms, sprigs of pussy willow, and potted azaleas from the hostess's garden rather than more formal cultivated flowers, and added antique tin children's toys and piles of shiny jelly beans for fun. The children were kept busy coloring eggs, which we displayed in egg cups and tiered baskets when they were finished. Another option would have been to ask each guest to bring a favorite decorated egg to add to the table.

Spring Ahead Dinner
for 10 to 12

***

DINNER

Halibut Topped with Olive Tapenade and
Zucchini "Scales"

Braised Veal Shanks with Parsnips and Carrots

Fiddlehead Ferns

Roasted Creamer Potatoes

Asparagus with Herb Dressing

Arugula, Vidalia Onion, and Blueberry Salad

Carrot and Fig Muffins
Whole-Wheat Focaccia with Dried Fruit

DESSERTS

Light and Fluffy Coconut Cake with
Fresh Strawberry or Mango Sauce

My Favorite Strawberry-Rhubarb Torte

Chocolate-Dipped Almond Macaroons

Fresh Strawberries with Whipped Cream

Halibut topped with olive tapenade and zucchini "scales."

Halibut Topped with Olive Tapenade and Zucchini "Scales"

Halibut is a mild ocean fish that is complemented by many different toppings. Substitute bass, snapper, grouper, or swordfish, if you prefer.

4½ to 5 pounds halibut fillets, skin removed

OLIVE TAPENADE:
2 cups imported black olives, pitted
10 cloves garlic
6 anchovy fillets in olive oil
20 fresh basil leaves

½ cup extra-virgin olive oil
2 cups bread cubes, from peasant-style or sourdough bread
¼ cup lemon juice

5 medium zucchini, cut into ⅛-inch-thick rounds
Extra-virgin olive oil

1. Arrange the halibut fillets in a lightly oiled baking dish. Preheat the oven to 375° F.

2. To make the tapenade, chop the olives, garlic, anchovies, and basil in a food processor. With the machine running, add the olive oil in a steady stream down the feed tube, alternating with the bread cubes and lemon juice. Process until you have a chunky paste.

3. Spread the tapenade evenly on each piece of halibut. Arrange the zucchini slices on top, overlapping slightly to create the illusion of fish scales. Brush lightly with olive oil. Bake about 20 minutes, until the fish flakes easily when tested with a fork.

Serves 10 to 12, as part of buffet.

PLANNING AHEAD: The tapenade will keep for at least 1 month in a covered container in the refrigerator.

Braised Veal Shanks with Parsnips and Carrots

This warm and comforting dish is really best when made a day ahead to allow the flavors to develop. Lamb shanks can be substituted if you prefer.

1 cup vegetable oil

12 to 15 veal shanks, trimmed and tied

1 bulb garlic, cloves peeled and chopped

15 sprigs fresh thyme, leaves picked

3 quarts chicken stock or broth

3 cups dry white wine

Coarse salt and freshly ground black pepper to taste

2 pounds carrots, peeled and diced

2 pounds parsnips, peeled and diced

LEMON GREMOLATA:

Zest of 2 lemons

8 cloves garlic, minced

¼ cup chopped flat-leaf parsley

½ teaspoon coarse salt

1. Heat ¼ cup of the oil in a heavy sauté pan. Add 3 to 4 of the shanks, and sear to brown over high heat. Repeat the browning process with the remaining shanks and oil.

2. Transfer the shanks to a braiser or roasting pan large enough to hold them all. Add the garlic, thyme, stock, wine, salt, and pepper, and bring to a boil. Cover the pan and simmer over medium-low heat on the stove or in a 350° F oven for about 1½ hours, until the shanks are tender. Fifteen minutes before the shanks are done, add the carrots and parsnips. Remove the pan from the heat and skim off any excess fat. Let cool, cover, and refrigerate for several hours or overnight.

3. Reheat the shanks in a 350° F oven or over medium heat on the stove.

4. To make the Lemon Gremolata, combine the lemon zest, garlic, parsley, and salt. Mound the gremolata on the veal shank bone and serve.

Serves 12, as part of buffet.

PLANNING AHEAD: The vegetables and herbs can be prepared up to 3 days ahead. The gremolata can be made up to 3 days ahead and kept covered and refrigerated. Cook the shanks up to 3 days ahead, and slowly reheat in cooking sauce before serving time.

Cooked veal shanks at the right, roasted creamer potatoes, fiddlehead ferns, and asparagus.

Fiddlehead Ferns

Fiddleheads are packed with vitamins and make a tasty addition to salads, pasta dishes, and vegetarian entrées. When you find them in markets in the spring, buy more than you need and store some, cooked, in the freezer.

2 pounds fiddlehead ferns, washed

1. Put the fiddleheads in a large bowl of cold water (they will float). With your fingers rub off any hairy coating and wash any really dirty ones again. Pick out the ferns with a skimmer and drain in a colander. Cut off any long stems on the diagonal (they are tough) so that the fiddleheads are uniformly coiled into their trademark "violin scroll" shape.

2. Bring a large pot of salted water to a boil over high heat, drop in the fiddleheads, and blanch about 2 minutes, until they are tender but still slightly firm. Drain in a colander and plunge into ice water to stop the cooking process. Drain immediately, as fiddleheads tend to absorb water.

Serves 10 to 12, as part of buffet.

NOTE: Don't plan on using the water the fiddleheads are cooked in for vegetable stocks or soups, as it turns an unappealing purple color and has little flavor.

PLANNING AHEAD: Fiddleheads can be blanched a day ahead and reheated in broth, oil, or butter just before serving.

Roasted Creamer Potatoes

These small, coin-sized potatoes are special to spring and early autumn. I think they are best simply roasted with herbs.

4 pounds creamer potatoes
1 cup vegetable or pure olive oil
Coarse salt and freshly ground black
    pepper to taste

1 tablespoon chopped fresh
    rosemary

1. Wash the potatoes and brush off any dirt. Place in a colander and drain well (excess water will make the oil spatter and cause the potatoes to steam rather than roast).

2. Preheat the oven to 450° F. Pour the oil into a roasting pan big enough to hold the potatoes in 1 layer. Heat the pan in the oven until the oil is hot, about 3 minutes. Remove the pan from the oven and add the potatoes, being careful that the hot oil doesn't spatter. Sprinkle the potatoes with salt, pepper, and rosemary and toss to coat them completely. Put the pan back in the oven and roast the potatoes for 25 minutes, until tender, shaking the pan once during the cooking process so the potatoes color evenly.

Serves 10 to 12, as part of buffet.

PLANNING AHEAD: These potatoes can be roasted up to 1 day ahead, left at room temperature or in the refrigerator, and then reheated in a 400° F oven close to serving time.

Asparagus with Herb Dressing

Another spring favorite, asparagus are always welcome on buffets. You will love them with this no-oil dressing.

Choose firm, green asparagus with stalks that aren't dried out or shriveled.

4 pounds asparagus

HERB DRESSING:
¼ cup honey
¼ cup Dijon-style mustard
¾ cup white wine vinegar
½ cup cold water
½ teaspoon freshly ground black pepper

2 cups chopped fresh herbs, any combination of the following: flat-leaf parsley, chives, dill, thyme, basil, or tarragon

Optional: **Chopped hard-cooked eggs (about 3 eggs)**

1. Peel the asparagus stalks if you are using large to jumbo-size (which I prefer). I find it easy to do this by holding the asparagus stalks by the tips against an inverted sauté pan (for balance), then peeling down the stalks with a vegetable peeler to remove their tough outer layer and little leaves. Cut off the tough ends of the asparagus (usually about 2 inches, less if you are using very thin, pencil asparagus) so that the stalks are of uniform length. Rinse in a colander under running water.

2. Bring a large pot of salted water to a boil over high heat, add the asparagus, and blanch for 1 to 2 minutes, until tender but still firm to the bite. Drain (see Note), then plunge into ice water to stop the cooking process. As soon as they are cool, remove the asparagus to a colander to drain.

3. To make the dressing, mix together the honey and mustard in a bowl. Whisk in the vinegar and water. Add the pepper and herbs and stir. Pour the dressing over the asparagus and toss lightly. If you are using the chopped egg, fold in half of it, then sprinkle the rest over the asparagus. Serve at room temperature.

Serves 10, as part of buffet.

NOTE: Save the water in which the asparagus are cooked to use as a base for a vegetable soup or stew; it is full of vitamins and very delicious.

PLANNING AHEAD: The dressing can be made a day ahead. The asparagus can be blanched the morning of the party, drained, and kept dry on layers of paper towels in a covered container in the refrigerator. Dress the asparagus right before serving so the vinegar doesn't discolor them.

Arugula, Vidalia Onion, and Blueberry Salad

Blueberry vinegar is easy to make and delicious on salads of fruit, smoked meat or fish, cheese, or garden lettuce. Marinating the Vidalias intensifies the taste and softens their raw texture.

BLUEBERRY VINEGAR:

1 cup fresh or frozen blueberries

¼ cup sugar

2 cups white wine vinegar, warmed

2 Vidalia onions (or other sweet onions, such as Walla-Walla or Maui)

2 tablespoons coarse salt

½ cup chopped fresh basil

Juice of 1 lemon

¼ cup extra-virgin olive oil

1 pint fresh blueberries

4 bunches arugula, washed

¾ cup vegetable oil

1. To make the blueberry vinegar, purée the blueberries and sugar with the warmed vinegar in a food processor or blender and strain through a fine-mesh strainer. Pour into glass bottles or jars and keep in the refrigerator until ready to use.

2. Peel the onions and cut into paper-thin slices. Place in a shallow dish and sprinkle with the coarse salt, followed by the basil, lemon juice, and olive oil. Cover the dish and marinate in the refrigerator for at least 2 hours, or up to 3 days.

3. Remove the onions from the refrigerator and toss them and their marinade with the fresh blueberries in a serving bowl. Add the arugula.

4. Whisk together ½ cup of the blueberry vinegar with the ¾ cup vegetable oil, and pour the vinaigrette over everything in the bowl. Toss again and serve.

Serves 12, as part of buffet.

PLANNING AHEAD: Blueberry vinegar will keep in the refrigerator for months. The onions can be marinated up to 3 days ahead. With the rest of the salad ingredients pre-washed and stored in sealable bags in the refrigerator, this salad can be assembled quickly.

Carrot and Fig Muffins

Moist and full of flavor, these muffins can be served at any meal, from breakfast to dinner.

4 cups all-purpose flour

2 teaspoons ground cinnamon

1 teaspoon nutmeg

2 teaspoons coarse salt

1½ teaspoons allspice

1½ teaspoons baking soda

3 cups sugar

2 cups vegetable oil

6 eggs

1 cup buttermilk

2 teaspoons vanilla extract

2 cups shredded carrots

2 cups Fig Preserves (recipe follows)

1. Sift together the flour, cinnamon, nutmeg, salt, allspice, and baking soda. In an electric mixer, using the whisk attachment, combine the sugar, oil, and eggs. Alternately add the dry ingredients and buttermilk in thirds, mixing well after each addition. Whisk in the vanilla. Fold in the carrots and fig preserves.

2. Preheat the oven to 350° F. Grease the muffin tins or line them with paper baking cups. Fill the muffin tins two-thirds full with batter, then bake approximately 30 minutes, until golden brown. Remove from the oven and let cool.

Makes 16 standard-size muffins or 36 mini-muffins.

PLANNING AHEAD: These muffins will keep for up to 5 days in a tightly covered container. Or they can be baked and frozen in sealable bags.

Fig Preserves

I adore figs and make lots of this when they are in season. Fig preserves are great to have on hand to spread over breads or scones, or to use in baking.

1 pint fresh or dried figs, stems
   removed

1 cup sugar

½ lemon, cut into thin slices

1. In a 1-quart saucepan, combine the figs and sugar and cook over low heat about 30 minutes until mushy and syrupy. Add the lemon slices and cook another 45 minutes, until the syrup thickens, skimming off any foam.

2. Pour the fig mixture into a ceramic or glass bowl and let cool. Transfer to an airtight container and store in the refrigerator until ready to use.

Makes 2 cups preserves.

PLANNING AHEAD: These preserves will last for 4 months in the refrigerator.

Whole-Wheat Focaccia with Dried Fruit

Focaccia is an Italian hearth bread that has become very popular. This is a basic whole-wheat recipe to which I have added dried fruits. Many other variations are possible—for example, using fresh herbs, olives, preserved lemons, or flavored oils.

1 package (2½ teaspoons) active dry
  yeast
3¼ cups warm (about 110° F) water
1 cup extra-virgin olive oil
2½ cups whole-wheat flour

2½ cups high-gluten flour
1 tablespoon coarse salt
2 cups dried mixed fruit, coarsely
  chopped

1. In an electric mixer, using the dough hook attachment, combine the yeast with half of the water. Allow to sit 10 minutes to activate the yeast and make it creamy. Add the remaining water, ½ cup of the olive oil, the whole-wheat and high-gluten flours, and salt and mix until a dough forms. Knead on low speed for 4 minutes, then add the dried fruit. Increase the speed to medium and knead for 4 more minutes. The dough should be firm yet elastic. Place the dough in an oiled bowl, cover with plastic wrap, and let rise in a warm place until doubled in size (or overnight in the refrigerator—see Planning Ahead).

2. Pour ¼ cup of the remaining olive oil in a 10½ × 15 × ½-inch rimmed baking sheet. Knead the dough, then stretch and punch the dough, spreading it over the pan until it completely covers it. Take your time; the dough will be stiff. When the pan is fully covered, brush the dough with the remaining ¼ cup oil. Let the dough rise in a warm place for about 1½ hours, until doubled in size.

3. Preheat the oven to 400° F. Bake the dough for approximately 20 to 25 minutes, until golden in color. Let cool, then cut into pieces.

Makes 1 bread, about 24 pieces 3 inches × 2 inches.

PLANNING AHEAD: The dough can be made up to 2 days ahead and left to rise the first time in the refrigerator. Or the dough can be frozen.

The baked bread can be successfully frozen; defrost and reheat in the oven before serving.

Light and Fluffy Coconut Cake

This light, lemon-soaked sponge cake covered with an old-fashioned boiled icing has been a popular favorite at my restaurant ever since we opened.

Be sure to use unsweetened coconut, which balances the sweetness of the boiled icing.

10 whole eggs
1 cup granulated sugar
2 cups all-purpose flour, sifted

LEMON SYRUP:
½ cup granulated sugar
1 cup water
1 cup fresh lemon juice
Zest of 1 lemon

BOILED ICING:
2 cups granulated sugar
½ cup water
2 tablespoons corn syrup
6 egg whites (about 1 cup)
Juice of 2 lemons

3 cups shredded unsweetened coconut (available in health-food stores)

1. Preheat the oven to 325° F. Line three 9-inch cake pans with parchment (see Note) or lightly oil them and dust with flour.

2. Using an electric mixer set on high speed, whip the eggs with the sugar until the mixture triples in volume, about 7 to 8 minutes. (This is important, as the batter must be light and airy.) Fold the flour into the egg-sugar mixture in three separate additions, working gently but making sure the flour is completely incorporated.

3. Divide the batter evenly among the three prepared pans, spreading it with a metal cake spatula. Bake for approximately 20 minutes, until the cake layers are golden and pulling slightly away from the pan. Remove the pans from the oven and let cool in the pans.

4. To make the lemon syrup, combine the sugar, water, lemon juice, and lemon zest in a saucepan. Bring to a boil and cook for 5 minutes, until the sugar is dissolved and the mixture is syrupy. Set aside to cool until ready to assemble the cake.

5. To make the boiled icing, combine the sugar, water, and corn syrup in a

The dessert buffet laid out on another round oak table. CLOCKWISE FROM LEFT: *Coconut cake with two fresh fruit sauces; fresh strawberries; chocolate-dipped almond macaroons; and strawberry-rhubarb torte.*

saucepan. Bring to a boil over high heat and cook for approximately 7 minutes, until the mixture reaches the "soft-boil" stage, or 230° F on a candy thermometer. To test, drop a teaspoon of the boiling sugar mixture into a cup of cold water; if it forms a soft ball in the water, the temperature is right.

6. About a minute before the boiling corn syrup mixture is ready, in an electric mixer, using the whip attachment, whip the egg whites on high speed about 4 minutes, until stiff but not grainy. With the machine still running, pour in the hot corn syrup mixture and continue beating. Add the lemon juice and beat 2 minutes more. The icing should be smooth and fluffy with a slight sheen. As soon as the icing is ready, the cake should be assembled.

7. To assemble the cake, put the bottom layer on a cake plate and brush with the cooled lemon syrup to lightly moisten (do not oversoak). Using a metal cake spatula, spread about a sixth of the icing evenly over the surface of the cake layer. Repeat the process with the second and third layers. Then frost the sides and top of the cake with the remaining icing.

8. Put the coconut in a bowl. Hold the cake plate in one hand over the bowl and use the other hand to press the coconut against the sides of the cake. Sprinkle the top with coconut. Serve with fruit sauces (recipe follows).

Makes one 9-inch, 3-layer cake, 12 to 14 servings.

NOTE: I always use parchment paper when baking and highly recommend keeping a box of it as standard equipment in your kitchen. The need to grease and flour a cake pan or cookie sheet is eliminated when it is lined with parchment, and baked goods can be removed easily. Parchment is also useful to line the baking sheet on which you place pies and tarts in the oven; it catches any leaks or spills and makes cleanup faster and easier.

PLANNING AHEAD: The cake layers can be made up to 2 days ahead, covered, and stored in a cool place. The frosting can be made a day ahead, but the cake must then be assembled immediately.

A slice of strawberry-rhubarb torte, accompanied by a chocolate-dipped almond macaroon cookie, fresh strawberries, and cream.

Fresh Strawberry and Mango Sauces

To make strawberry sauce, wash and hull 2 pints of strawberries. Place in a food processor with ¼ cup sugar and ¼ cup of either orange or lemon juice. Purée until smooth. Strain through a fine-mesh strainer, if desired.

To make mango sauce, peel 4 mangoes and cut a slice off the top and bottom of each one. Holding the fruit upright, pare the flesh off the fruit, cutting lengthwise around the long, flat seed. Purée all of the flesh in a juicer or blender until you have a thick and pulpy juice. Add a little lemon juice or cold water if the puree is too thick. If the mangoes are nice and ripe, sugar isn't necessary. Mango juice freezes well, so if you find a good buy on mangoes when they're in season, make up several batches and freeze in plastic containers, ready to use with desserts or in homemade sorbets. I also use mangoes to make fresh salsas and vinaigrettes.

My Favorite Strawberry-Rhubarb Torte

I love this version of a European torte because the buttery sweet crust blends so well with the fruit. Using the basic pastry, I have made many variations depending on the season. For example, I have used figs and raspberries, blueberries and peaches, cherries and bananas.

PASTRY:
1½ cups all-purpose flour
¾ cup confectioners' sugar
6 ounces (1½ sticks) unsalted butter

FILLING:
2 pints strawberries, washed, hulled,
   and sliced
1½ pounds rhubarb, peeled, halved
   lengthwise, and sliced

4 eggs
1½ cups granulated sugar
1 tablespoon vanilla extract
1 teaspoon baking soda
¼ teaspoon coarse salt

Whipped cream, for serving

1. Line a 9- or 10-inch cake pan with parchment or wax paper.
2. To make the pastry, sift together the flour and sugar. Cut the butter into small cubes and work into the flour-sugar mixture with your fingers (or a food processor), until a dough is formed. Press about two-thirds of the dough into the bottom of the

cake pan and 1 inch up the sides. Cover and refrigerate the pan and the remaining dough for at least 1 hour or up to 2 days.

3. Preheat the oven to 425° F. Bake the chilled dough for 8 to 10 minutes, until light golden. Let cool. Reduce the oven temperature to 375° F.

4. Form the remaining dough into 1-inch-long cigarlike rolls and press them vertically along the sides of the pan, carefully sealing the dough to the prebaked crust.

5. To make the filling, combine the strawberries and rhubarb in a large bowl. Beat together the eggs, sugar, vanilla, baking soda, and salt, then pour over the fruits. Toss gently. Pour the filling into the pastry shell and bake for about 45 minutes, until the center is cooked through and lightly puffed. Remove from the oven and let cool in the pan.

6. Loosen the sides of the torte with a knife. Invert a large plate on top and quickly flip the torte over onto it. Remove the cake pan. Take the cake plate on which you want to serve the torte and gently place it on top. Flip the torte back onto it. Serve with whipped cream.

Makes one 9- or 10-inch torte, 12 servings.

PLANNING AHEAD: This cake keeps very well. You can make it up to 4 days ahead, store it in the cake pan in the refrigerator, and reheat in a low (275° F) oven for about 20 minutes before serving.

Chocolate-Dipped Almond Macaroons

Delicate and light with soft chewy centers, these cookies can also be studded on top with chopped almonds or pine nuts before baking.

16 ounces almond paste

1 cup granulated sugar

1 cup confectioners' sugar

2 to 3 egg whites

CHOCOLATE GLAZE (GANACHE):

½ cup heavy cream

1 tablespoon corn syrup

4 ounces semisweet chocolate

1. Using a mixer with a paddle attachment, combine the almond paste and granulated sugar. With the mixer on low speed, add the confectioners' sugar followed by the egg whites, one at a time, and beat until the mixture has the consistency of toothpaste. Increase the speed to high and whip the mixture for about 1 minute to lighten it. Scoop the batter by teaspoonfuls onto a baking sheet or pipe on using a pastry bag fitted with a plain metal tip. Smooth the cookies with a finger moistened with water or egg white.

2. Preheat the oven to 425° F. Bake the macaroons for about 7 to 8 minutes, until golden and the tops crack slightly. Remove from the oven and let cool.

3. To make the chocolate glaze, combine the cream and corn syrup in a small saucepan and bring to a boil. Coarsely chop the chocolate in a food processor. With the motor running, pour the hot cream over the chocoalte and process until smooth. Transfer the glaze to a bowl. Cool slightly and dip the cookies into it one at a time. Let set a few minutes before serving.

Makes 3 dozen macaroons.

PLANNING AHEAD: These cookies will keep for 2 weeks in an airtight container.

Flower Garden Party

A dear friend of mine lives near my house on a thirty-acre farm. A truly gifted organic gardener, she is well known locally for the heirloom apples she grows in her orchard, as well as the currants, berries, baby beans, arugula, Swiss chard, sorrel, zucchini, lettuces, and other vegetables and fruits she grows in the gardens on her property. She has more than enough produce for herself, her family and friends, and local farmers' markets.

This informal buffet party was held in the spring in her flower garden. The food was all portable and fit neatly inside sturdy white paper paint buckets. Chinese take-out containers were used to hold the salad; small galvanized buckets were perfect for the soup (squares of vinyl were rubber-banded across the tops to secure them); and ordinary aluminum take-out containers with plastic lids were just the right size for the dessert. Also tucked inside the buckets were plastic utensils, flower-patterned paper napkins in cocktail and luncheon sizes, a paper cup, and—as whimsical party favors in keeping with the garden theme—pastel or printed cotton garden gloves and a flower seed packet. Many kinds of "to go" containers can be found at restaurant supply stores, and paper paint buckets can be found at hardware stores (paper ice buckets, used by hotels, also work well).

The lunch buckets were set out on a table in the garden. Guests simply picked one up and took it with them as they strolled around the garden to admire my friend's spectacular display of spring blooms. Iced herb tea was set out on an old chair, and guests helped themselves. Chilled white and rosé wines and sparkling and still mineral waters were also offered. We used garden chairs, picnic benches, and stone walls for seating. Folding chairs and quilts might have been another option.

The portable buffet: White paper paint buckets filled with light summer fare were set out on an old table in the middle of the hostess's garden.

This light vegetarian menu is ideal for even the hottest day because no mayonnaise is used. Some of the dishes were chosen to take advantage of the abundance of produce at this property—the green beans, tomatoes, cherries, currants, mint, basil, chives, and geranium leaves used in the recipes were all homegrown—but the menu can easily be adapted to showcase whatever fruits, vegetables, herbs, and edible flowers you have growing in your garden at this time of year. The point is to keep the menu simple, fresh, light, and seasonal—in keeping with the garden theme.

Flower Garden Party

for 12

Chilled Cherry Soup

Blue Cheese Poppy Seed Shortbreads

Artichoke Pasta, Vegetable, and Wheat Berry Salad

Rose Geranium Cakes with Black Currant Sauce

Garden Fresh Herb Tea

Chilled Cherry Soup

I usually make this light and refreshing summer soup when cherries are in season, but dried cherries can also be used (use half the amount of fresh cherries).

2 quarts water
4 bags cherry herb tea (see Note)
4 pounds cherries, washed, stemmed, and pitted
½ cup sugar
2 cinnamon sticks
1 teaspoon allspice
½ teaspoon freshly ground black pepper

2 tablespoons cornstarch
¼ cup raspberry vinegar
Juice of 2 lemons

Garnishes: Halved cherries
Plain yogurt or sour cream

1. Bring the water to a boil in a 3-quart saucepan over medium heat. Add the tea bags, all of the cherries (except for 2 cups), sugar, cinnamon sticks, allspice, and pepper, and simmer for 20 minutes. Remove the tea bags.

2. Combine the cornstarch, vinegar, and lemon juice, then add the mixture to the soup. Bring the soup back to a boil and cook over medium heat until it thickens, about 2 to 3 minutes. Remove from the heat. Discard cinnamon sticks.

3. Using a blender or food processor, puree the soup until smooth. Pour through a very fine strainer. Serve chilled, garnished with halved cherries and a dollop of plain yogurt or sour cream.

Makes 2 quarts.

NOTE: If you can't find, or don't like, cherry herb tea you can substitute 1 quart red wine for the tea and reduce the quantity of water to 1 quart.

PLANNING AHEAD: This soup can be made up to 5 days ahead and kept in the refrigerator. It can also be frozen.

Chinese take-out containers filled with artichoke pasta, vegetable, and wheat berry salad fit neatly inside the paint buckets. A small galvanized bucket held the cherry soup, and the dessert tin was at the bottom.

Blue Cheese Poppy Seed Shortbreads

These savory shortbreads can be varied by using a different kind of soft, pungent cheese and by rolling the logs in sesame seeds or chopped nuts instead of poppy seeds. They are great to have on hand for snacking and to serve with beverages.

4 ounces (1 stick) unsalted butter
2 ounces blue cheese or Roquefort
2 ounces sharp cheddar cheese
1 cup all-purpose flour, sifted

¼ teaspoon cayenne pepper
1 teaspoon coarse salt
¼ cup poppy seeds

1. Combine the butter and cheeses in a food processor. Add the flour, cayenne, and salt, and process until a dough ball is formed.

2. Shape the dough into 2-inch-diameter logs. Roll in the poppy seeds. Wrap the logs in plastic and chill thoroughly, at least 1 hour or up to 2 days.

3. Preheat the oven to 375° F. Remove the dough from the refrigerator and cut into ¼-inch-thick slices. Arrange the slices about 1 inch apart on a baking sheet and bake for 12 to 15 minutes, until golden.

Makes about 30 shortbreads.

PLANNING AHEAD: Baked and stored in a tightly covered container, these short-breads will keep up to 1 month. The worked dough logs can be frozen for up to 6 weeks and cut and baked as needed.

Artichoke Pasta, Vegetable, and
Wheat Berry Salad

This is a delightful pasta and grain salad with lots of texture and flavor. I chose corn, tomatoes, and green beans because these vegetables are so fresh and abundant at this time of year, but other seasonal vegetables and herbs can be substituted easily.

3 cups wheat berries (available in
   health-food stores)
2 tablespoons tamari soy sauce
1½ pounds artichoke pasta
   (see Note)

VINAIGRETTE:
¾ cup wine, sherry, or balsamic
   vinegar
1½ cups extra-virgin olive oil or
   grapeseed oil
Coarse salt and freshly ground black
   pepper to taste

½ cup vegetable oil
3 cups fresh corn, cut from cob
1½ pounds baby green beans or
   sugar snap peas
1½ cups imported black olives,
   pitted
2 pints cherry tomatoes or red and
   yellow pear tomatoes, halved
24 fresh basil leaves, finely shredded
30 chive stalks, snipped
Coarse salt and freshly ground black
   pepper to taste

1. To reduce the cooking time of the wheat berries, soak them in water to cover for about 6 hours. Drain, cover with cold fresh water in a 2½-quart saucepan, and bring to a boil over high heat. Reduce the heat and simmer for 2 hours, until the water is completely absorbed and the wheat berries are tender. Add the tamari and let cool.

2. While the wheat berries are cooking, cook the pasta in rapidly boiling salted water until al dente, about 20 minutes, depending on the shape and size. Drain.

3. To make the vinaigrette, whisk together the wine (or sherry or balsamic) vinegar, olive (or grapeseed) oil, salt, and pepper. Combine the pasta and wheat berries in a bowl and pour the vinaigrette over them. Set aside.

4. To make the vegetables, heat the vegetable oil in a large skillet over high heat. When hot, add the corn and sauté until it colors and chars slightly. Remove to a large salad bowl and let cool.

5. Blanch the green beans or peas in a pot of boiling salted water until just tender. Drain, immediately plunge into ice water, and drain again. Combine with the corn in the bowl. Add the olives, tomatoes, basil, and chives, and toss. When ready to serve,

add the pasta and wheat berries in the vinaigrette, then correct seasoning and toss again.

Serves 10 to 12.

Note: I use *quatraflore* artichoke pasta for this salad, which I buy from a specialty pasta store. I like the four-sided shape because it is easy to pick up with a fork, especially handy for picnics.

Planning Ahead: The pasta can be cooked a few days ahead, cooled, and stored using the method on page 282. The wheat berries can be cooked up to 3 days ahead and stored in the refrigerator or freezer in a covered container or plastic bag. The salad can be made up to 8 hours ahead.

Rose Geranium Cakes

The rose geranium is a pretty leafy geranium plant that smells good, repels mosquitoes, and, best of all, has edible leaves. In this recipe, the leaves are used to line the bottoms of the pans in which the cakes are baked. The dessert can be served with either side up, but I like to see the pattern and texture of the leaves.

This is a basic pound cake, which means that the ingredients can be increased or decreased as long as the weights of the butter, sugar, eggs, and flour are always equal. It's what the French call a quatre-quatre *recipe.*

Unsalted butter, for greasing pans
Sugar, for sprinkling
12 geranium leaves
8 ounces whole eggs (approximately 4 large eggs)
2 teaspoons rose water

1 teaspoon vanilla extract
8 ounces (2 sticks) unsalted butter
8 ounces (approximately 1¼ cups) sugar
8 ounces (approximately 2 cups) flour

1. Preheat the oven to 350° F. Lightly grease with butter a 12-inset muffin pan or one 9- to 10-inch round cake pan. Sprinkle the bottom(s) with sugar and line with geranium leaves.

2. Break the eggs into a cup and weigh. Combine the rose water and vanilla in a medium bowl, add the eggs, and beat lightly.

(CONTINUED)

The dessert—rose geranium cake with black currant sauce—was presented in an aluminum take-out container.

3. Using an electric mixer, cream together the butter and sugar until light in color. With the machine running on low speed, slowly add the egg mixture and mix well. Fold in the flour.

4. Pour the batter into the prepared pan and bake: 20 to 25 minutes for muffins and 30 to 35 minutes for a cake. Let cool, loosen around the edges, and invert to remove. Cool on a wire rack. Serve with Black Currant Sauce (recipe follows).

Makes 12 individual cakes or one 9- to 10-inch round cake.

PLANNING AHEAD: These cakes can be made up to 3 days ahead and kept in a covered container.

Black Currant Sauce

Black currants are a very special fruit that is not easy to find but worth the effort. In northwestern Connecticut black currants are in season in July and are available at local farm stands. When I can get these currants, I freeze them in plastic containers to use as needed throughout the year. They are sour and need quite a bit of sugar, but their flavor is wonderful. When cooked, currants give up a lot of liquid and pectin, making them a good choice for preserves and sauces.

If you cannot find fresh black currants, there is a frozen black currant puree that you can buy in markets that is useful for sauces like this one, as well as for sorbets.

2 pints fresh black currants   **2 cups granulated sugar**

1. Wash the currants in a large bowl of water, picking all the leaves off the top of the water. Drain.

2. Place the currants in a medium saucepan with the sugar, stir, bring to a boil, and cook for 20 minutes, until the currants open. Remove to a large-hole china cap (conical sieve) or food mill with a receptable for the liquid underneath. Push the fruit against the sides of the cap, catching as much liquid (sauce) as possible.

Makes 2 cups.

PLANNING AHEAD: This sauce can be kept in the refrigerator for up to 2 weeks, or it can be frozen for up to 6 months.

(CONTINUED)

An old wooden orchard box was filled with ice and used to hold the wine and sparkling waters. Iced tea was served from a glass cookie jar.

VARIATION: If you can't find black currants, you can substitute red or black raspberries. To make a simple uncooked sauce, wash and drain the fresh berries and puree them with a little sugar and lemon juice in a food processor. Strain through a fine-mesh strainer if desired, to remove the seeds.

Garden Fresh Herb Tea

What the French call tisanes, *or herbal infusions, are often served hot after a meal as a digestive aid or restorative. Iced, these concoctions are delightful on a warm afternoon. I brewed mint tea for this buffet, but many other herbs and edible flowers can be used, including angelica, chamomile, catmint, dill, fennel, rosemary, sage, lemon verbena, lemon balm, hyssop, lavender, linden flowers, marigolds, rose hips, and violets.*

**6 sprigs fresh mint or other fresh
    herbs or flowers
8 cups boiling water**

Optional: **Sugar
Citrus slices and mint sprigs, if
    serving iced**

1. Put the mint in a large heatproof jug or pitcher. Pour in the boiling water, stir, and let sit for 5 to 10 minutes, depending on how strong you want the infusion. Make the tea a little stronger if you plan to serve it over ice.
2. Strain the tea into cups or a serving pitcher. Add sugar if you like.
3. For iced tea, chill the tea and serve over ice with slices of citrus and a mint sprig.

Makes 2 quarts.

Buddha's Delight:
An Asian Buffet

This party was held in early June in a friend's Japanese-inspired garden here in Woodbury, Connecticut. A beautiful serene setting, the garden has traditional meditative areas, pagodas for sitting and dining, magnificent rock formations, and a waterlily pond. Something is always blooming during the growing season. At this time of year exquisite heirloom single peonies, with scarlet flowers and vibrant yellow centers, were in full bloom, along with masses of daylilies that we used in bouquets.

Typical of most Asian feasts, this meal is quite extensive and offers many different tastes and choices. Because it is so flexible the menu can easily be scaled down for a smaller group. Whatever the number of guests, I find this party works best with good friends who love Asian flavors and are comfortable returning to the buffet table several times to sample all the dishes. This menu is also ideal for vegetarians because there are many dishes—such as lo mein noodles, sesame eggplant, and asparagus stir-fry— for them to enjoy.

All of the dishes have their own character and complement each other. Only a few need to be served warm; the rest are fine at room temperature. The desserts are delicious and quite easy to make, but if you're short on time, you could substitute store-bought fortune cookies. Ginger tea, hot or cold, is a refreshing and energizing drink with this feast.

I suggest cooking many of the dishes on this buffet in a wok. I have a professional black steel wok in my restaurant kitchen that we use almost exclusively for our quick-cook items—from vegetables, rices, and noodles to seared fish and meats. At home I also find a good-quality domed wok indispensable for cooking foods requiring rapid,

A "dress rehearsal" of all the tableware for this buffet: Plates of different sizes and shapes, bowls, platters, cups, glasses, goblets (for fruit salad), mugs (for tea), teapots, cotton napkins, and, of course, chopsticks.

even heat. I clean my woks with a bamboo or natural bristle brush dipped in water (no soap), and then put them back on the burner over high heat for a few seconds to dry them completely before putting away. With this method my woks remain seasoned and do not rust.

I also use a variety of other Asian equipment in my kitchen. I like the feel and control of Asian cleavers, with their wide, flat, shorter blades, and prefer them over a traditional chef's knife for certain cutting techniques. I have several Asian cleavers in different sizes and weights. Besides being indispensable for cutting and chopping, they are handy for crushing garlic and lemongrass, flattening meats, and lifting chopped foods from the cutting board. I recommend cleavers to my students in cooking classes, and after a quick demonstration they see how versatile and efficient they are in the kitchen.

Chinese bamboo steamers are also a favorite of mine, and I have them in various sizes for cooking and serving. They work wonderfully and do not impart a metallic taste to food the way other steamers can.

Asian ladles and skimmers, with metal bowls and bamboo handles, are essential in my kitchen. I use the ladles for soups and sauces and for scooping foods because of the deep shape of their bowls. I use the skimmers for blanching and deep-frying because they skim faster and more efficiently than their Western counterparts; their deep shape and open mesh baskets allow more liquid to flow through.

And, of course, I use Asian spatulas to help break up, lift, and turn foods while I am stir-frying in a wok.

Keep in mind that there are many Asian markets around, and good-quality equipment and supplies, as well as Asian ingredients, can readily be found. Asian markets are also a good source for inexpensive table decorations and party favors.

At this Asian buffet, I set out chopsticks and forks, but almost everyone chose chopsticks; because of the way it is prepared Asian food is very easy to pick up and eat. The cloth we used on the table had a "Marco Polo" design and was an ideal background for the colorful food. I bought yards of this fabric on sale a few years ago and have used it on a number of occasions. For this buffet I cut a length of cloth with pinking shears to make a quick and simple table covering. The buffet plates, in vibrant pinks, blues, and greens, looked great on the cloth. I frequently scout import housewares stores for fun or funky tableware at a good price—it's hard to go wrong when plates cost only a dollar or two, which is comparable to renting.

In keeping with the Asian theme, invitations were sent out on postcards of Asian landscapes, and inexpensive trinkets I bought in New York's Chinatown were given to everyone to take home.

Buddha's Delight:
An Asian Buffet

for 30

Barbecued Duck Legs

Lo Mein Noodle Salad

Chili Beef, Tomato, and Minted Onion Salad

Peppered Sautéed Squid

Shrimp and Peas in Pink Coconut Sauce

Pineapple Fried Rice

Sesame Grilled Eggplant

Asparagus, Shiitake, and Red Pepper Stir-Fry

Mizuna, Bean Sprout, and Crispy Wonton Salad
with Miso Dressing

Sesame Scallion Bread

———

Kiwi, Apricot, Lychee, and Mango Salad

Almond Cookies

Ginger Iced Tea

Bite-Size Coconut Tartlets

Barbecued Duck Legs

These succulent duck legs just melt in your mouth. The same recipe can be used for duck breasts. If you prefer to serve smaller portions, or wish to serve more people, cut the duck legs into 2 pieces at the leg joint after cooking.

MARINADE:

2 cups brown sugar

2 cups fresh orange juice

1 cup soy sauce

1 cup rice vinegar

½ cup oyster sauce

¼ cup chopped fresh garlic

¼ cup chopped fresh gingerroot

6 stalks lemongrass, thinly sliced

Optional: **About 10 Kiefer lime leaves (available at Asian markets)**

25 duck legs

Lo Mein Noodle Salad, for serving (recipe follows)

1. Combine the brown sugar, orange juice, soy sauce, vinegar, oyster sauce, garlic, ginger, lemongrass, and lime leaves (if using) in a large bowl. Add the duck legs and turn to coat completely. Transfer the duck and marinade to a covered container and marinate in the refrigerator for at least 12 hours, and up to 24 hours.

2. Preheat the oven to 300° F. Remove the duck from the refrigerator and arrange in 1 layer in 2 large baking pans. Pour the marinade on top. Bake the duck legs 1 hour 15 minutes, then turn them over and bake for 1 hour more, until the meat is very tender and has pulled away from the knuckle bone. Remove from the oven and transfer the duck legs to a clean container, discarding the marinade. Set aside.

3. Close to serving time, preheat the oven to 400° F. Place the duck legs on a baking sheet and reheat for about 8 to 10 minutes. Serve with Lo Mein Noodle Salad.

Serves at least 25, as part of buffet.

PLANNING AHEAD: These duck legs can be cooked up to 5 days ahead and kept in the refrigerator. Reheat as instructed in the recipe.

Lo Mein Noodle Salad

Fresh lo mein noodles are a great addition to soups or stir-fried dishes. They can also be crisped in hot oil and tossed into salads for extra crunch. You can vary this dish by adding other ingredients, such as tatsoi or mizuna, snowpeas, mushrooms, seafood, or meats.

3½ pounds fresh lo mein noodles (see Note)
1½ cups vegetable oil
½ cup soy sauce
½ cup pure Asian sesame oil
½ cup light brown sugar
½ cup rice vinegar
2 bunches scallions, thinly sliced

1½ cups unsalted cashews, coarsely chopped
3 medium to large carrots, peeled and shredded
2 cucumbers, peeled and shredded
1 large daikon, peeled and shredded
Optional: **1 bunch cilantro, coarsely chopped (about 1 cup)**

1. Bring a large pot of salted water to a boil. Add the noodles, stir with a cook's fork to separate, and cook until al dente, about 7 minutes. Drain, then toss lightly in ½ cup of the vegetable oil. Lay out on a sheet pan to cool.

2. Combine the remaining oil, soy sauce, sesame oil, brown sugar, vinegar, scallions, cashews, carrots, cucumbers, daikon, and cilantro (if using) in a large bowl. Add the noddles and toss.

Serves 30, as part of buffet.

NOTE: Fresh lo mein noodles are available in the produce section of larger markets. They sometimes come in one continuous strand; if so, clip to desired length with scissors before cooking.

PLANNING AHEAD: The noodles can be cooked, and the vegetables cut up and kept in separate covered containers in the refrigerator for up to 3 days. Assemble and toss the salad up to 6 hours ahead and serve at room temperature.

The entire buffet. CLOCKWISE FROM UPPER FAR LEFT: *Scallion bread; peppered sautéed squid; sesame grilled eggplant; pineapple fried rice; barbecued duck legs with lo mein noodle salad; chili beef, tomato, and minted onion salad; asparagus, shiitake, and red pepper stir-fry; shrimp and peas in pink coconut sauce; mizuna, bean sprout, and crispy wonton salad.*

Chili Beef, Tomato, and Minted Onion Salad

This combination of tender spicy beef and crunchy vegetables is irresistible and will have everyone coming back for seconds.

I prefer to use sirloin strip steaks with all the fat removed, but beef tenderloin works just as well.

6 pounds boneless beef steaks, each
   about 1 inch thick
3 cups thinly sliced onions
10 medium tomatoes, each cut into
   10 wedges
6 cucumbers, peeled, halved, seeded,
   and sliced
3 tablespoons minced fresh garlic
1 bunch fresh cilantro, coarsely
   chopped (about 1 cup)

1 bunch fresh mint, leaves picked
   (about 1 cup)
2 cups diagonally sliced scallions

DRESSING:
1 cup Asian fish sauce (see Note)
1 cup fresh lime juice
4 tablespoons Asian chili paste
Sugar to taste

1. Grill or broil the steaks to medium-rare. Remove, let cool, and cut into thinly sliced pieces across the grain.

2. Combine the onions, tomatoes, cucumbers, and garlic in a salad bowl. Add the cilantro, mint, and scallions and mix gently. Add the beef slices.

3. Make the dressing by whisking together the fish sauce, lime juice, and chili paste. Taste, and if you find it too acidic, add a small amount of sugar. If it's not hot enough, add more chili paste. Pour the dressing over the salad and toss gently.

Serves 30, as part of buffet.

NOTE: Fish sauce is made with fermented anchovies, and can be found in Asian markets and the Asian sections of many supermarkets. It is imported from Thailand (where it is called *nam pla*), Vietnam (*nuoc nam*), and other Asian countries. The country of origin doesn't really matter.

PLANNING AHEAD: The beef can be grilled, and the salad ingredients prepared and stored in separate covered containers in the refrigerator up to 24 hours in advance. Assemble the salad up to 4 hours ahead and serve at room temperature.

Peppered Sautéed Squid

Squid is truly a "fast food" dish—it's usually cleaned when you buy it, and requires only minutes to cook.

5 pounds fresh squid with tentacles, cleaned

¾ cup Asian fish sauce (see Note, page 44)

½ cup light soy sauce

SAUCE:

24 cloves garlic

½ cup chopped scallions

2 fresh jalapeño peppers, or 3 or 4 serrano chilies, seeded

¾ cup Asian fish sauce

¾ cup fresh lime juice

¼ cup sugar

1 cup shredded fresh basil

½ cup chopped fresh cilantro

½ to 1 cup vegetable oil, for frying

3 red, yellow, or green bell peppers, finely diced or julienned

1. Cut the squid into the shape you prefer, either in rounds or in a crisscross Asian cut. Combine the fish and soy sauces in a large bowl. Add the squid and marinate at least 30 minutes, and up to 24 hours.

2. To make the sauce, put the garlic, scallions, and chili peppers in a food processor and chop finely. Add the fish sauce, lime juice, sugar, basil, and cilantro and process to combine. Set aside.

3. Heat a wok or large skillet over high heat. When very hot, add 2 to 3 tablespoons of oil to the pan. Add one-fourth of the squid and stir-fry quickly. When the squid begins to curl and whiten in color, add one-fourth of the red peppers and stir-fry a minute or two. Add one-fourth of the sauce and stir-fry another minute. Remove to a serving platter and repeat with the remaining 3 batches of squid, peppers, and sauce. Note that when stir-frying it is always better to have a small quantity of ingredients in the wok at one time so that they will cook quickly.

Serves 30, as part of buffet.

PLANNING AHEAD: The sauce can be made up to 1 day ahead, and the peppers and squid cut up and kept in separate covered containers in the refrigerator. It is best to stir-fry this dish just before the party begins and to serve it at room temperature. However, it can be cooked earlier and reheated in a roasting pan covered with foil in a low (300° F) oven for about 10 minutes.

Shrimp and Peas in Pink Coconut Sauce

Shrimp is so popular that I always plan to cook more rather than less for a buffet. You won't believe how good this typically Asian tomato-coconut sauce is with shrimp.

SAUCE:

3 large (28-ounce) cans plum tomatoes in their juice

½ cup vegetable oil

8 to 10 cloves garlic, peeled and finely chopped

1 cup finely shredded fresh basil

½ cup finely shredded fresh mint

1 tablespoon Asian chili paste

6 cups unsweetened coconut milk

¾ cup cornstarch mixed with ¾ cup water

1 cup fresh lime juice (from about 8 to 10 limes)

*

8½ pounds medium-large shrimp, peeled and deveined

2 cups vegetable oil

8 to 10 cloves garlic, peeled and finely chopped

1 cup finely shredded fresh basil

½ cup finely shredded fresh mint

6 cups frozen green peas

Garnish: 1½ cups chopped scallions

1. To make the sauce, puree the tomatoes and their juice in a food processor or blender. Strain to remove seeds or excess pulp. Heat the oil in an 8-quart pot over high heat. Add the garlic, basil, mint, and chili paste, and sauté just until the garlic is soft. Add the tomato puree, stir, and bring the mixture to a boil. Stir in the coconut milk, bring back to a low boil, and add the cornstarch-water mixture. Remove from the heat, stir in the lime juice, and set aside.

2. To cook the shrimp, in a large wok or skillet, heat ¼ cup of the oil. Add a batch of shrimp and sauté over high heat for about 2 minutes, until just barely pink. Add some of the garlic, basil, mint, and peas and cook 1 minute more. Repeat with the remaining shrimp and vegetables.

3. Put the pot with the sauce back on the stove and heat over medium heat. Toss in the shrimp mixture from the wok. Transfer to a serving casserole or chafing dish and sprinkle with the sliced scallions.

Serves 30, as part of buffet.

PLANNING AHEAD: The sauce can be prepared up to 3 days ahead and kept in the refrigerator. Close to serving time, sauté the shrimp and add them to the reheated sauce. Keep warm on the buffet table over Sterno heat or on a hot plate.

Pineapple Fried Rice

Fresh pineapple really perks up the rice in this dish. If you prefer, halve the pineapples, leaving the plumes on, remove the fruit, and use the empty shells as serving vessels.

This dish can be embellished with other ingredients, such as broccoli, corn, bean sprouts, shrimp, and so on.

3 ripe pineapples
½ cup vegetable oil
18 cups cooked long-grain white or
    brown rice (about 9 cups raw
    rice)
1½ cups rice vinegar
½ cup Asian fish sauce (see Note,
    page 44)

1 cup soy sauce
½ cup sugar
1 cup chopped fresh cilantro
½ cup sliced or slivered almonds
2 teaspoons freshly ground black
    pepper

1. Cut off the ends and tops of the pineapples and pare off the skin. Cut the pineapples in fourths lengthwise and remove the core. Cut the flesh into small chunks.

2. In a wok or large skillet, heat the oil over high heat. Add the rice, 2 cups at a time, and stir-fry for about 2 minutes, using a Chinese spatula to break the rice apart. When the rice is completely coated with oil, add the pineapple chunks and stir-fry another minute. Add the vinegar, fish sauce, soy sauce, sugar, cilantro, almonds, and pepper, and continuing stir-frying another few minutes, until everything is well mixed.

Serves 30, as part of buffet.

PLANNING AHEAD: This dish can be made up to 2 days ahead. It is fine served at room temperature, but if you prefer it hot you can transfer it to a covered baking dish and reheat in a 400° F oven for about 20 minutes.

Sesame Grilled Eggplant

A nice vegetable accompaniment to all kinds of grilled meats and fish. I prefer thin white or purple Asian eggplants for this dish because they are almost seedless, never bitter, and do not soak up a lot of oil when cooked.

MARINADE:

1½ cups soy sauce

1½ cups dry sherry

¾ cup pure Asian sesame oil

10 cloves garlic, peeled and finely chopped

1 tablespoon Asian chili paste

*

18 to 20 Asian eggplants (or 8 to 10 American eggplants)

½ cup unhulled, or hulled and toasted, sesame seeds

1. In a saucepan combine the soy sauce, sherry, sesame oil, garlic, and chili paste. Heat over medium heat a few minutes. Let cool slightly.

2. Cut the tops from the eggplants. Cut the Asian eggplants in half, the American eggplants in 4 lengthwise slices. Pour the marinade into a shallow pan and arrange the eggplant slices in a single layer on top, cut side down. Let marinate at least 1 hour.

3. Prepare a grill or broiler. Remove the eggplant from the marinade, reserving the marinade, and grill or broil close to the heat for about 3 minutes. Turn the eggplant over, brush with marinade, and cook 3 minutes more. Remove to a platter and sprinkle with sesame seeds.

Serves 30, as part of buffet.

PLANNING AHEAD: The eggplant slices can be left in the marinade in the refrigerator for up to 3 days before cooking. This dish is good at room temperature, but if you prefer it can be reheated in a 300° F oven for 5 minutes.

Asparagus, Shiitake, and Red Pepper Stir-Fry

A simple and pure tricolor vegetable stir-fry.

9 to 10 pounds asparagus

3 pounds fresh shiitake mushrooms

5 large red bell peppers

1 bulb garlic

¾ cup Asian oyster sauce

½ cup water

1½ cups pure Asian sesame oil

½ cup thin pickled ginger slices

Optional: Coarse salt or soy sauce

1. To prepare the vegetables, break off tough ends of asparagus and slice stalks on the diagonal into 2-inch pieces. Trim and discard the shiitake stems and cut the shiitakes into ¼-inch slices. Quarter the red peppers, remove the seeds and white ribs, and cut into ⅛-inch slices. Peel the garlic cloves and chop.

2. Whisk together the oyster sauce and water.

3. Divide the vegetables into 3 batches for stir-frying. For each batch, heat ½ cup of the oil in a wok or large skillet until very hot and smoking. Add a third of the asparagus and stir-fry over high heat for 2 minutes. Add a third of shiitakes and stir-fry 2 minutes more. Toss in a third of the red pepper, garlic, and ginger and stir-fry for 1 more minute. Pour in a third of the oyster sauce-water mixture, stir, and cook another minute. Taste for seasoning, and add salt or a little soy sauce if necessary. Remove to a serving dish and repeat stir-fry process for the next two batches.

Serves 30, as part of buffet.

PLANNING AHEAD: The vegetables can be prepared ahead and stored raw in separate covered containers in the refrigerator up to 3 days. Stir-fry up to 3 hours before the party and serve the dish at room temperature.

Mizuna, Bean Sprout, and
Crispy Wonton Salad with Miso Dressing

Mizuna is a tasty Asian green that is becoming very popular. It is healthy, easy to grow, and similar to arugula. Delicious in a salad, mizuna can also be quickly stir-fried and served as a side dish.

1 package fresh wonton wrappers

4 cups vegetable oil (peanut or soy), for frying

1 tablespoon coarse salt and 1 teaspoon Asian five-spice powder, combined

1 to 1½ pounds mizuna, washed and dried

2 pounds fresh bean sprouts

Optional: 1 tablespoon unhulled (or hulled and toasted) black sesame seeds

Miso Dressing, for serving (recipe follows)

1. Cut a stack of wonton wrappers into 1-inch-wide pieces and separate into single strips. In a wok or 6-quart pot, heat the oil over high heat to about 350° F. Drop in the wonton strips, moving them around with a wire skimmer to keep them separate. Fry until golden, then transfer to paper towels or a wire rack to drain. While the noodles are still hot, sprinkle them with the combined salt and Asian five-spice powder. Set aside.

2. Toss the mizuna in a large salad bowl with the bean sprouts and wontons. Sprinkle with sesame seeds (if using). Serve with Miso Dressing on the side.

Serves 30, as part of buffet.

PLANNING AHEAD: The wontons can be fried, and the mizuna washed and dried and stored in the refrigerator, up to 3 days ahead. Assemble the salad close to serving time or serve the dressing on the side so the salad doesn't get soggy.

Miso Dressing

There are several types of miso made from different combinations of fermented soy beans, rice, and grains. For this recipe I prefer a mellow white barley miso, but you can experiment with other flavors.

Our always-popular Good News Salad, which has been on the menu since we opened, consists of crunchy seasonal vegetables, such as sugar snap peas, carrots, fennel, and green beans, combined with tofu and black beans and tossed in this dressing, "à la M. Perna."

2 large carrots, peeled and roughly chopped
1 small onion, peeled and roughly chopped
3 tablespoons honey

2 tablespoons soy sauce
1 cup barley miso
½ cup cider or rice vinegar
1½ cups water
1½ cups vegetable oil

In a food processor, finely chop the carrot and onion. With the motor running, one by one, add the honey, soy sauce, miso, vinegar, water, and oil through the feed tube. Process until all of the ingredients are incorporated and the dressing is emulsified.

Makes 4 cups.

Planning Ahead: Miso dressing will keep for 2 weeks in the refrigerator.

Sesame Scallion Bread

This fried flatbread is made with very simple ingredients. The trick is to roll the dough correctly so all the seasonings are incorporated.

3 cups all-purpose flour, sifted
1 cup boiling water
⅓ cup cold water
¼ cup pure Asian sesame oil
¼ cup sliced scallions
¼ cup chopped fresh cilantro

¼ cup unhulled, or hulled and
    toasted, sesame seeds
3 teaspoons coarse salt
1 cup peanut or vegetable oil, for
    frying

1. Place the flour in a large bowl. Pour the boiling water over it and immediately mix until smooth with chopsticks or a wooden spoon. Let cool about 3 minutes, then pour in the cold water. Knead the dough thoroughly, until smooth (it should feel like an earlobe). Cover the dough with plastic wrap and let rest for 30 minutes.

2. Place the dough on a floured surface and cut into 6 equal pieces. Knead each piece briefly and roll out into a 10-inch circle about ½-inch thick, as if you were making pizza dough. Rub or brush the rounds with sesame oil and sprinkle with scallions, cilantro, sesame seeds, and salt. Roll up each piece like a jelly roll, pinching the ends firmly closed. Then curl each piece of dough into a spiral (snail) shape, tucking the end into the center of the dough. Flatten with a rolling pin until the pieces are ¼ inch thick and about 8 to 10 inches in diameter. Wrap the dough in plastic and store on a plate in the refrigerator until ready to cook.

3. Heat 2 tablespoons of the oil over high heat in a frying pan until very hot, about 350° F. Fry a piece of dough for 2 minutes on one side, then flip over, being careful not to spatter the oil. Add another tablespoon of oil down the sides of the pan, and continue to fry another minute or two, until the bread is golden and crispy. Remove the bread, using tongs or a skimmer, and drain on paper towels or a wire rack. Repeat the process with the remaining pieces of dough, adding more oil for each batch. *Hint:* If you shake and jiggle the pan while frying, the bread will be flakier.

4. Cut each bread into 8 wedges and serve.

Makes 6 round breads, 8 to 10 inches in diameter.

PLANNING AHEAD: The pieces of dough can be kept in the refrigerator for up to 3 days before frying. Once fried, this bread is best served within 4 hours.

Kiwi, Apricot, Lychee, and Mango Salad

Lychees are an ancient Chinese fruit with an illustrious history. They are in season during the summer months, when you will find them in markets still on their branches. Peel the red shells, and you will discover the lychee's plump milky white fruit, which can be pulled away from the inner pit.

Mangoes are also a centuries-old fruit. For this salad be sure the mangoes, as well as the kiwis and apricots, are perfectly ripe. They should be slightly soft to the touch when gently squeezed.

7 kiwis, peeled and cut into sixths
**11 apricots, pitted and cut into
    quarters or sixths**
**36 to 40 lychees, peeled and pitted
    (see Note)**

**3 to 4 mangoes, peeled and cut from
    the seed into ⅛-inch slivers**

Gently toss all of the fruit together in a bowl.

Serves 30.

NOTE: Canned lychees can be substituted for fresh.

PLANNING AHEAD: This fruit salad can be assembled up to 5 hours ahead and kept covered in the refrigerator.

A huge tray of desserts ended the feast: Kiwi, apricot, lychee, and mango salad served from a watermelon half carved with Chinese designs; coconut tartlets; and almond cookies.

Almond Cookies

Light and delicious, almond cookies are a nice accompaniment to fruit salad.

3 cups lard, solid vegetable shortening, or unsalted butter

2 cups sugar

4 eggs

2 teaspoons almond extract

4½ cups all-purpose flour, sifted

1½ cups ground almonds

1½ teaspoons baking powder

1 teaspoon salt

1 egg yolk mixed with 1 teaspoon
   water

Garnish: 30 whole almonds

1. Using an electric mixer with a paddle attachment, cream the shortening with the sugar until light and fluffy. Add the eggs one at a time, beating well after each addition. Add the almond extract and mix to incorporate.

2. In a large bowl, combine the flour, ground almonds, baking powder, and salt. A little at a time, add the dry ingredients to the creamed mixture, mixing well. The dough should be moist.

3. On a floured board, knead the dough until smooth, adding a little flour from the board if the dough seems too sticky. Roll the dough into 2 logs and chill at least 1 hour.

4. Preheat the oven to 350° F. Line baking sheets with parchment. Remove the dough from the refrigerator and cut each log into 15 pieces. Roll each piece into a ball, then flatten into 2½-inch-diameter cookies. Place ½ inch apart on baking sheets and brush with the egg wash. Place a whole almond in the center of each cookie. Bake for approximately 18 to 20 minutes, until the cookies are golden. Remove and let cool on baking sheet.

Makes 30 cookies.

PLANNING AHEAD: The dough can be refrigerated up to 5 days ahead or frozen for up to 2 months. The baked cookies will keep for up to 2 weeks in a tightly covered container.

Ginger Iced Tea

Ginger tea is refreshing and healthy. I drink it year-round, hot and cold.

10 quarts water

2 cups sugar

2 (4-inch) pieces fresh ginger, washed
   and cut into ¼-inch-thick slices
   (peeling not necessary)

Optional: Thinly sliced lemon or
   lime

1. In a large pot, combine the water, sugar, and ginger. Stir to dissolve the sugar, and bring to a boil over high heat. Turn the heat down to medium and simmer for 1 hour, until the tea is reduced to 8 quarts.

2. Remove the tea from the heat, strain, and let cool. Serve over ice. If you like, float lemon or lime slices on top.

PLANNING AHEAD: This tea can be made up to 2 weeks in advance and kept in the refrigerator. It can also be frozen.

Bite-Size Coconut Tartlets

This traditional, not-too-sweet Chinese dessert is made with two pastry crusts, one placed inside the other, making the tartlets flaky yet crisp.

PASTRY 1

2½ cups all-purpose flour, sifted

⅔ cup water

3 ounces lard, melted

PASTRY 2

1½ cups all-purpose flour, sifted

4 ounces lard, melted

COCONUT FILLING:

¾ cup sugar

½ cup water

1 ounce unsalted butter

1½ cups shredded unsweetened
   coconut

2 eggs, beaten

1 tablespoon milk

½ teaspoon baking powder

¼ teaspoon vanilla extract

1. To make Pastry 1, place the flour in a mixing bowl and make a well in the center. Combine the water and lard, pour into the well, and work into the flour with your fingers until you have a soft dough. Turn out onto a board and knead until smooth.

(CONTINUED)

Gingered iced tea, refreshing on a hot day.

2. To make Pastry 2, place the flour on a board and make a well. Pour in the lard and work with your fingers until the dough is smooth (don't knead). Add a few teaspoons of water if the dough is too dry and will not hold together.

3. Wrap both doughs in wax paper or plastic and set aside in the refrigerator until ready to use.

4. To make the filling, combine the sugar and water in a medium saucepan, bring to a boil, and let cook for 4 minutes over medium heat, until a light syrup is formed. Add the butter and stir until melted. Pour the mixture into a bowl and let cool. Add the coconut, eggs, milk, baking powder, and vanilla, and mix well.

5. Preheat the oven to 400° F. Roll out each pastry to a thickness of ⅛ inch. Place one on top of the other and cut into 2-inch rounds with a regular or fluted cutter. Lightly press the pastry into greased mini-muffin tins. Spoon in the filling until each cup is three-fourths full. Bake approximately 12 to 15 minutes, until the pastry is golden and the filling is firm to the touch.

Makes 36 bite-size tartlets.

PLANNING AHEAD: Both the dough and the filling can be made up to a week ahead and kept in the refrigerator; if the filling is cold, you will need to bake the tartlets a little longer. Baked tartlets can be prepared up to 2 days ahead and stored in a covered container in the refrigerator.

Summer Cookout

This menu has "summer" written all over it. When the weather is hot and "the livin' is easy," as the Gershwin song goes, entertaining is easier too. Friends and family are around more in summer, everyone is in a relaxed and happy mood, and menus can be planned around summer's splendid array of fresh produce. Especially if you have a garden, it is possible to cook up a very satisfying meal for a lot of people with little effort. The key to summer cooking is to keep menus simple and flexible, use fruits and vegetables of the season, and beat the heat by grilling foods outdoors as much as possible.

Once humans discovered fire they began grilling, learning the art over a thousand centuries to create succulent feasts. There are many different ways to grill, but essentially it comes down to using an open grill or a covered one. Open grills are best for quick-cooking foods such as seafood, vegetables, and meats. Covered grills, which create an oven effect, are efficient for smoking and roasting foods. Open grills range in size from single hibachis to barrel grills, open pits, campfires, and hearths. For best flavor, I prefer a fire made with fruitwoods, hickory, or other fine-scented woods. In this part of Connecticut there is such an abundance and variety of wood that building wonderful cooking fires is no problem. When I am cooking on the open brick grill in my home kitchen I have the luxury of using wood gathered from trees on my own property. My second choice is to use real wood or "lump" charcoal. It is a bit more expensive than common charcoal briquettes, but does not contain chemicals or other additives. Another option is to add wood chips (such as mesquite) to the coals for added flavor.

To start a fire I usually use paper logs and place them under the wood or charcoal. Once lighted, they burn long and hot enough to ignite the fuel. Other methods

The tables set up under the tent were draped with a fun flag-pattern cloth. Centerpieces were simple field daisies in painted tin cans.

include pressed wood starter logs, electric starters, and metal starter chimneys. Of course you can also use lighter fluid, but I find that it gives food a chemical taste.

Keep in mind that cooking temperatures on the grill will vary depending on the arrangement of the wood or coals. When the coals are spread out evenly the hottest area of the grill will be in the center, and the outer edges will be less hot. When I grill meat, for example, I first put it in the center to sear the meat and lock in the juices, moving it out to the edges of the grill to finish cooking. This technique works well when grilling for a crowd, as it allows you to cook food in stages. Bunching up the wood or coals in one area of the grill is another way to create a "hot spot" and give you greater cooking flexibility.

For this cookout we rented a five-foot-long portable Big John grill, firing it up early to char the eggplant and peppers for the dip and the corn for the salad. We kept the grill hot by adding more fuel to the fire as necessary. Since this was a large party we grilled the vegetables ahead for the large platter and also precooked the foil-wrapped flank steaks, which require a longer cooking time; both were served at room temperature on the buffet. When the guests arrived I grilled the chicken and then the swordfish, which took only a few minutes. I find that a large grill always becomes a focal point at cookouts, with friends curiously sniffing around offering advice and help. A big grill also makes it possible for everyone to sit down to eat at the same time.

On a hot summer day I always set up some kind of protection from the sun—umbrellas, awnings, cabanas, or a tent. For this party the large expanse of lawn by the pool was the perfect spot for a colorful blue-and-white striped tent. The nearby pool house served as a bar area that we set up ahead of time. Tables were covered with a flag-print cloth that I use throughout the summer, not just on Independence Day. The table decorations were simple—bunches of daisies in red-painted tin cans and white "flag-folded" napkins. I prefer to use cloth napkins because they don't fly away when it's breezy or tear the way paper napkins do. I served the buffet on red and blue granite-ware dishes, which have just the right casual look for picnics and barbecues and are sturdy and unbreakable.

At the bar set up in the pool house we served classic summertime drinks—margaritas, gin and vodka tonics, beers, and wine spritzers—along with lots of fresh watermelon juice, sodas, and sparkling waters, very welcome on such a hot day.

After lunch, and a spirited game of volleyball, everyone headed for the pool. Late in the afternoon we served the desserts—a double berry cobbler with whipped cream and a refreshing summer fruit bowl—which no one could refuse.

Summer Cookout

for 16 to 20

MUNCHIES

Fresh and Light Crab Cakes

Charred Eggplant and Tofu Dip with Garlic Pita Chips

Boiled Shrimp with Homemade Cocktail Sauce

Garden-Fresh Radishes ✦ French Baguettes

Fresh Watermelon Juice

COOKOUT

Marinated Grilled Chicken

Grilled Swordfish with Fresh Tomato Vinaigrette

Flank Steak Rolled with Swiss Chard

Goat Cheese–Stuffed Poblano Chilies

Garden Tomatoes and Mozzarella

A Simple Potato and Green Bean Salad

Grilled Vegetable Platters

Fresh Peach, Corn, Jicama, and Lola Rosa Salad

DESSERT

Double Berry Cobbler

Summer Fruit Bowl

Fresh and Light Crab Cakes

These are delectable Maryland-style crab cakes. Mayonnaise is the secret to their lightness and soft texture. Make plenty—they are a real favorite.

1 pound fresh crabmeat
1 cup Homemade Mayonnaise
(recipe follows)
½ cup chopped flat-leaf parsley

1½ tablespoons Dijon-style mustard
¾ cup all-purpose flour (see Note)
⅛ teaspoon cayenne pepper
½ cup vegetable oil, for frying

1. Drain the crabmeat of any excess liquid and place in a small mixing bowl. Fold in the mayonnaise, parsley, mustard, flour, and cayenne pepper, working quickly to avoid breaking apart the crab nuggets. Store covered in the refrigerator until ready to cook.

2. Generously coat a heavy-bottomed skillet with some of the oil and heat over medium-high heat. Gently form the crab mixture into silver dollar–size pancakes. Cook them, a few at a time, in the hot oil, turning once with a spatula to brown evenly on both sides. Add more oil as needed to cook the rest of the crab cakes. If you are cooking a large quantity, you will need to clean off the spatula often so the cakes won't stick to it.

Makes 30 silver dollar–size crab cakes.

NOTE: The amount of flour may vary slightly, depending on the wetness of the crabmeat. If the mixture seems too wet, add more flour and cook 1 cake to test.

PLANNING AHEAD: The crab mixture can be kept in the refrigerator for 3 days. The cakes can be cooked a couple of hours before you plan to serve them, then reheated on a baking sheet in a 250° F oven for about 8 to 10 minutes.

Homemade Mayonnaise

This is a basic mayonnaise recipe. Try experimenting with different flavored oils and vinegars to create your own variations. Just remember that since the oils in mayonnaise are not cooked, it is important to use the highest quality for the best flavor.

1 egg yolk (see Note)
2 tablespoons lemon juice or good
   white vinegar
1 cup vegetable oil or pure olive oil

Coarse salt and freshly ground black
   pepper to taste
Optional: 2 tablespoons cold water

In a food processor or blender combine the egg yolk and lemon juice or vinegar. With the motor running add the oil in a slow, steady stream and process until the mayonnaise is thick and emulsified. Correct the seasoning with the salt and pepper. If the mayonnaise is too thick, whisk in a few drops of water to thin it.

Makes 1 cup.

NOTE: Quality farm-fresh eggs will make a big difference in the flavor of homemade mayonnaise. Try to buy them from reliable local farms or health-food stores rather than from large supermarkets.

PLANNING AHEAD: Homemade mayonnaise will keep for 5 days in a covered container in the refrigerator.

Charred Eggplant and Tofu Dip

The blending of charred eggplant, peppers, and tahini gives this dip a wonderful mellow, smoky taste. Tofu gives it a creamy texture without dairy, fat, or oil.

5 medium eggplants
  (about 3 pounds)
2 red bell peppers
6 cloves garlic, chopped
1 piece tofu (about 7–8 ounces),
  preferably medium-firm
½ cup tahini

Juice of 1 lemon
12 large basil leaves, shredded
½ cup chopped flat-leaf parsley
Coarse salt and freshly ground black
  pepper to taste
Optional: **3 medium tomatoes,**
  peeled, seeded, and chopped

1. Prepare a fire in a grill or preheat the broiler. Wash the eggplants and pierce near the stem (to allow steam to escape while cooking). Place the eggplants on the hot grill or under the broiler about 2 inches from the heat. Cook for about 8 to 10 minutes, until the skin is charred on all sides and the flesh is tender, turning with tongs. Remove the eggplants and place in a colander held over a bowl to drain excess liquid and cool.

2. While the eggplants are cooling, wash the peppers and place them on the grill or under the broiler. Roast about 2 to 3 minutes, turning, until the skin is blackened and charred on all sides. Peel off the skin, pull out the stem, remove the seeds, and cut into medium dice. Set aside.

3. Holding the eggplant by its stem and working over a bowl, peel off the skin and discard. Pull open and remove as many of the seeds as you can. Cut off the stem. Place the eggplant flesh in a food processor, add the garlic, and process briefly to mix. Add the tofu, tahini, and lemon juice and mix just until you have a thick chunky paste.

4. Remove the eggplant mixture to a bowl and fold in the red pepper, basil, and parsley. Taste for seasoning, and add salt and pepper. Fold in the tomatoes if you are using them, or garnish the dip with tomatoes. Serve with Garlic Pita Chips (recipe follows).

Makes 3 cups.

NOTE: The eggplants can also be charred by holding them over a gas flame on the stove. Finish cooking by putting in a 425° F oven for 10 minutes.

PLANNING AHEAD: This dip will keep for 5 days in an airtight container in the refrigerator.

Garlic Pita Chips

I find so many uses for these crispy chips that I always make them in large quantities. I serve them as an accompaniment to dips and salads, and by themselves as a snack. Sprinkled with cinnamon sugar, they can even be served with ice cream and puddings.

3 packages small pita breads
½ cup olive oil
6 cloves garlic, minced
1 teaspoon coarse salt
1 pinch freshly ground black pepper

Optional: **1 tablespoon chopped fresh basil or flat-leaf parsley**

With a sharp knife cut each pita into 2 half moons. Then cut each half into 3 triangular pieces. To save time, I often stack the pitas and cut through the stack. Gently pull apart each triangle to separate it into 2 pieces. You should get at least 12 chips from each pita bread.

Preheat the oven to 375° F.

In a large mixing bowl combine the oil and other ingredients, including the herbs if you are using them. Add the pitas and quickly toss to coat them. Remove and lay out on baking sheets. Bake in the oven approximately 7 minutes, until the pitas begin to color. Remove from the oven and turn the pitas over with a metal spatula. Return to the oven and continue baking another 5 minutes, until the chips are golden brown and crispy. Remove from the oven and let cool. Store in airtight containers or Ziploc bags.

Makes approximately 200 pita chips.

VARIATIONS: There are many variations of these pita chips, depending on the flavorings you prefer. Try the following ingredients combined with coarse salt:

Sesame seeds (use sesame oil instead of olive oil)
Fennel or anise seeds
Fresh herbs of your choice
Hot red pepper flakes
Grated Parmesan or Romano cheese
Curry powder and spices
Finely diced shallot or onion

You can also make sweet pita chips, by tossing the pitas in melted butter combined with sugar and cinnamon.

PLANNING AHEAD: These chips can be made up to 3 weeks ahead and kept in an airtight container.

Boiled Shrimp with Homemade Cocktail Sauce

A simple hors d'oeuvre that is a classic favorite. As a rule, if you are serving shrimp before a full meal, allow 3 to 4 per person; for a long cocktail party, plan 6 to 7 per person.

1 lemon, cut in half
12 sprigs flat-leaf parsley
2 tablespoons coarse salt
1 teaspoon crushed black pepper

3 to 3½ pounds large raw shrimp
    (16-20 count size), unpeeled
    (see Note)
Homemade Cocktail Sauce, for
    serving (recipe follows)

1. Fill a 10-quart pot with water, squeeze in the juice of the lemon, and drop the cut lemon halves into the water. Add the parsley, salt, and pepper. Bring to a boil over high heat and let boil for 3 minutes.

2. Add the shrimp and cook 1½ to 2 minutes over high heat, until just pink. Remove them with a skimmer, or pour into a colander to drain. Cool immediately in an ice bath, then drain.

3. To peel shrimp, hold by the shell closest to the tail. Using your other hand remove the shell from the head down, breaking at the natural segments. Leave the tail on or carefully remove it and pull off the end of the tail shell to expose the meat.

4. Holding the shrimp between your thumb and index finger like a clamp, scrape down the center of the shrimp, and remove and discard the intestine. Place the cleaned shrimp in a covered container and store in the refrigerator until ready to serve.

5. Serve with Homemade Cocktail Sauce.

Serves 16 to 20, as part of buffet.

NOTE: I prefer to cook shrimp with their shells on to retain their shape. Pre-peeled and deveined shrimp are a convenience, but I dislike the way they curl when cooked. Be careful not to overcook shrimp, as they become dry and rubbery.

PLANNING AHEAD: Shrimp can be cooked up to 2 days ahead and stored in a sealable plastic bag over ice in the refrigerator. Do not store in ice water; the shrimp will get soggy and lose their flavor.

Homemade Cocktail Sauce

You can make this with commercial ketchup, of course, but the taste is much better with homemade.

2 cups ketchup, preferably homemade (recipe follows)
¼ cup grated horseradish, fresh or prepared

Juice of 2 lemons
Tabasco or red chili paste to taste

In a small bowl, mix together the ketchup with the horseradish and lemon juice. Taste for seasoning, then add the Tabasco or chili paste a little at a time. Remember that the sauce will get hotter after a few minutes.

Makes 2 cups.

PLANNING AHEAD: The sauce will keep in a covered container in the refrigerator for at least 2 weeks.

Homemade Ketchup

In summer, when tomatoes are plentiful, this is a great way to use soft or bruised fruits. It may not be as thick as commercial ketchup, but it is all-natural, especially if you use organic tomatoes.

18 medium tomatoes, cored and
  quartered
3 tablespoons Dijon-style mustard
½ cup brown sugar or honey
1 cup red wine vinegar or balsamic
  vinegar

1 fresh jalapeño pepper or
  ¼ teaspoon cayenne pepper
Optional: ⅛ teaspoon ground mace

1. Place the tomatoes, mustard, sugar or honey, vinegar, jalapeño or cayenne pepper, and mace (if using) in a 6- to 8-quart pot. Stir and bring to a boil over high heat. Turn the heat down and simmer for at least 30 minutes, until the tomatoes have exuded all their juice and the pulp is dissolved.

2. Remove from the heat, transfer to a blender or food processor, and puree until smooth. Strain through a fine conical strainer or food mill into a container and refrigerate until ready to use.

Makes 1 to 1½ quarts.

PLANNING AHEAD: This ketchup will keep for 2 weeks in a covered container in the refrigerator. It can also be frozen for up to 8 months, so make extra batches in the summer and enjoy homemade ketchup 12 months a year.

Garden-Fresh Radishes

When I was in my twenties and I met my husband, Bernard, he introduced me to the classic "French picnic"—garden radishes, stems left on and just lightly scraped with a paring knife, served on a bed of ice; coarse salt; a fresh baguette; and sweet butter. I hated radishes as a child, but this combination—what a meal! Try it, and you will see. This is the way the French do it: a bite of radish dipped in salt, a bite of buttered bread, repeat. Aim to use just-picked, perfectly fresh radishes from the garden for fullest flavor.

Fresh Watermelon Juice

Watermelons are so juicy that 1 large one will yield 20 cups of juice. The technique is simple: Just slice the watermelon in half or quarters, cut out the flesh, and juice using a juice extractor. Don't worry about the seeds, as they will be strained out. Pour into a serving pitcher, chill if desired, and serve.

Marinated Grilled Chicken

Remember to use the best chicken you can find. Free-range and other natural chickens have a taste that is incomparable to commercially raised chickens.

6 whole fresh chickens (about 2½ to 3 pounds each), cut into 6 pieces
20 cloves garlic, peeled and smashed
2 tablespoons coarse salt
1 tablespoon freshly ground black pepper
6 lemons, cut in half
2 cups fresh herb leaves (any combination of oregano, marjoram, basil, thyme, flat-leaf parsley, chervil, or cilantro)
2 cups pure olive oil or good vegetable oil

1. Remove the backbone from each chicken, then cut each chicken into 6 pieces: Cut in half at the breastbone, cut between the leg and breast, then disjoint the thigh and drumstick. Cut off the wing tip and first joint and save to use in another dish.

2. Place the chicken pieces in a baking pan, sprinkle with the garlic, salt, and pepper, and toss to coat. Squeeze lemon juice over the chicken, using a small mesh strainer

to catch the seeds. Add the lemon halves and fresh herbs, and toss again. Pour the oil over the chicken and toss one more time to coat the chicken.

3. Refrigerate the chicken for at least 24 hours.

4. Prepare a barbecue grill. When hot, place the chicken on the grill, skin side down, and cook approximately 12 minutes, depending on the heat of the fire, then turn over and cook another 12 minutes on the other side. Test for doneness by piercing the flesh with the tip of a knife to see if the juices run clear.

Serves 16 to 20, as part of buffet.

VARIATIONS: There are many ways to vary the flavor of the basic marinade.

For Southwestern flavor: Add chili peppers, cumin, cilantro or epazote, and coarsely chopped peanuts; substitute fresh lime juice for the lemon.

For Spanish flavor: Add sliced onions and paprika or saffron; substitute fresh orange juice for the lemon.

For Indian flavor: Add curry powder, ginger, and ground cinnamon; substitute fresh orange juice for the lemon.

For Asian flavor: Add chili peppers, lemongrass, ginger, scallions, brown sugar, and soy sauce; substitute fresh lime juice for the lemon, and sesame oil for the olive oil.

PLANNING AHEAD: The chicken can be left in the marinade in the refrigerator for up to 4 days before grilling. Serve the chicken hot off the grill, or grill ahead and serve at room temperature.

Grilled Swordfish with Fresh Tomato Vinaigrette

Swordfish is a universal favorite for grilling because of its fine, firm texture. Other good grilling fish include salmon, marlin, tuna, grouper, pompano, sea bass, mahimahi, mako shark, bluefish, and sardines.

½ cup chopped fresh dill, thyme, or
  flat-leaf parsley, or ¼ cup
  chopped fresh rosemary
1 cup pure olive or vegetable oil
¼ cup fresh citrus juice or white
  wine or balsamic vinegar
20 (4- to 5-ounce) fresh swordfish
  steaks (about 5 to 5½ pounds
  whole swordfish)

Coarse salt and freshly ground black
  pepper to taste
Fresh Tomato Vinaigrette, for serving
  (recipe follows)

1. In a small bowl, mix together the herbs, oil, and juice or vinegar. Pour half of the mixture into a rimmed baking pan large enough to hold the swordfish. Place the fish in the baking pan, sprinkle with salt and pepper, and pour the remaining marinade on top. Cover and refrigerate for at least 4 hours.

2. Prepare a barbecue grill. When hot, remove the fish from the marinade and grill about 2 to 3 minutes. Turn over and grill 2 to 3 minutes on the other side. Fish should be white and firm. Serve with Fresh Tomato Vinaigrette.

Serves 16 to 20, as part of buffet.

PLANNING AHEAD: The swordfish can be left in the marinade in the refrigerator for up to 2 days before grilling.

The barbecue buffet. COUNTERCLOCKWISE FROM LOWER RIGHT: *Grilled swordfish; goat cheese–stuffed poblano chilies; marinated grilled chicken; flank steak rolled with Swiss chard; peach, corn, jicama, and Lola Rosa salad.*

Fresh Tomato Vinaigrette

Another great way to use the extra garden tomatoes that always seem to pile up in summer. I prefer to keep this vinaigrette simple, but there's no reason not to add fresh herbs and other seasonings if you like.

6 ripe medium tomatoes, cored and coarsely chopped
½ cup good-quality balsamic or red or white wine vinegar

1 cup vegetable oil
Coarse salt and freshly ground black pepper to taste

1. Place the tomatoes in a food processor or blender. With the motor running, add the vinegar and oil in a steady stream and blend until smooth. You can also do this in a bowl using an immersion blender. Taste for seasoning, and add salt and pepper as needed.

2. Pass the tomatoes through a fine conical strainer or food mill. Store in the refrigerator until ready to use.

Makes at least 1 quart.

PLANNING AHEAD: This vinaigrette will keep for up to 7 days in a covered container in the refrigerator.

Flank Steak Rolled with Swiss Chard

Flank steak is delicious simply marinated and grilled, but here I serve it stuffed with Swiss chard, which is so abundant in summer. These vegetables add flavor to the meat and keep it moist and juicy during cooking.

Cleo, our Saint Bernard, who ordinarily never takes food from counters or tables, couldn't resist the succulent smell of this flank steak cooking on the grill. When no one was looking she swiped a slice from the platter and wolfed it down in less than a minute. She was heading back for another piece when we caught her. Trust me, this dish is a real crowd pleaser!

2 whole flank steaks, about 2 pounds each, fat removed
1 tablespoon vegetable oil
2 cups diced onions, leeks, or scallions
Optional: 1 pound mushrooms, cleaned and diced
8 cloves garlic, peeled and minced
Coarse salt and freshly ground black pepper to taste

36 large leaves Swiss chard, washed, stems removed, and coarsely shredded
4 tablespoons Dijon-style mustard
3 tablespoons fresh thyme leaves (from about 20 stems)
¾ cup finely grated aged goat cheese or Parmesan, or 3 cups coarsely grated provolone or jack cheese

1. Put the steaks on a clean board, cover with plastic, and pound to an even 1-inch thickness. Set aside in the refrigerator.

2. Heat the oil in a large skillet over high heat, add the onions, and cook about 2 to 3 minutes, until soft. Add the mushrooms, if you are using them, and garlic and cook briefly. Sprinkle with salt and pepper. Using a skimmer or slotted spoon, transfer the mixture to a bowl, leaving the liquid in the skillet.

3. Add the Swiss chard to the skillet and sauté over high heat for a minute or two just to wilt. Season with salt and pepper, then mix with the onions in the bowl. Set aside to cool.

4. Place the steaks on a board. Spread the mustard on each piece and sprinkle with thyme leaves. Squeeze the Swiss chard mixture with your hands to get rid of excess liquid, then spread over each steak, leaving a border of about 1½ inches on all sides. Sprinkle the cheese over the Swiss chard. Roll up the short end of the meat like a jelly roll. Tear off about 20 inches of heavy aluminum foil. Put the meat in the middle, and bring the edges of the foil together over the top, like a tent. Crimp the foil down until the meat is completely enclosed in a tight packet. Tuck the ends in.

5. Prepare a barbecue grill, or preheat the oven to 400° F. Cook over the hot center part of the grill for about 10 minutes, then move out to the cooler edges to cook for 25 minutes more. If cooking in the oven, roast the meat rolls for approximately 30 to 35 minutes.

6. Let the meat rest for about 30 minutes before unwrapping and slicing.

Serves 16 to 20, as part of buffet.

PLANNING AHEAD: The meat can be pounded and wrapped in plastic, and the filling made, up to 2 days ahead and kept separately in the refrigerator. The rolls can be assembled and wrapped in foil up to 24 hours before grilling or roasting.

Goat Cheese–Stuffed Poblano Chilies

Beautiful dark green in color and rich in flavor, the poblano chili ranges from mildly hot to very hot. It must be roasted when used fresh. When dried, poblanos are called ancho chilies.

Paired with a mole sauce or fresh chopped salsa, these peppers also make a good first course or vegetarian entrée.

16 to 20 poblano chilies
2 tablespoons vegetable oil
1½ pounds fresh goat cheese
6 stalks fresh cilantro or epazote,
   leaves picked and coarsely
   chopped

6 scallions (white part and most of
   green stalk), coarsely chopped
3 cups yellow or blue cornmeal, for
   dredging
½ cup vegetable oil

1. Char the poblanos over a hot grill or gas flame. Or roast them in a 450° F oven using this method: Wash the poblanos and toss in the 2 tablespoons oil. Place in a single layer on a baking sheet or in a roasting pan. Roast for about 5 to 6 minutes to quickly blacken and blister the skins, turning to color evenly on all sides. Let the poblanos cool. Wearing rubber gloves or plastic bags on your hands to protect yourself, rub off the skin, leaving the stem intact. Using a sharp knife, make one long slit down the length of each pepper and carefully remove the seeds.

2. In a medium bowl, mash the goat cheese to soften it. Stir in the cilantro or epazote and scallions. Shape the cheese into cylinders and fit one inside each pepper. Wrap the pepper around the cheese, overlapping the edges. Roll in cornmeal to coat well. Keep the peppers in the refrigerator on a bed of cornmeal, covered, until ready to cook.

3. Preheat the oven to 400° F. Coat a roasting pan with ¼ cup of the vegetable oil, arrange the peppers on top, then sprinkle the peppers with the remaining oil. Cook about 8 to 10 minutes, until the peppers are hot and the cornmeal coating crisps.

Serves 16 to 20, as part of buffet.

PLANNING AHEAD: The cornmeal-coated peppers can be left in the refrigerator for up to 4 days. They can be cooked up to 6 hours ahead and served at room temperature, or reheated in a low (300° F) oven for about 3 minutes.

Garden Tomatoes and Mozzarella

Yes, another tomato recipe! But who can resist tomatoes at this time of year? And this recipe is so easy and delicious. Be sure to use fresh, soft mozzarella, packed in water, from a good cheese shop, rather than the hard, prepackaged supermarket kind.

3 to 4 balls fresh or homemade mozzarella (about 6 to 8 ounces total)
Coarse salt and freshly ground black pepper
1 cup fresh basil leaves, shredded

2 cups extra-virgin olive oil or good-quality herb-flavored oil
8 to 10 beefsteak tomatoes, cored
Optional: **Good-quality red wine vinegar or balsamic vinegar**

1. Cut the mozzarella into ¼-inch-thick slices and arrange them, overlapping, in a pan. Sprinkle with a generous amount of salt and pepper and half of the basil and olive oil. Cover and refrigerate for at least 4 hours.

2. Cut the tomatoes into slices ¼ to ½ inch thick. Arrange on a serving platter,

A luscious platter of garden tomatoes layered with slices of fresh mozzarella.

alternating every 2 or 3 slices with mozzarella. Sprinkle the whole platter with a little salt and pepper and the remaining basil and oil. If you wish, sprinkle with vinegar.

Serves 16 to 20, as part of buffet.

PLANNING AHEAD: The mozzarella can be marinated up to 3 days ahead in the refrigerator. The whole platter can be assembled up to 6 hours before serving and kept cool.

A Simple Potato and Green Bean Salad

I make this dish all summer long. Small new potatoes and fresh green beans from the garden tossed with a little dressing—who needs more?

40 small new potatoes (see Note)
2½ to 3 pounds fresh green beans, ends snapped off
2 tablespoons Dijon or whole-grain mustard
¾ cup balsamic or red wine vinegar
1½ cups olive or vegetable oil

Coarse salt and freshly ground black pepper to taste
1 medium red onion or 6 shallots, finely diced
1 cup coarsely chopped flat-leaf parsley

1. Cook the potatoes by one of the following methods:

    a. Put the potatoes in a large pot, sprinkle with salt, and add water to cover. Bring to a boil over high heat and cook about 15 minutes, until tender. Drain in a colander.

    b. Arrange the potatoes in a lightly oiled pan and roast in a 425° F oven for about 20 minutes, until soft.

2. While the potatoes are cooking, blanch the green beans: Bring a pot of salted water to a boil, add the beans, and cook over high heat for about 2 to 3 minutes, until just tender, or al dente ("to the bite"). Drain, then plunge into an ice bath to cool. Drain and set aside.

3. To make the dressing, whisk together by hand or in a food processor the mustard and vinegar, then add the oil in a steady stream until the dressing is thickened and emulsified. Season to taste with salt and pepper.

4. Pour 1¾ cups dressing into a serving bowl, add the hot potatoes and the onion or shallots, and toss lightly. Set aside.

5. No more than 3 hours before serving, add the green beans and parsley and toss with the remaining dressing.

Serves 16 to 20, as part of buffet.

NOTE: I usually cut a band around the center of small new potatoes before cooking because I find it keeps the jackets from bursting, but this step is not crucial. If potatoes are larger, cut them in halves or quarters.

PLANNING AHEAD: The potatoes can be cooked, combined with the onion and dressing, and kept in the refrigerator for up to 2 days. Before proceeding with the recipe, let them come to room temperature; cold potatoes have much less flavor than room temperature ones. The green beans can be blanched and kept refrigerated for up to 1 day. Don't combine the beans with the dressing and potatoes more than 3 hours before serving because the dressing will darken the beans' bright color.

Grilled Vegetable Platters

Use your garden as a guide for choosing vegetables to grill, but if you don't have one, here are some suggestions. For sixteen to twenty people, select six different vegetables from the list, and the quantities will be about right.

I cut the vegetables into large pieces so they don't fall through the grill grates into the fire. Another option is to use a long-handled grill basket.

3 medium eggplants	2 heads broccoli
5 medium zucchini or yellow squash	2 pounds asparagus
3 fennel bulbs	4 bell peppers, any color
6 onions, peeled, or 9 to 10 leeks, washed and stems removed	2 pounds mushrooms, cleaned, preferably portobellos or shiitakes
2 pounds carrots or parsnips, peeled	20 unhusked ears of corn
8 medium tomatoes, red or green	2 cups vegetable oil

1. Choose your vegetables and wash them. Cut the eggplants, zucchini, fennel, onions, and carrots or parsnips into large straight or diagonal pieces about ¼ to ½ inch thick. Make the pieces big enough so they don't fall through the grill. Cut the tomatoes into halves or slices. Cut the broccoli into large florets with some stem, and break off the tough ends of the asparagus. Cut the peppers in half, remove the seeds and white pith, and slice into large strips or diamonds. Leave the mushrooms whole, but cut off the stems. Remove the silk from the corn, but leave the husks on; the husks will prevent the corn from burning and will add a smoky flavor.

2. Toss all of the vegetables, except the corn, in the oil. Dip the corn in water. Prepare a barbecue grill, and when it is hot, put the vegetables on top, turning them to cook on both sides. Depending on the heat of the grill, most vegetables, except corn, will probably take 2 to 5 minutes to cook; corn will usually take about 10 to 15 minutes.

Serves 16 to 20, as part of buffet.

PLANNING AHEAD: Once the vegetables are prepared and tossed in the oil, they can be kept in separate covered containers in the refrigerator for up to 2 days before grilling.

A closer look at the platter of grilled vegetables.

Fresh Peach, Corn, Jicama, and Lola Rosa Salad

Here in the Litchfield hills we are fortunate to have wonderful peach orchards. For this salad I like to mix yellow and white peaches with crunchy jicama, smoky fresh corn, and frilly Lola Rosa leaves.

I usually don't make a dressing for this salad because the corn and peaches are juicy and release liquid. However, guests can use some of the Fresh Tomato Vinaigrette that is served with the swordfish (page 74). A light vinaigrette dressing made with fresh lime or lemon and olive oil would also be nice.

6 to 8 ears fresh corn
2 large jicamas, peeled and julienned
6 large ripe peaches, washed and
    peeled (see Note)
Coarse salt and freshly ground black
    pepper to taste

4 to 6 heads Lola Rosa or other
    lettuces, such as Bibb, butter,
    mizuna, or tatsoi
30 sprigs fresh basil, leaves picked

1. To give a nice smoky flavor to the corn, dip the ears in water, then grill them in their husks. Let cool, then cut the kernels off the cobs. Or, cut off the raw kernels and sear in a hot skillet or wok to char them lightly.

2. Put the corn kernels in a large salad bowl, then add the jicama. Cut the peaches in half, pull out the pits, and slice into wedges. Add to the bowl. Sprinkle with salt and pepper, and toss.

3. Wash and dry the lettuce leaves and basil. Just before serving, toss with the rest of the ingredients in the bowl.

Serves 16 to 20, as part of buffet.

NOTE: White or orchard-ripe peaches can usually be peeled with a paring knife. To peel other peaches, dip them in boiling water for a second, and their skins will come right off.

PLANNING AHEAD: All of the ingredients can be prepared 1 day ahead and kept in separate covered containers in the refrigerator. Assemble and toss the salad just before serving.

Double Berry Cobbler

When berry season hits I am bombarded with juicy fat berries of all kinds. This simple, homey dessert is a great way to take advantage of the summer bounty.

The basic cobbler pastry can be used with any kind of seasonal fruit. Serve with whipped cream or ice cream, homemade or store-bought.

PASTRY:

8 cups all-purpose flour

1 cup sugar

1 tablespoon baking powder

½ teaspoon coarse salt

4 ounces (1 stick) unsalted butter, cut into cubes

Zest and juice of 1 orange

Optional: ½ cup crystallized ginger, chopped

3½ cups heavy cream

*

8 pints (about 16 cups) fresh berries (blueberries, raspberries, huckleberries, gooseberries, strawberries, or blackberries), stems removed and picked over to remove any rotten ones or debris

2 cups sugar

8 tablespoons cornstarch

Juice of 2 lemons

1 egg beaten with 1 tablespoon water

1. To make the dough, sift together the flour, sugar, baking powder, and salt. Using a pastry cutter, work in the butter until the mixture resembles coarse crumbs. Add the orange zest and the ginger, if you are using it. Work in the cream and orange juice to make a smooth dough. Divide into 2 parts, wrap in plastic, and chill at least 1 hour.

2. On a floured surface, roll out each piece of dough to a ¼-inch thickness. Cut the dough to fit the size of 2 baking pans, either a 9 × 11-inch rectangular pan or 10-inch round pan.

3. Remove the stems from the berries, lightly rinse with water, and dry in batches in a salad spinner. If you are using large strawberries, slice them after drying; leave other berries whole. Put the berries in a large mixing bowl.

4. Sift together the sugar and cornstarch and sprinkle over the berries. Sprinkle with the lemon juice and toss to mix. Divide the berries between the 2 baking pans. Place a piece of rolled dough over each pan, tucking the edges in. Cut a steam hole in the center and brush the dough with the egg wash. If you like, cut any excess dough into decorative shapes and place on top; brush the decorations with the egg wash. Refrigerate at least 1 hour.

5. Preheat the oven to 400° F. Bake the cobbler, uncovered, for approximately 35

to 40 minutes, until cooked in the center with a golden crust. Let rest at least 1 hour before serving.

Makes 2 cobblers; serves 16 to 20.

PLANNING AHEAD: The dough can be made up to 4 days ahead and kept wrapped in plastic in the refrigerator. The unbaked cobbler can be refrigerated for up to 24 hours.

Summer Fruit Bowl

In summer, when there is such an abundance of fresh locally grown fruit—peaches, plums, berries, melons, and more—it couldn't be easier to put together a fruit bowl. Just let Mother Nature or the local farmstand be your guide. Wash the fruit, remove stems, seeds, or pits if necessary, cut up, toss together in a serving bowl, and keep refrigerated until ready to serve.

For this barbecue I combined 5 medium peaches, 4 plums, 2 cups mixed berries, and 1 cut-up cantaloupe, which was plenty for 16 to 20 people.

Dishes of the Sun:
A Mediterranean Buffet

The Mediterranean is an almost landlocked sea between southern Europe and Africa, connected to the Atlantic Ocean by the Strait of Gibraltar and to the Red Sea by the Suez Canal. The foods of this region are often referred to as the "cuisine of the sun," because of the area's hot, dry summers and warm, wet winters. Mediterranean cuisine dates back to ancient times and is deeply rooted in the history, culture, and traditions of the Mediterranean people. Each country or region has developed its own unique variations, but the basic character of Mediterranean cuisine has remained the same for centuries. Recipes are based on the bounty of the land and sea: vegetables and herbs from the garden, fruits from the orchards and vineyards, wheat from the fields, fish and seafood from the sea, and a small amount of meat from farms or the wild. "The cuisine of the soul," I like to call it, because Mediterranean food is so comforting in its rustic simplicity.

Twenty-five years ago, when I was training as a chef at the Culinary Institute of America, we were taught classical French cuisine, and very little attention was paid to Italian, Greek, or any other world cuisine. But after graduation, as my career started to take hold, I developed a passion for learning about different cuisines. By the early 1980s I had opened a restaurant called La Provence in Austin, Texas. Back then Provençal cooking was not well known in this country, especially in Texas. But people came, and loved the food we served: fish flown in from the Mediterranean, such as *loup*, or wolf fish, with a fresh tomato, olive, and rosemary sauce on a bed of couscous; monkfish cooked in retsina wine, cinnamon, and raisins; seafood salads; layered

The dinner buffet. COUNTERCLOCKWISE FROM LOWER LEFT: *Swiss chard, currant, and rabbit pie; garlic, tomato, and zucchini casserole; cucumber, feta, and pomegranate salad; Mediterranean seafood salad; saffron orzo, fava bean, and artichoke salad; whole-wheat focaccia; lamb stew with tomatoes and green olives; polenta with eggplant and peppers.*

vegetable terrines; "barigoule" of artichokes; and Mediterranean hors d'oeuvres, similar to tapas, varied nightly and brought into the dining room on a cart.

A few years later I became chef at a restaurant in New York called Cafe Greco, one of the first upscale Mediterranean restaurants in the city. There we focused on the foods of Greece, Africa, Italy, and France, featuring lamb shanks, duck soup with orzo and fava beans, olive tapenade–stuffed rabbit loin, grilled whole fish, and slow-roasted tomatoes with goat cheese.

Now at the Good News Café I have the opportunity to be as global as I like, and I find that the Mediterranean dishes we have on the menu are always popular. When I consult with clients about parties or weddings we often decide to offer at least a few Mediterranean dishes because they please so many people, especially vegetarians, and are light and healthy. Mediterranean food also stands up well to hours on a buffet because of the limited use of butter, mayonnaise, and cream.

Mediterranean ingredients are generally easy to find, but they need to be chosen carefully, with freshness and taste in mind. Olive oil, for example, which is used extensively in Mediterranean cooking, can vary considerably in quality and price. I use Italian, Spanish, and Greek olive oils, choosing extra-virgin oil for its richness and strength when the oil will be drizzled on a dish, and pure or virgin olive oil for many dressings and for cooking. Students in my cooking classes always want to know which is "the best" olive oil. There are many brands available, and the array can be confusing, but I always tell them that taste is the only judge. A good olive oil should be smooth, mellow, and fruity. I recommend buying a small quantity of different brands and having a tasting at home. Keep trying until you find an oil you really like. Price doesn't matter; olive oil prices fluctuate constantly depending on the crops, and an expensive oil does not necessarily guarantee quality. Olive oil can turn rancid after a few months in a kitchen cabinet, so if you don't use it often keep it in the refrigerator. It will turn cloudy and solidify, but will liquify at room temperature.

This casual buffet was photographed at my friend Susan's sun-filled home overlooking beautiful Lake Waramaug in Connecticut. We arranged the buffet on simple wood and marble tables, using Susan's extensive collection of handmade Provençal dishes and serving pieces. In keeping with the simplicity and earthiness of Mediterranean food, we used whole fruits and vegetables in our table arrangements, and even a couple of fragrant lemon trees as a backdrop. Many of the fresh vegetables and herbs used in the recipes were picked from my friend's large summer garden. During the warm-weather months here in Connecticut it is easy to put together just the right elements for a Mediterranean feast.

Dishes of the Sun:
A Mediterranean Buffet
for 20

SALADS
Cucumber, Feta, and Pomegranate Salad with Pita Croutons

Mediterranean Seafood Salad

Saffron Orzo, Fava Bean, and Artichoke Salad

SAVORY ENTRÉES
Swiss Chard, Currant, and Rabbit Pie

Baked Garlic, Tomato, and Zucchini Casserole

Seasoned Lamb Stew with Tomatoes and Green Olives

Baked Polenta with Eggplant and Peppers

Roasted Whole Garlic

Whole-Wheat Focaccia (page 16)

DESSERTS
Wine-Poached Fruits

Anise Cake

Lavender Ice Cream

White Sangria with Fruits

Fresh Grape Juice

Cucumber, Feta, and Pomegranate Salad
with Pita Croutons

Sometimes called Chinese apples, pomegranates are such an old fruit—they appear in Egyptian art as early as the 16th century B.C.—that no one is quite sure of their place of origin, probably somewhere in the Middle East. Today they appear in markets for a few months, from early September to January, and are well worth waiting for. I use their crimson seeds in many dishes, from salads to desserts, and the juice for marinades and drinks.

Bread salads are popular in Mediterranean countries, and are typically made with a coarse-textured whole-grain loaf. To add texture and crunch to this light salad, I like to use pita croutons, a variation of the Garlic Pita Chips on page 66.

PITA CROUTONS:
2 tablespoons vegetable or pure
   olive oil
2 teaspoons ground cumin
2 teaspoons coarse salt
6 small pitas, separated and cut into
   2-inch squares

DRESSING:
½ cup fresh lemon juice (from about
   4 lemons)
1 cup extra-virgin olive oil
Coarse salt and freshly ground black
   pepper to taste

*

6 large cucumbers, peeled, cut in
   half, seeded, and cut into ½-inch
   diagonal pieces
3 cups pomegranate seeds (about
   2 large fruits) (see Note)
2 bunches fresh mint, leaves picked
   and coarsely chopped
   (about 1 cup)
1 pound feta cheese, diced or
   broken into small chunks

1. To make the croutons, preheat the oven to 400° F. Combine the oil, cumin, and salt in a medium bowl. Add the pita bread and toss to coat. Arrange in a single layer on a baking sheet and toast in the oven until lightly browned, about 10 minutes, checking after 5 minutes to shake the pan a bit to loosen the pitas and to make sure the pitas are coloring evenly.

2. To make the dressing, whisk together the lemon juice and olive oil. Season with salt and pepper to taste (remember that the feta is already salty).

3. Combine the cucumbers, pomegranate seeds, mint, and feta in a salad bowl. Add the croutons, dress, and toss.

Serves 20, as part of buffet.

NOTE: To extract pomegranate seeds: use a sharp knife to cut off the blossom end of the fruit, then cut the fruit into quarters. Pull the skin back and pick the seeds out of the white pith. Some cooks prefer to score the fruit and break it open with their fingers to avoid puncturing the kernels with a knife and spilling the juice. Personally, I feel there is no getting around the fact that cooking is messy work. Stains usually wash out, but if you hate the mess, you really shouldn't cook!

PLANNING AHEAD: Pomegranate seeds can be picked from the fruit up to 3 days ahead and kept covered in the refrigerator.

Pita croutons will keep for at least 3 weeks in a tightly covered container. But don't add them, or the dressing, to the salad bowl more than 1 hour before serving.

Mediterranean Seafood Salad

To make the scrumptious dressing for this typically Mediterranean salad, the shellfish cooking liquid is combined with olive oil. I favor extra-virgin oil for this recipe because its strong flavor stands up well to the seafood juices.

If you like this salad, try embellishing it with octopus, langoustines, or chunks of firm-textured fish.

½ cup plus 1 tablespoon pure olive
   oil
1 large onion, finely diced
4 sprigs fresh thyme, leaves picked
1 tablespoon chopped fresh garlic
3 pounds fresh mussels, cleaned and
   drained
2 cups white wine
40 clams, shells washed (top or
   middle neck size)
2 pounds peeled rock shrimp or
   medium peeled shrimp
2 pounds squid, cleaned, bodies cut
   into ½-inch rings, tentacles left
   whole and uncut

1 cup capers, drained
3 large red bell peppers, oven
   roasted (see technique on page
   102) and sliced
1½ cups imported Greek or Italian
   olives, pitted
Freshly ground black pepper to taste
½ cup extra-virgin olive oil, for
   dressing
1 head romaine lettuce or other
   coarse greens, leaves washed and
   dried, shredded

(CONTINUED)

The three cold salads offered on the buffet. FROM TOP TO BOTTOM: *Saffron orzo, fava bean, and artichoke salad;*
Mediterranean seafood salad; and cucumber, feta, and pomegranate salad.

1. Heat 1 tablespoon of the olive oil in an 8-quart pot. Add the onion, thyme, and garlic, and cook over high heat for 1 minute, until softened. Add the mussels and wine and shake the pan. Cover and cook over high heat until the mussels begin to open, approximately 2 to 3 minutes. When they are all open, pour the mussels and the cooking liquid into a colander set over a large bowl. Set the mussels aside and return the liquid to the pot. See Note.

2. Add the clams to the pot and cook them over high heat until they open, approximately 4 to 5 minutes. Strain, as you did the mussels. Set the clams aside, reserving the cooking liquid.

3. Heat ½ cup of the olive oil in a skillet. Add the shrimp and sauté quickly over high heat for approximately 2 minutes, until just pink. With a skimmer, transfer the shrimp to a large bowl. Sauté the squid in the same oil over high heat, approximately 2 minutes. Add to the bowl with the shrimp and toss in the capers, bell peppers, and olives.

4. Remove the mussels and clams from their shells and add to the bowl. Pour the cooking liquid into a small saucepan and reduce by half over high heat. Season with freshly ground black pepper. Whisk in the extra-virgin olive oil and blend to make a dressing. Let cool, then toss into the seafood salad. Just before serving, add the lettuce and toss.

Serves 20, as part of buffet.

NOTE: Discard any mussels or clams that do not open with the others.

PLANNING AHEAD: The seafood can be cooked, and the salad (without the lettuce or dressing) assembled, up to 2 days ahead and kept in the refrigerator. Add the lettuce and dressing 1 hour before serving.

Saffron Orzo, Fava Bean, and Artichoke Salad

Saffron-flavored orzo, fresh favas, and artichokes—what could be more delectable? Only the addition of preserved lemons!

Fava beans are typically Mediterranean, but baby lima beans also work well in this salad.

3 pinches saffron threads
1 pound Greek orzo (see Note)
¼ cup pure olive oil
10 pounds fresh fava beans (about
   3 cups shelled)
6 large artichokes
1 lemon, cut in half

DRESSING:

1½ cups extra-virgin olive oil
Juice of 2 fresh lemons
6 quartered Preserved Lemons,
   finely diced (recipe follows)

3 bunches lettuces or other greens,
   such as arugula, radicchio, dandelion, trevise, or purslane, washed
   and dried

1. Fill a 6-quart pot with salted water, add the saffron, and bring to a boil. Add the orzo and cook until al dente, about 15 minutes. Remove from the heat and drain in a colander (do not rinse). Sprinkle the orzo with the olive oil and spread out on a baking sheet to cool. Set aside.

2. Shell the fava beans. Bring a pot of salted water to a boil, add the beans, and cook until tender, about 5 minutes. Drain in a colander and cool under cold water. Remove the outer skin by squeezing each bean between your thumb and forefinger over a bowl. Set aside.

3. Cut off the stems of the artichokes and pare off all the leaves down to the bottoms. Rub the artichokes with the cut lemon halves to prevent discoloration. Add the artichokes to a pot of salted water, toss in the lemon halves, cover with a clean towel (the towel holds the artichokes down, and they cook evenly), and cook over high heat until the artichokes are tender, about 15 minutes. Test by piercing the artichokes with the point of a knife. Drain in a colander and refresh with cold water. Scoop out and discard the chokes and set aside the bottoms.

4. To make the dressing, whisk together olive oil, lemon juice, and preserved lemons.

5. Cut the artichoke bottoms into eighths and place in a salad bowl. Pour the dressing over the artichokes, then add the favas and orzo and toss. Just before serving, toss in the lettuces or greens.

Serves 20, as part of buffet.

NOTE: I prefer Greek orzo for this dish because it is plumper and firmer than Italian orzo.

PLANNING AHEAD: The artichokes can be cooked and stored in their cooking liquid in the refrigerator for up to 5 days. The orzo and favas can be cooked, cooled, and stored in airtight containers in the refrigerator for up to 2 days. The dressing can be made up to 2 days ahead.

Preserved Lemons

Preserved lemons are an important flavoring in Morrocan cooking. Don't be tempted to substitute fresh lemon peel; the flavor will not be the same.

6 whole fresh lemons
⅔ cup coarse salt

1¼ cups fresh lemon juice

1. Wash the lemons and dry well. Cut into quarters and toss with the salt. Place the lemon quarters in a sterilized 1-quart Mason jar; they should fit tightly. Add the lemon juice and enough water to cover. Put the lid on the jar and shake to dissolve the salt.

2. Leave the lemons to cure in this solution for at least 2 weeks, at room temperature, shaking the jar each day. The lemons should be softened all the way through, without any bitter lemon pith taste.

3. Before using preserved lemons, rinse with cold water to remove excess salt. Pull out the pulp, discard, and use the skins only.

Makes 1 quart.

PLANNING AHEAD: These lemons will keep for 3 to 6 months, covered with olive oil, in the refrigerator.

Swiss Chard, Currant, and Rabbit Pie

Every cuisine has its own savory pie. This one has a distinctly Mediterranean flavor. Chicken can be substituted for the rabbit if you prefer, and the filling can be embellished with pitted imported olives and/or chopped hard-boiled eggs.

DOUGH:

3 cups all-purpose flour

¼ teaspoon salt

8 ounces (2 sticks) cold unsalted
   butter, cut into small pieces

Juice and zest of 1 lemon

2 eggs, beaten

FILLING:

¼ cup pure olive or vegetable oil

3 large leeks, washed and diced

1 cup pistachios, shelled

2 bunches fresh dill, chopped (about
   1 cup)

1 cup dried currants or raisins

1 cup chopped fresh or dried
   apricots

2 tablespoons ground cinnamon

Optional: 1 teaspoon mace

Zest and juice of 1 orange

4 cups cooked and coarsely chopped
   rabbit meat (from a 2- to 2½-
   pound rabbit)

Coarse salt and freshly ground black
   pepper to taste

3 bunches Swiss chard, stems
   removed, washed, dried, and
   shredded

2 cups plain yogurt

1 egg beaten with 1 teaspoon water,
   for glaze

1. To make the dough, sift the flour with the salt into a large bowl. Work in the butter with your fingers or a pastry cutter until the mixture resembles coarse meal. Add the lemon juice, zest, and eggs, and mix until a pliable dough is formed. Divide the dough into 4 parts, roll each into a ball, and flatten. Wrap in plastic and refrigerate at least 1 hour.

2. To make the filling, heat the oil in a wok or large skillet over high heat. Add the leeks and cook for 1 minute just to soften. Add the pistachios and cook 2 minutes more. Add the dill, currants or raisins, apricots, cinnamon, mace (if using), and orange zest, toss, and cook another 2 minutes. Add the rabbit, mix, and cook for 3 minutes more, until meat is just cooked. Season to taste with salt and pepper and remove from the heat.

3. Wilt the Swiss chard by either searing it briefly over high heat in a pan coated with a small amount of oil or by quickly blanching it in a small amount of water. Drain

in a colander, then press to squeeze out any excess liquid. Transfer to a large bowl and break apart with your fingers. Add the rabbit mixture and mix well. Whisk the yogurt and the orange juice together and fold into the filling mixture.

4. Remove the dough from the refrigerator. Roll out each piece into a circle or square slightly larger than 2 tart pans (9 or 10 inches round or square). Fit a circle or square of dough into each pan, allowing a little to overlap the edge. Divide the filling in half and fill each pan. Brush the edges of the dough with some of the egg glaze. Place another circle or square of dough on top, leaving a small amount overlapping. Cut off the excess and tuck the dough into each pan to seal the pie. Cut a steam hole in the center and brush the top with the remaining egg glaze. Put the pies in the refrigerator and let them rest at least 1 hour and up to 24 hours.

5. Preheat the oven to 375° F. Bake the pies approximately 40 minutes, until the crust looks golden and the filling is bubbling at the steam hole. Remove from the oven and let cool for at least 20 minutes before serving.

Makes two 9- to 10-inch pies.

PLANNING AHEAD: The dough will keep up to 1 week in the refrigerator, or up to 3 months in the freezer. The filling can be prepared 3 or 4 days ahead and kept in the refrigerator. Once the pies are filled, they can rest in the refrigerator for up to 24 hours before baking. I like this kind of savory pie served at room temperature, but it can also be reheated in a low (300° F) oven for 20 to 25 minutes before serving.

Baked Garlic, Tomato, and Zucchini Casserole

Garlic and tomatoes are the base for so many "dishes of the sun" that it's easy to forget how exquisite they can be simply baked. The secret is using perfectly fresh garden-ripe produce.

Extra-virgin olive oil
8 large or 16 medium tomatoes,
    cored and cut into ½-inch slices
6 medium zucchini, stems removed,
    cut on the diagonal into ½-inch
    pieces
12 cloves garlic, peeled and sliced
10 sprigs fresh basil, leaves picked
    and finely shredded

Coarse salt and freshly ground black
    pepper to taste
Aged goat cheese grating stick (see
    Note) or other good grating
    cheese, such as Parmesan or
    Asiago

1. Coat a large, shallow casserole with a thin layer of olive oil. Layer the zucchini slices alternately with the tomato slices, overlapping slightly. Sprinkle the garlic slices and shredded basil on top and season to taste. Finish with a thin layer of grated cheese.

2. Preheat the oven to 400° F. Bake the casserole for about 30 minutes, until the vegetables are tender.

Serves 20, as part of buffet.

NOTE: The Coach Farms goat cheesemaker ages cheese into grating sticks. Because the flavor is stronger and more intense, you will need to use less of these sticks than other hard grating cheeses.

PLANNING AHEAD: This dish, without the final sprinkling of cheese, can be assembled 1 day ahead, covered, and kept in the refrigerator. When ready to bake, top with the grated cheese. Serve hot or at room temperature.

Slices of fresh tomatoes and zucchini sprinkled with garlic and basil, ready to be baked.

A dinner plate filled with portions of the four hot buffet dishes: Swiss chard, currant, and rabbit pie; garlic, tomato, and zucchini casserole; lamb stew with tomatoes and green olives; and polenta with eggplant and peppers.

Seasoned Lamb Stew with
Tomatoes and Green Olives

Green olives are simply unripe olives. When cooked, they impart a unique flavor to many Mediterranean dishes.

2¼ cups pure olive oil

3 sprigs fresh rosemary, leaves picked, finely chopped

10 sprigs fresh savory or thyme, leaves picked, finely chopped

1 tablespoon chopped fresh garlic

1 tablespoon chopped fresh chilies or 1 teaspoon dried chili flakes

1 tablespoon coarse salt

½ teaspoon freshly ground black pepper

2 tablespoons each coriander seeds and fennel seeds, ground in a spice grinder

1 teaspoon allspice

1 boneless leg of lamb (about 7 to 8 pounds), trimmed and cut into 2-inch cubes

4 pounds fresh ripe tomatoes, or 2 large (28-ounce) cans plum tomatoes in puree or their own juice

2 medium onions, finely chopped

6 sprigs fresh basil, leaves picked

½ cup balsamic vinegar

3 cups large green imported olives, pitted

4 tablespoons honey, if needed to counteract acidity of tomatoes

1. Combine 1 cup of the olive oil with the rosemary, savory or thyme, garlic, chilies or chili flakes, salt, and pepper in a large bowl.

2. Combine the coriander, fennel, and allspice in a sauté pan and heat over medium heat until they begin to "bloom" and smell fragrant. Let cool, then combine with the other herbs and spices in the large bowl. Add the lamb cubes, toss to coat, and marinate in the refrigerator for 24 to 48 hours.

3. Remove the lamb from the marinade. Heat 1 cup of the remaining oil in a large sauté pan set over high heat. Add the lamb in batches and brown quickly and evenly. The lamb can also be browned by spreading the cubes out on a baking sheet and browning in a 450° F oven, then turning over to brown the other side.

4. If using fresh tomatoes, wash and core them, then blanch them rapidly in boiling water to make it easy to remove the skins. Cut the skinned tomatoes in half, squeeze out the seeds, and hand chop or coarsely chop in a food processor. If using canned tomatoes, drain in a colander over a bowl, saving the juice. Break the tomatoes

open over the bowl to catch their juice, then chop as above. Strain the reserved tomato liquid and add to the chopped tomatoes.

5. Heat the remaining ¼ cup oil in an 8-quart stockpot over high heat. Add the onions and cook for 2 to 3 minutes to soften them. Add the basil and vinegar and cook for 2 minutes more. Add the chopped tomatoes and liquid. Stir in the lamb. Bring the mixture to a boil, then reduce the heat and simmer for 20 minutes. Add the olives and cook approximately 25 minutes more, until the meat is tender. Halfway through the cooking process taste the stew and add a little honey for sweetness if the tomatoes are very acidic.

Serves 20, as part of buffet.

PLANNING AHEAD: Like most stewed dishes, this one improves in flavor when made a day or two ahead and kept in the refrigerator. Simmer slowly for about 15 to 20 minutes to reheat, stirring occasionally.

Baked Polenta with Eggplant and Peppers

Polenta is an Italian version of cornmeal porridge. Baked with vegetables and cheese and sliced into wedges, this firm-textured polenta dish is perfect for buffets and can also be used as a vegetarian main course.

2 medium eggplants or 5 small
    eggplants, cut into 1-inch cubes
2 tablespoons coarse salt
4 large bell peppers in assorted
    colors, such as green, red, yellow,
    or purple
1¼ cups extra-virgin olive oil
1 tablespoon chopped fresh garlic

8 sprigs fresh thyme, oregano, or
    basil, leaves picked
4 quarts water or stock (chicken or
    vegetable)
4 cups dried quick-cooking polenta
    (see Note)
10 ounces fresh mozzarella, cut into
    1-inch cubes

1. Place the eggplant cubes in a large colander, sprinkle with coarse salt, toss, and let rest for at least 30 minutes to drain excess moisture.

2. Preheat the oven to 450° F. Toss the peppers in ¼ cup of the oil and place in an ovenproof skillet or roasting pan. Roast about 8 minutes to blister and blacken the skins. Using tongs, turn the peppers over and roast 7 minutes more. Do not over-

roast. When cool enough to handle, pull out the top stem and remove the seeds and skin. Pat dry. Cut into 1-inch dice and set aside.

3. Pour the remaining oil into a large skillet and heat over high heat. Add the drained eggplant and cook for 2 minutes, stirring. Add the garlic and fresh herbs and cook 2 minutes more, until the eggplant is soft. Remove from the heat and add the roasted peppers.

4. Fill a 6-quart pot with salted water or stock and bring to a boil. Add the polenta in a steady stream, whisking until smooth. Cook over medium-low heat for 15 minutes, stirring frequently with a wooden spoon or spatula. Pour into a large baking dish or casserole. Spread the eggplant-pepper mixture evenly over the polenta, pressing it down with a wooden spoon. Top with the mozzarella cubes, pressing lightly.

5. Preheat the oven to 375° F. Bake the casserole for approximately 25 minutes, until the cheese is melted.

Serves 20, as part of buffet.

NOTE: I prefer to use quick-cooking polenta because it requires less water and has a mellower flavor than regular cornmeal.

PLANNING AHEAD: This dish can be assembled 1 day ahead, kept in the refrigerator, and baked close to serving time. Increase the baking time by about 20 to 25 minutes if the unbaked casserole is cold.

Roasted Whole Garlic

Roasting gives garlic a creamy mellow taste. For this buffet we cut the roasted bulbs in half so guests could squeeze the soft pulp onto bread or use it to enhance the flavor of other dishes.

20 whole bulbs garlic   **Olive oil**

1. Prepare the garlic for roasting in one of 3 ways:
    a. Rub the bulbs with oil and wrap each one individually in foil.
    b. Place the bulbs in a terra-cotta garlic roaster.

c. Place the bulbs in a roasting pan big enough to fit them snugly, and sprinkle with a small amount of oil. Cover the pan with foil.

2. Preheat the oven to 325° F. Roast the garlic for about 1 hour, until soft.

Serves 20, as part of buffet.

PLANNING AHEAD: Garlic can be roasted up to 5 days ahead and kept covered in the refrigerator. Serve cold or reheated.

Wine-Poached Fruits

Poached in wine, lemon, and spices, this fragrant compote is truly sublime.

2½ cups sweet white wine, such as a
 Greek retsina
½ cup honey
Juice and zest of 1 lemon
2 cinnamon sticks

2 bay leaves
5 large ripe pears, peeled, cored, and
 cut into eighths
40 seedless grapes
10 to 15 fresh figs

1. In a 6-quart pot combine the wine, honey, lemon juice and zest, cinnamon, and bay leaves. Bring to a boil over high heat, then reduce the heat, add the pears, and simmer until pears are tender, about 10 minutes.

2. Remove the pot from the heat and immediately add the grapes and figs. Let the mixture cool to room temperature. The grapes and figs will cook in the hot poaching liquid.

Serves 20.

PLANNING AHEAD: This dessert can be made up to 1 week ahead and kept in the refrigerator.

Anise Cake

Anise has a pleasant licorice taste and lovely fragrance and is commonly used in Mediterranean cooking. Here I've used it to flavor a simple sponge cake that I serve with poached fruits and ice cream. But if you are short on time, you can always substitute ready-made biscotti.

3 cups all-purpose flour, sifted, or cake flour	**12 eggs**
	¼ cup anisette liqueur
1½ teaspoons ground aniseed	**1¾ cups sugar**
1 teaspoon ground fennel seed	

1. Prepare two 4 × 8-inch loaf pans or two 9-inch cake pans by lining with parchment paper or greasing and flouring. Preheat the oven to 300° F.

2. Sift together the flour, aniseed, and fennel. In the bowl of an electric mixer, combine the eggs, liqueur, and sugar. Whip until tripled in volume and very airy and light. Fold in the flour-spice mixture, working quickly, until completely incorporated.

3. Pour the batter evenly into the pans. Bake immediately for approximately 25 to 35 minutes, until the cake is golden in color and springs back when touched with your finger. Let cool in the pans.

Makes 2 loaves or 9-inch round cakes.

VARIATION: Instead of using parchment paper, grease the pans with butter and sprinkle the bottoms with finely chopped nuts. Pour the batter in and bake the cakes in a 325° F oven for about 40 minutes.

PLANNING AHEAD: This cake is best served the same day it is baked. However, if wrapped tightly in plastic wrap, it will keep for 1 day.

Lavender Ice Cream

Lavender grows wild on the hillsides of the Mediterranean region and is used in various dishes, mostly desserts.

2 teaspoons fresh or dried lavender flowers (see Note)
1½ cups sugar
1½ cups milk

12 egg yolks
1½ cups heavy cream or Crème Fraîche (page 273)

1. Place the lavender flowers and sugar in a food processor and blend well, until the lavender becomes powdery. This can also be done with a mortar and pestle.

2. In a large mixing bowl, combine the lavender sugar and milk, stirring to dissolve the sugar. In another large bowl, whisk together the egg yolks and cream or crème fraîche until thoroughly combined. Pour the milk mixture into the egg-cream mixture and blend well.

3. Pour the mixture into an ice cream freezer and freeze according to the manufacturer's instructions, at least 4 hours.

Makes 20 scoops.

NOTE: Do not confuse fresh or dried lavender flowers with the scented lavender flowers used in potpourri, which are not meant to be eaten. Buy unscented lavender for cooking purposes in a health-food or good spice store.

PLANNING AHEAD: This ice cream can be made up to 1 week ahead and kept in the freezer.

The dessert table. COUNTERCLOCKWISE FROM LOWER LEFT: *Slices of anise cake; fresh grapes and figs; lavender ice cream in stemmed glasses; wine-poached fruit compote.*

White Sangria with Fruits

In the summer white sangria is a refreshing change from white wine. Be sure to serve it very cold.

4 bottles white wine
3 cups raspberries or blackberries
3 cups fresh peaches, peeled, pitted, and thinly sliced
¾ cup sugar

Optional: **1 cup peach brandy**
¾ cup fresh orange juice
¼ cup fresh lime juice
1½ quarts sparkling water, well chilled

1. Stir together the wine, berries, peaches, sugar, optional brandy, orange juice, and lime juice in a large pitcher. Keep refrigerated.
2. Just before serving, stir in the sparkling water.

Serves 20.

PLANNING AHEAD: You can combine all the ingredients, except the sparkling water, 1 day ahead.

Fresh Grape Juice

This is healthy nonalcoholic juice for children and adults alike. You can use any kind of grape you prefer, but don't use Concord or sour grapes unless you want to add sugar, which I think defeats the purpose of fresh juice.

6 pounds grapes

1. Wash the grapes and feed whole into a juice extractor. The machine will strain out all the skin, seeds, and pulp.
2. Pour the juice into a serving pitcher and chill if desired.

Makes about 2 quarts juice.

PLANNING AHEAD: This juice can be made 1 day ahead and kept chilled in the refrigerator.

A Wedding Celebration

Weddings are a time of union and reunion: the joyous union of two sweethearts and the reunion of their families and friends. With everyone coming together to celebrate love, marriage, and happily ever after, how could the spirit of a wedding party be anything but upbeat?

I have staged many wedding parties over the years and love doing them. Each one is challenging in its own way. Talking to the couples, listening to their ideas, and creating a party that meets their hearts' desire and budget is exciting. There are always stressful moments, but overall I find weddings great fun.

Although I do full sit-down dinners, I find that most couples want a buffet when their wedding is at home or in a rented location. If they want a sit-down meal, they generally choose a hotel, club, or restaurant. Buffet wedding receptions have many advantages, among them:

—A wider variety of foods can be offered, with more choices for guests.

—It's easy to accommodate the person who wants seconds, or an unexpected guest or two.

—Less service staff is required than for a plated dinner.

—Guests tend to mingle more freely, and dancing is more spontaneous.

—A beautifully designed buffet table can be a focal point for the party.

—The buffet table doubles as a space to serve cake, sweets, coffees, and teas.

The wedding photographed here, for 140 guests, was held on a Saturday in midsummer in Washington, Connecticut. The bride wanted to be married at sunset on her family's property and to have the reception at the Washington Club, a charming old country school building on the town green. Guests parked at the club and were brought to the house by hired mini-buses around 6:15 P.M. Here they were offered drinks and passed hors d'oeuvres, and invited to snack from an appetizer table. It was a beautiful day, but we had a tent ready "just in case" for the cocktail reception and ceremony. At about 7:45 the sun went down, and the ceremony took place. Afterward, guests departed for the club while the family lingered to take some photographs.

For many weddings, the ceremony is followed by a receiving line, hors d'oeuvres, and then the reception. But in other situations, like this one, it makes sense to offer hors d'oeuvres first so when the guests arrive at the reception they are not completely ravenous. At the Washington Club we offered an open bar and had a platter of cheeses and other small snacks set out for those who needed a little something more before the buffet. The wedding party arrived about 8:30, and everyone took their assigned seats. On the tables were preset salads as well as assorted breads, butters, and herbed oil. After a champagne toast to the bride and groom, the meal began.

At about 9:00 we opened the double-line buffet. Although the food was identical on both sides of the buffet, I used different platters and serving pieces, mixing silver, brass, copper, and porcelain to give the tables a rich and textured look.

After the meal the dancing really kicked in. At about 10:30 the cake—beautifully made to the couple's tastes by my colleague Terry Karpen—was cut. Guests went through the buffet line again for cake with fresh fruits and a few bite-sized sweets. We used one side of the buffet for these desserts and the other side for coffees, teas, and liqueurs.

The decorations for this wedding were simple and beautiful. I work with a rental company called Affairs of the Heart that offers linens in many different colors and patterns. In one of my early meetings with the family we decided on a blue-and-white color scheme, in part because these colors would seem so refreshing and cool on a summer day, and also because the family wanted to use the handsome antique Chinese ginger jars they had been collecting over the years. These jars made beautiful table centerpieces and gave the wedding a unique look. The tables were a generous 60 inches round, so the flower arrangements needed to be tall to be in proportion with not only the tables but also the soaring height of the room's ceiling. Some people worry that it will be difficult for guests to converse over a tall flower arrangement, but the truth is that people rarely try to talk across such a large table anyway. And if you notice, I cinched the flowers in the vase so guests could see around them.

For this double-line buffet we covered two long tables with layers of white and cream banquet cloths, which we swagged and tied with cobalt blue ribbons. The round center table dividing the two buffet lines was covered with a blue floral chintz fabric swagged with grapevines. The flower arrangement on this table consisted of white

At the house before the ceremony a great gnarled basket filled with vegetables and cheeses was set out for guests to nibble on with drinks.

Antique Chinese ginger jars filled with flowers and fruits were placed on each set table.

roses, delphiniums, daylilies, and freesias mixed with champagne grapes, Queen Anne cherries, and wild greens.

The menu for this country wedding was designed to be simple and to appeal to a broad range of people of all ages and tastes. There was plenty of food, and lots of choices, but it wasn't overwhelming. You really don't need to have thirty different elaborate dishes for a wedding buffet; I much prefer a simple, pretty buffet table with six to eight dishes. More than that seems like overkill to me. When I plan a wedding menu, I tailor it to the season and generally include these elements:

1. An appetizer table and/or four to six hors d'oeuvres of various types passed on trays.

2. A preset appetizer on tables, usually salad or soup.

3. Two entrées, usually fish, poultry, or meat. A sliced beef tenderloin is classic and always popular, but I find I'm asked for beef less and less these days.

4. One or two starch dishes: pasta, rice, grains, or polenta.

5. Two vegetable dishes, one of which is completely vegetarian (with no cheese or dairy).

6. Sauces or condiments on the buffet table near the dishes they are meant to complement.

7. Bread, rolls, biscuits, and a variety of flavored butters and/or herbed oils. I prefer to put breads in baskets on the guest tables rather than on the buffet table, especially when there is a preset appetizer. It's awkward to try to balance bread on top of buffet plates.

8. Wedding cake. People love different flavored cakes, especially chocolate. Some favorites include, for example, triple chocolate cake with chocolate mousse filling and white chocolate buttercream frosting, or hazelnut cake with apricot and blackberry mousse filling and buttercream frosting.

9. Other sweets or desserts, such as fresh berry salads, dipped fruits, bite-sized cookies, or tartlets.

10. Coffees, teas, and liqueurs.

When you are planning a wedding reception, whether at home or in a rented space, whether working with a caterer or doing it yourself, there are myriad details to consider. Although it's unnecessary to run a party with the precision of the Swiss railway, it is very important to be organized. Keep a notebook for lists, floor plans, and miscellaneous ideas. Start with a basic plan, and build from there. Here is the framework I use in the early stages of planning wedding parties and other large celebrations.

The reception room at the Washington Club set up before the guests arrived.

Basic Considerations

—Budget.

—Season of the year, date, and time of party.

—Location. Will tents be needed?

—Number of guests. Will there be children?

—Type of menu: Luncheon, dinner, hors d'oeuvres only?

—Open or limited bar. (See pages xii–xiii for details on bar setup.)

—Music and dancing.

After these questions have been answered, I move on to other details, such as:

Rented Sites

—Does the site fit the style of the wedding?

—How many guests can be accommodated comfortably? Is the site large enough?

—Parking—is it adequate? Will attendants be needed?

—What furniture and tableware is included? What will need to be rented?

Tents

—Is the terrain suitable for tents?

—How many will be needed, and what size?

—What about electricity and water? Lavatory facilities?

—How will tent poles and walls be decorated? Sprays of flowers, greens, grapevines, streamers, fabric swags, large plants?

Setup

—Draw a floor plan of the room, detailing placement of bars, buffet tables, and guest tables, as well as the dance floor area and other tables that might be needed for the cake and gifts. Assign guests to specific tables.

—Keep in mind that it takes professional crews two to three hours to set up completely, including tables, chairs, linens, tableware, flowers, and decorations. If you are doing it yourself, allow three-and-a-half to four hours to set up a party for one hundred people so you will have time to take care of any unexpected details before guests arrive.

—Make sure the lighting in the room is adequate, not too dim or too harsh. Will candles be used? What type—votive or stem?

LINENS AND TABLEWARE

—Order extra linens for the tables, especially the buffet table. Once the buffet dishes are cleared a fresh cloth can be laid on top, and the table can be used again for desserts and coffee.

—Allow two to two and a half cocktail glasses per person if there will be an open bar throughout the party. An all-purpose stemmed glass is simplest. For each place setting, you will need to have water and wine goblets, and a champagne flute if you are having a toast.

—Flatware depends on the menu, but usually includes a salad fork or soup spoon; dinner fork and knife; dessert fork and teaspoon. Butter knives are optional. Always allow 10 percent more dessert flatware than there are guests because by the end of a wedding there is a lot of table-hopping.

—Plates also depend on the menu, but usually include appetizer or salad plates; dinner or oversized buffet plates; bread-and-butter plates; dessert plates; and cups and saucers or mugs.

—Don't forget salt and pepper shakers on the tables, sugars and creamers (these can also be placed on the buffet table with the coffee service), and, if you choose, wedding favors, disposable cameras, and so on.

DECORATIONS AND FLOWERS

—Personal touches can be charming. If you love ribbons and lace, by all means use them. White on white can be a lovely color scheme, as can a vivid palette of colors.

—For a different look, instead of premade skirting, try using ribbons and fabric to bunch and swag table coverings.

—Use local, in-season flowers, even roadside flowers, for a more natural look with less expense. I often combine flowers with fruits and vegetables, which can make a spectacular display and highlight some of the foods guests will be tasting on the wedding menu. For this summer wedding, I used champagne grapes and Queen

The buffet table arrangement of flowers, fruits, and vegetables also included "something old, something new, something borrowed, something blue."

Anne cherries with garden flowers. For an autumn wedding, I might use squashes, whole eggplants, and tomatillos, for example, combined with fall flowers.

STAFF

—Keep a detailed list of paid staff, including kitchen helpers, serving staff, bartenders, parking attendants, and clean-up crew, noting their rates and contracted hours. Clearly outline each person's job.
—Coordinate the duties of the photographer, caterer, and band or DJ so that the timing of announcements, toasts, and other events is smooth.

Last, if all of this seems like too much work, do what my husband and I did instead—get married at city hall and have a quiet romantic dinner afterward! Good luck!

A Wedding Celebration
for 50

HORS D'OEUVRES
A Cheese and Vegetable Basket

Zucchini Squash Pancakes

Fresh Crabmeat and Cheese Triangles

Seared Tuna Niçoise

Grilled Grape-Leaf-Wrapped Peanut Beef

PRESET APPETIZER
Field Greens Salad with Local Tomatoes and Radish Curls

Creamy Whole-Grain Mustard Dressing

BUFFET DINNER
Horseradish-Crusted Sea Bass Fillets

Dilled Cucumbers

Trio of Rices and Beans with Fresh Apricots

Breast of Chicken Venus

Crunchy Vegetable Medley ◆ Fresh Chive Vinaigrette

Herbed Cheese Polenta Hearts

DESSERT
"Queen of Hearts" Chocolate Buttermilk
Wedding Cake with Mixed Berries and Peaches

Zucchini Squash Pancakes

These delicious vegetable pancakes are an excellent showcase for zucchini, which is so abundant during the summer.

25 medium zucchini, washed and
   stems cut
Zest of 3 lemons
2 tablespoons coarse salt
2½ cups grated Parmesan cheese
2 cups chopped fresh flat-leaf
   parsley
1 cup chopped fresh basil leaves
1 teaspoon freshly ground black
   pepper

4½ to 5 cups all-purpose flour
2½ cups vegetable oil, for cooking

TOPPING:
Goat cheese, roasted tomatoes, or
   fruit chutney

Optional garnish: Nasturtium leaves

1. Using the large-hole side of a hand grater or the medium blade setting on a mandoline, slice the zucchini into julienne strips, rotating the zucchini to use only the flesh and not the seeds. Place the zucchini in a large mixing bowl.

2. Toss the zucchini with the lemon zest and salt and let sit for approximately 8 minutes, until the zucchini starts to soften. Add the Parmesan cheese, parsley, basil, and pepper and toss well.

3. Start adding the flour a little at a time, mixing well after each addition. When you have added about 4½ cups flour, make a test pancake about the size of a silver dollar in your hand. If the ingredients bind together but aren't too pasty the pancake is ready to cook.

4. Heat a few tablespoons of oil in a large skillet over high heat. Reduce the heat to medium and fry the pancakes in batches for approximately 2 to 3 minutes per side, until golden. Remove to absorbent towels to drain. Repeat the process with the remaining pancakes, adding more oil for each 1 or 2 batches.

5. Just before serving, top the pancakes with goat cheese, roasted tomatoes, or fruit chutney. Garnish each pancake with a nasturtium leaf if you like.

Makes 90 to 100 1½-inch pancakes.

PLANNING AHEAD: The zucchini can be shredded, and the herbs chopped, up to 1 day ahead and kept covered in the refrigerator. Mix the ingredients together up to 1 hour before you plan to cook the pancakes. The cooked pancakes can be made up

One of the passed hors d'oeuvres: Zucchini squash pancakes topped with goat cheese and nasturtium leaves on a simple basket tray.

to 8 hours before you plan to serve them and reheated on a baking sheet in a 250° F oven for about 3 minutes. Garnish right before serving.

Fresh Crabmeat and Cheese Triangles

This is just a simple grilled crab and cheese sandwich cut into bite-size pieces—a delectable hors d'oeuvre.

3 pounds fresh crabmeat
1 cup mayonnaise, preferably
   homemade (page 64)
1 tablespoon Dijon-style mustard
½ cup chopped fresh parsley
Optional: 12 sprigs fresh tarragon,
   leaves picked and chopped
Coarse salt and freshly ground black
   pepper to taste

6 ounces (1½ sticks) unsalted butter,
   softened
1 loaf thinly sliced white or whole-
   wheat bread (26 to 28 pieces)
26 to 28 pieces thinly sliced Swiss
   cheese

1. Drain the crabmeat, discard any shell, and squeeze lightly to remove excess liquid.

2. In a large bowl, combine the mayonnaise with mustard, parsley, and tarragon (if using). Carefully and quickly fold in the crabmeat. Taste for seasoning and correct with salt and pepper if needed. Cover the bowl and set aside in the refrigerator.

3. Divide the bread slices into two stacks. Carefully spread a thin layer of butter on one side of all the pieces in one stack, and arrange the bread, buttered side down, on parchment- or plastic-covered baking sheets. Place a piece of Swiss cheese on top, spread evenly with 2 tablespoons of the crabmeat mixture, and top with another slice of cheese. Butter the other stack of bread and place 1 piece, buttered side out, on top of each sandwich. If not grilling immediately, set aside in the refrigerator.

4. In a large, heavy-bottomed skillet over medium heat, grill the sandwiches, in batches, until golden on one side, about 2 to 3 minutes. Flip over and grill on the other side. Remove the sandwiches to a cutting board, slice off the crusts, and cut each sandwich into 4 triangles.

Makes 52 to 56 triangles.

PLANNING AHEAD: The sandwiches can be assembled up to 1 day ahead and refrigerated. They can be grilled up to 3 hours ahead and reheated in a 250° F oven for about 2 to 3 minutes before serving.

Seared Tuna Niçoise

This tasty canapé, which features fresh tuna, olives, and garlic, captures the spirit of Provence.

1 tablespoon pure olive oil

2 pieces (6 to 8 ounces each) fresh tuna, approximately 1½ inches wide by 4½ inches long

12 small new potatoes, roasted until tender and cooled (see technique on page 12)

Optional: 15 ripe cherry tomatoes

25 green beans, blanched until just tender

½ cup Garlic Aioli (recipe follows)

1 cup Olive Tapenade (page 8)

1. Heat the oil in a large skillet over high heat. Add the tuna and sear quickly on all sides, leaving it rare. Set aside.

2. Cut each potato into 5 slices. Cut each piece of tuna into 30 slices. If using cherry tomatoes, cut each one into 4 slices. Slice the green beans on the diagonal into 1-inch pieces.

3. Lay out the potato slices on a tray and spread with a small amount of Garlic Aioli. Top each with a slice of tuna and cherry tomato, a dab of Olive Tapenade, and 2 pieces of green bean.

Makes 60 hors d'oeuvres.

PLANNING AHEAD: The fish, potatoes, and green beans can be cooked up to 1 day ahead. Assemble the hors d'oeuvres up to 2 hours ahead and keep covered in the refrigerator until ready to serve.

Garlic Aioli

Aioli is simply mayonnaise to which blanched garlic has been added.

10 cloves garlic, peeled   **1 cup Homemade Mayonnaise**
                                                      (page 64)

1. Place the garlic in a small saucepan, cover with water, and bring to a boil over high heat. Drain. Add more cold water to cover, bring back to a boil, and drain. Add water a third time, boil, and drain one more time. This process mellows the garlic and makes it more digestible.

2. Let the garlic cool. Place the mayonnaise in a food processor. With the motor running, drop the garlic down the feed tube and puree until smooth.

Makes 1 cup.

PLANNING AHEAD: Aioli can be prepared up to 1 week ahead and kept in a covered container in the refrigerator.

Grilled Grape-Leaf-Wrapped Peanut Beef

This recipe is inspired by the Vietnamese dish called Bo La Lot. In the summertime in Connecticut I pick fresh wild grape leaves, which have a wonderful flavor. I blanch them in water and vinegar to soften them. Commercial grape leaves packed in brine can also be used.

**50 grape leaves, fresh and blanched,
   or packed in brine**
2 pounds fresh lean chopped beef
1 cup ground roasted peanuts
3 medium carrots, finely minced
10 cloves garlic, finely minced
1 large onion, finely minced
Zest of 2 lemons, chopped
**1 tablespoon Asian fish sauce
   (see Note on page 44)**

1 tablespoon soy sauce
2 teaspoons sugar
**½ teaspoon freshly ground black
   pepper**
**Approximately ¾ cup pure Asian
   sesame oil, for grilling**

Garnish: **2 bunches scallions, finely
   chopped**

1. Wash the grape leaves packed in brine in cold water to remove the saltiness. Cut off the stems with a sharp knife, working carefully so you don't tear the leaves.

2. In a large mixing bowl, combine the beef, all but 2 tablespoons of the peanuts, the carrots, garlic, onion, chopped zest, fish sauce, soy sauce, sugar, and pepper. Mix well to incorporate all of the ingredients completely. Let mixture rest for 30 minutes.

3. Lay the grape leaves out on a worktable. Place approximately 1 tablespoon of the beef mixture on the narrow part of each leaf. Fold the sides in and over, then roll up to form a neat envelope-like packet.

4. Prepare a grill. Brush the packets with sesame oil and grill over medium heat for approximately 5 minutes, turning once, until meat inside feels firm to the touch. Remove to a platter, brush with a little more oil, and sprinkle with the reserved peanuts and the scallions.

Makes 50 hors d'oeuvres.

PLANNING AHEAD: The grape leaves can be stuffed up to 2 days ahead and kept covered in the refrigerator on a platter or tray brushed with oil. Grill them up to 6 hours ahead, and reheat in a low (250° F) oven for about 2 minutes. Garnish right before serving.

Another passed hors d'oeuvre: Grilled grape-leaf-wrapped peanut beef with a peanut dipping sauce.

Field Greens Salad with Local Tomatoes
and Radish Curls

There's nothing better than garden tomatoes. For this wedding I served them with mixed field greens.

4 pounds baby lettuce leaves
6 bunches arugula
6 bunches other mixed greens, such
   as curlycress, mizuna, tatsoi,
   chicory, Lola Rosa, or purslane
2 medium heads radicchio, shredded
1 cup chopped fresh herbs, such as
   chervil, parsley, basil, or tarragon

5 bunches (about 50 to 60) radishes
12 tomatoes, each cut into 8 wedges
Creamy Whole-Grain Mustard
   Dressing, for serving (recipe
   follows)

1. Wash all of the lettuces in cold water in the sink or a large basin. Lift out and dry using a salad spinner, basket, or absorbent towels. Place the greens in a large tub, cover with a damp cloth, and keep in the refrigerator until ready to use.

2. Clean the radishes, trim the ends, and cut into curls with an Asian spiral cutter. Leave in cold water until ready to use.

3. Toss the greens with the radicchio and herbs in a large bowl. Divide the salad among individual plates, and top with radish curls and tomato wedges. Serve with Creamy Whole-Grain Mustard Dressing on the side.

Serves 50.

PLANNING AHEAD: The lettuce can be washed, dried, and stored in the refrigerator up to 2 days ahead. Curl the radishes up to 1 day ahead, and leave in water in the refrigerator.

Creamy Whole-Grain Mustard Dressing

This creamy dressing is a longtime favorite of mine. It really enhances the flavor of a green salad.

2 cups mayonnaise, preferably
   homemade (page 64)
2 cups plain yogurt
2 cups buttermilk
½ cup whole-grain mustard

¼ cup Dijon-style mustard
½ cup fresh lemon juice
Coarse salt and freshly ground black
   pepper to taste

In a large mixing bowl, whisk together the mayonnaise, yogurt, and buttermilk. Add the whole-grain and Dijon-style mustards and whisk again. Finish with lemon juice, and add salt and pepper to taste.

Makes 7 cups.

PLANNING AHEAD: This dressing will keep for up to 2 weeks in the refrigerator. Whisk again before using.

Horseradish-Crusted Sea Bass Fillets

I have made this simple recipe for numerous parties and always get raves. If bass is not available, substitute another firm-textured fish, such as salmon, grouper, mahimahi, Chilean bass, or walleye pike.

6 (2½- to 3-pound) sea bass fillets,
   skin removed
30 cups unseasoned bread crumbs
   (see Note)
6 cups prepared horseradish, excess
   moisture squeezed out
Juice of 10 oranges
Zest of 3 oranges

20 sprigs fresh tarragon, leaves
   picked and finely chopped
20 sprigs fresh rosemary, leaves
   picked and finely chopped
2½ cups pure or extra-virgin olive
   or grape seed oil
Coarse salt to taste

1. Check the fillets for any bones, and cut or pull them out with needle-nose pliers. Wash the fillets and pat dry. Set aside in the refrigerator until ready to use.

(CONTINUED)

Horseradish-crusted sea bass fillets, garnished with fresh chervil, nasturtiums, and whole shrimp.

2. Place the bread crumbs in a large mixing bowl and add, one ingredient at a time, the horseradish, orange juice, tarragon, rosemary, oil, and salt, mixing well after each addition. The crumbs should hold together, and not be too dry or too wet and pasty.

3. Preheat the oven to 425° F. Lay out the fish fillets on a parchment-lined baking sheet. Pat the crumbs evenly over the fish, completely covering the tops. Bake for approximately 20 to 25 minutes, until the fish is cooked through and the crumbs have colored. Remove from the oven and serve either hot or at room temperature. To serve, either arrange the fillets on a platter and offer a portion to each guest, or cut each fillet into 8 or 9 pieces and let the guests serve themselves.

Serves 50, as part of buffet.

NOTE: To make your own bread crumbs, use at least day-old bread, preferably peasant, sourdough, or whole-grain, or French baguettes. Grate with the grater blade in a food processor. I often keep the ends of bread in the freezer; when I have enough, I make crumbs.

PLANNING AHEAD: The bread crumb mix can be made up to 8 days ahead and stored in a covered container in the refrigerator. The coated fish can be baked up to 1 day ahead, refrigerated, and then reheated in a 300° F oven for about 20 minutes.

Dilled Cucumbers

This is a traditional Eastern European recipe from my grandmother. In this menu the cucumbers go particularly well with the fish, but they are also good on their own as a salad or cold plate.

30 European or 40 domestic cucumbers	**2 cups plain yogurt**
Coarse salt	**2 cups fresh chopped dill**
24 large cloves garlic, peeled and finely chopped	**Zest and juice of 2 lemons**
2 cups sour cream	**2 teaspoons freshly ground black pepper**

1. Peel the cucumbers and cut in half lengthwise. Scrape out any seeds and slice into $\frac{1}{16}$-inch pieces with a sharp knife or mandoline. Place a colander over a bowl. Put a layer of cucumbers in the bottom of the colander, sprinkle liberally with salt, and continue layering until all of the cucumbers are in the colander. Cover with plastic

wrap, put a plate on top, and weight down with a can for up to 12 hours. This procedure will remove a lot of liquid from the cucumbers. Drain and discard the liquid as often as necessary.

2. Place the cucumbers in a large bowl and toss with the garlic, sour cream, yogurt, dill, lemon juice and zest, and pepper. Taste for seasoning. Refrigerate until ready to serve.

Serves 50, as part of buffet.

PLANNING AHEAD: The cucumbers can be prepared up to 3 days in advance and kept covered in the refrigerator. Don't mix them with the other ingredients too far in advance, however, because cucumbers, even when pressed, continue to give off more liquid, which will dilute the dressing.

Trio of Rices and Beans with Fresh Apricots

I like to use different combinations of grains and legumes for flavor and texture in this recipe. Vegetables and fruit embellish the dish and add even more texture.

WILD RICE:

½ cup vegetable oil

2 medium onions, diced

12 sprigs fresh thyme, leaves picked

2 pounds wild rice

4 quarts cold water

2 teaspoons coarse salt, or to taste

BASMATI RICE:

1½ cups vegetable oil

4 pinches saffron threads

6 cups basmati rice

9 cups salted water

WHITE BEANS:

½ cup vegetable oil

3 bunches (about 4 to 6) leeks, washed, trimmed, and finely diced

2 tablespoons fresh chopped garlic

2 bunches fresh oregano, leaves picked and chopped (about 1 cup)

3 sprigs fresh rosemary, leaves picked and chopped

2 bunches fresh thyme, leaves picked and chopped (about ½ cup)

4 cups dried white beans, soaked in water from 3 to 24 hours to soften, and drained

7 cups water seasoned with salt and pepper, or vegetable stock

OTHER INGREDIENTS:

2 bunches celery, cut into small diagonal pieces

24 fresh apricots, pitted and sliced into 4 to 6 pieces

6 bunches fresh chervil, chopped (about 3 cups)

2 cups sherry vinegar

3 cups vegetable or pure olive oil

1. To cook the wild rice, heat the oil in a 6-quart pot over high heat. Add the onions and thyme and cook until the onions are wilted. Stir in the wild rice. Cook 3 minutes, stirring to coat the rice. Add the cold water and salt and cover the pot. Bring to a boil over high heat, then reduce the heat to medium and cook for 35 to 40 minutes, until the liquid is evaporated and the rice begins to "bloom" or pop open. Set aside.

2. To cook the basmati rice, heat ½ cup of the oil in a 4-quart pot over high heat. Add the saffron and let "bloom" for 30 seconds. Add the basmati rice and stir to coat with the saffron and oil. Add the salted water, stir, and bring to a boil over high heat. Stir in the remaining 1 cup oil, and let the rice simmer for 12 to 15 minutes, until cooked through and dry. Remove from the heat and spread out on a tray to cool. Set aside.

3. To cook the white beans, heat the oil in a 4-quart pot. Add the leeks and cook over high heat for 2 minutes, until wilted. Add the garlic, oregano, rosemary, and thyme and cook for 1 to 2 minutes more. Add the white beans and stir to coat. Pour in 7 cups seasoned water or vegetable stock, stir, cover, and bring to a boil over high heat. Reduce the heat to a simmer and cook approximately 40 minutes, until the beans are tender but not mushy. Remove from the heat and let cool.

4. In a large bowl, combine the wild and basmati rices. Toss in the beans, then the celery, apricots, and chervil. Whisk together the sherry vinegar and oil and sprinkle over the dish to your taste.

Serves 50, as part of buffet.

PLANNING AHEAD: The rices and beans can be cooked up to 4 days ahead, cooled, covered, and refrigerated. The dish can be assembled up to 8 hours ahead.

Breast of Chicken Venus

Boneless chicken pieces tossed with fresh and roasted vegetables make a simple yet impressive entrée for a large gathering. This dish is delicious served warm, cold, or at room temperature.

15 pounds boneless, skinless chicken breasts
2 bunches fresh tarragon, leaves picked and chopped (about 2 cups)
Coarse salt and freshly ground black pepper to taste
2 cups vegetable oil, for cooking
3 cups extra-virgin olive oil
16 cloves garlic
15 sprigs fresh thyme
5 pounds cremini mushrooms, stems removed

12 large red bell peppers, oven roasted (see technique on page 102) and cut into large dice
12 medium or 24 small artichoke hearts or bottoms, blanched
5 bulbs fennel, thinly slivered, sprinkled with lemon juice
4 large bunches fresh basil, leaves shredded (about 4 cups)
3 cups balsamic vinegar
4 bunches broccoli, florets only, blanched

1. Cut the chicken into 2-inch pieces, removing the excess fat and tendons. Sprinkle with the tarragon, salt, and pepper.

2. Heat a small amount of the vegetable oil in a large skillet. Add the chicken in batches and cook over high heat for approximately 10 to 12 minutes per batch, until seared and cooked through. Or lay out the chicken pieces on an oiled sheet pan and bake in a 400° F oven approximately 20 minutes. Remove to a large mixing bowl.

3. Preheat the oven to 400° F. Pour 1 cup of the olive oil into a rimmed baking sheet and sprinkle with the garlic, thyme, salt, and pepper. Lay the mushrooms on top, gill side down, and sprinkle with the remaining oil. Roast for approximately 10 to 12 minutes. Remove from the heat and let cool in the pan.

4. Toss the mushrooms and their liquid with the chicken in the bowl. One by one, add the bell peppers, artichokes, fennel, and basil, tossing after each addition. Toss with the balsamic vinegar and taste for seasoning. Just before serving, add the broccoli (don't add it earlier or it will lose its color).

Serves 50, as part of buffet.

PLANNING AHEAD: The peppers and mushrooms can be roasted, and the artichokes blanched, up to 4 days ahead. The chicken can be cut into pieces up to 2 days ahead and kept in a covered container in the refrigerator. The whole dish can be made up to 1 day ahead and refrigerated. Add the blanched broccoli just before serving.

The same foods were offered on two different tables for this double-line buffet. Visually separating the two buffets was an impressive flower and fruit arrangement on a round chintz-covered table.

Crunchy Vegetable Medley

You can make this medley with many different vegetables, such as asparagus, broccoli, or zucchini.

10 cups fresh corn kernels (about 24 ears)

3 pounds sugar snap peas, ends picked

3 cups fresh English peas

3 pounds baby green beans (*haricots verts*), ends picked

3 cups shelled and shucked fresh fava beans

6 pounds medium carrots, peeled and julienned

6 cups fresh bean sprouts

3 large jicama, peeled and julienned

Optional: 25 small beets, cut in half or julienned

Fresh Chive Vinaigrette, for serving (recipe follows)

1. In separate pots, steam or blanch the corn, peas, green beans, and fava beans, until each is cooked but still crunchy. Plunge the vegetables into an ice bath, drain, and store in the refrigerator until ready to use.

2. In a large bowl, combine the cooked vegetables with the julienned carrots, bean sprouts, jicama, and optional beets. Just before serving, toss with the Fresh Chive Vinaigrette or offer dressing on the side.

Serves 50, as part of buffet.

PLANNING AHEAD: The vegetables can be prepared up to 2 days ahead, and cooked up to 1 day ahead. Do not toss them with the dressing until right before serving because the acid in the vinaigrette will discolor the green vegetables.

Fresh Chive Vinaigrette

A vibrant green, mild-flavored vinaigrette that can accompany many different salads and vegetables.

Approximately 60 fresh chive stalks, or 3 bunches scallions, coarsely chopped
2 cups white wine vinegar or champagne vinegar

6 cups grape seed oil or vegetable oil
Coarse salt and freshly ground black pepper to taste

1. Place the chives or scallions in a blender (see Note), add the vinegar, and blend briefly to combine. Add the oil in a steady stream and blend until emulsified. Season with salt and pepper. Alternatively, you can put all the ingredients in a mixing bowl and blend with an immersion blender.
2. Pour the dressing through a fine-mesh conical strainer or food mill.

Makes 8½ cups.

NOTE: Don't try to use a food processor to combine the ingredients for the vinaigrette; only a blender will work.

PLANNING AHEAD: This vinaigrette can be made up to 3 days ahead and kept in the refrigerator. Whisk or reblend briefly before serving.

Herbed Cheese Polenta Hearts

A sweet accompaniment to the Chicken Venus on this menu.

10 cups water
3 bunches fresh basil, leaves
   shredded (about 3 cups)
Coarse salt and freshly ground black
   pepper to taste

2½ cups dried quick-cooking
   polenta (see Note on page 103)
1½ pounds fresh goat cheese

1. Bring the water to a boil over high heat in a 4-quart pot. When boiling, add basil, salt, and pepper. Whisk in the polenta in a steady stream, stirring with a wooden spoon. It will start to thicken immediately. Reduce the heat to low, add the goat cheese, and cook, stirring, another 6 to 8 minutes; the polenta will be firm.

2. Pour a ¾-inch-thick layer of polenta onto a large sheet pan with at least a 1-inch rim. Make sure the pan is covered evenly. Let cool, then cut into shapes with a 3-inch heart-shaped cutter.

Makes 50 hearts.

PLANNING AHEAD: The polenta can be made up to 3 days ahead, cut into shapes, wrapped in plastic, and stored in the refrigerator. Reheat in a low (250° F) oven for a few minutes before serving.

"Queen of Hearts" Chocolate Buttermilk Wedding Cake

My colleague Terry Karpen, owner of Queen of Hearts in Redding, Connecticut, is an expert pastry chef who creates many of the cakes for the wedding parties I do. She makes them specifically to the couple's tastes, and they are always delicious. This wedding cake—a three-tiered chocolate buttermilk layer cake with a choice of dark chocolate truffle filling, cherry mousse filling, or a combination of both—is rich and moist. The cake serves 60, but there is rarely any left. Guests always ask for seconds.

We have divided the recipe into parts to make it easier to understand. Terry's advice: "Read through the entire equipment list, the ingredients lists, and the recipe instructions before you begin. Plan ahead. Allow plenty of time. Have every component ready before assembling the cake. Don't forget to breathe. And—have fun."

Equipment Needed
(available in cookware shops or cake decorating stores)

3 round cake pans with 2-inch-high sides: 6-inch, 9-inch, and 12-inch

1 6-inch round cardboard

1 9-inch round cardboard

Sturdy base, at least 14 inches round, for wedding cake: 1 cake platter or decorative foil-covered board

5-quart stand-up electric mixer, with 2 bowls if possible

Cake decorating turntable or lazy susan

Metal icing spatula

Plastic drinking straws to support cake tiers

Pastry bag fitted with a plastic coupler

#66 leaf tip

#69 leaf tip

Chocolate Buttermilk Layer Cake

Each tier of this wedding cake consists of 2 layers of cake separated by filling. In her bakery kitchen Terry has a professional 20-quart mixer and extra cake pans, so she can make a double batch of batter and bake all 6 of the layers at the same time in her oven.

(CONTINUED)

The tiered wedding cake—chocolate buttermilk layer cake with dark chocolate truffle filling—simply decorated with roses and ivy.

In a home kitchen, with a standard 5-quart mixer and one set of cake pans, you will need to make the recipe twice.

The following ingredients are for ONE batch of batter.

3 cups all-purpose flour

¾ cup unsweetened cocoa powder

½ teaspoon salt

1½ teaspoons baking soda

1½ teaspoons baking powder

12 ounces (3 sticks) unsalted butter,
   at room temperature

2¼ cups granulated sugar

3 eggs

1½ teaspoons vanilla extract

2¼ cups buttermilk

1. Preheat the oven to 350° F. Butter and flour a 6-inch, 9-inch, and 12-inch round cake pan with 2-inch-high sides.

2. Sift together the flour, cocoa, salt, baking soda, and baking powder. Set aside.

3. In the bowl of an electric mixer cream the butter and sugar together until light and fluffy. Add the eggs, one at a time, beating well after each addition and scraping down the sides of the bowl. Mix in the vanilla.

4. Alternately add the flour mixture and the buttermilk in 2 parts each. Beat on low speed to blend after each addition.

5. Distribute the batter evenly in the prepared pans. Bake 30 minutes, or until the center of the cake springs back when lightly touched.

6. Cool the cakes in the pans on a wire rack. When cool, remove the cakes, wrap in plastic, and chill in the refrigerator until cold.

7. Wash, and then butter and flour the same 6-inch, 9-inch, and 12-inch cake pans.

8. Make a second batch of batter, and proceed as above.

Two batches batter makes two 6-inch, two 9-inch, and two 12-inch round layers; the cake serves 60.

PLANNING AHEAD: The cake layers can be made up to 2 days ahead and kept in the refrigerator. They can also be frozen for several weeks if well wrapped in plastic and foil.

Filling I: Dark Chocolate Truffle

This filling is rich and delicious by itself, or it can be layered with the cherry mousse filling (recipe follows). If you want to use two fillings, divide this recipe in half.

Any leftover filling can be rolled into truffle candies. Dust with cocoa powder if you like.

1½ pounds best-quality bittersweet chocolate
3 cups heavy cream

Optional: **½ cup Grand Marnier or other liqueur**

1. Finely chop the chocolate. Set aside in a large bowl.
2. In a saucepan bring the cream to a simmer. Remove from the heat and pour over the chocolate in the bowl. Stir gently until the chocolate is melted, and the mixture is completely smooth. Stir in the liqueur, if using.
3. Set the filling aside until it is thick enough to spread. This can take from 3 to 12 hours, depending on the room temperature. This filling can remain unrefrigerated for 24 hours. At room temperature it remains spreadable. On a warm day or to save time, place filling in refrigerator. Stir occasionally.

Makes 6 to 6½ cups.

PLANNING AHEAD: This filling can be made up to 3 days ahead and stored in the refrigerator, covered, where it will set. It can also be frozen up to 2 months. Bring to room temperature before using. If filling is too thick to spread, set bowl above a saucepan half filled with hot water over low heat. Stir often.

Filling II: Cherry Mousse

The flavor of this light cherry filling is perfect with the chocolate cake. Divide the recipe in half if you want to spread the layers with some of the dark chocolate truffle filling (above) as well.

Leftover cherry mousse filling can be frozen and served later as a dessert.

1½ pounds fresh cherries, pitted and chopped
¾ cup granulated sugar
8 tablespoons cold water

2 envelopes unflavored gelatin
6 tablespoons cherry preserves
3 tablespoons Kirschwasser liqueur
3 cups heavy cream

1. Combine the cherries with the sugar and 6 tablespoons of the water in a saucepan and bring to a boil over medium heat. Boil for 1 minute, then pour through a strainer held over a bowl. Set the cherries aside and return the liquid to the saucepan. Simmer over medium heat until reduced to 1 cup. Remove from the heat.

2. Moisten the gelatin with the remaining 2 tablespoons water, and let it absorb for 5 minutes. Add to the reduced cherry liquid and stir. Return the saucepan to medium heat and stir until the gelatin is completely dissolved. Stir in the cherries, cherry preserves, and Kirschwasser.

3. In an electric mixer whip the cream until soft peaks form. Gently fold in the cherry mixture, mixing just until combined. Refrigerate for at least 4 hours.

Makes approximately 8 cups.

PLANNING AHEAD: This mousse can be made up to 2 days ahead and kept in a covered container in the refrigerator. It can also be frozen up to 2 months.

Vanilla Buttercream Frosting

When making buttercreams remember to use the best-quality unsalted butter and pure flavorings to get a shiny, stable icing.

To frost this wedding cake you will have to make 2 batches of buttercream. The following ingredients are for ONE batch.

NOTE: It's helpful to have 2 bowls for your electric mixer on hand so you don't waste time washing one out for the second part of the recipe, but it's not absolutely essential.

1 cup milk
1 vanilla bean, split and scraped
2½ cups granulated sugar

14 egg yolks
2¼ pounds unsalted butter, at room temperature

1. In a 4-quart stainless pot combine the milk, vanilla, and half of the sugar. Scald over medium heat. Set aside.

2. In a standing 5-quart electric mixer with the wire whisk attachment beat the egg yolks and remaining sugar until they turn a pale yellow color and a thick ribbon forms from the beater.

3. With the mixer running at medium speed, pour in a third of the milk mixture.

When incorporated, whisk the egg mixture back into the pot with the remaining milk. Bring to a boil over high heat, whisking constantly.

4. Remove from the heat and strain through a fine mesh strainer back into the mixing bowl. With the mixer running on medium speed beat until the mixture doubles in volume. Set aside.

5. In another mixing bowl (or the same one, if you remove the contents and wash it out) beat the butter (with the paddle attachment) 3 to 5 minutes, until it whitens in color and holds soft peaks. With the mixer running, pour the egg/milk mixture in a steady stream down the sides of the bowl. Continue beating on medium speed until the lower part of the bowl is cool, and the buttercream is shiny and silky in texture. The buttercream may separate, but keep beating and it will come back together (see Note below).

Makes 8 cups buttercream.

NOTE: Do not attempt to make buttercream under very hot conditions, because it will separate and not come together even with continual beating.

PLANNING AHEAD: The buttercream can be made up to 1 week ahead and kept in the refrigerator. It can also be frozen up to 2 months; let the buttercream defrost and then re-beat before using.

Assembling the Cake Layers

1. Put one of the 6-inch cake layers on a 6-inch cardboard round. Spread evenly with 1 cup of the truffle filling or 1 cup of the cherry mousse filling or ½ cup of each. If you wish to use two fillings, do this: first spread the cake layer with truffle filling and refrigerate until firm, about 15 minutes. Then spread with the cherry mousse filling. Place the second 6-inch cake on top and gently press the layers together.

2. Put one of the 9-inch cake layers on a 9-inch cardboard round. Spread evenly with 1¾ cups of the truffle filling or 1¾ cups of the cherry mousse filling or a little less than 1 cup of each. Place the second 9-inch cake on top and gently press the layers together.

3. Put one of the 12-inch cake layers on a sturdy cake base. Spread evenly with 3¼ cups of the truffle filling or 3¼ cups of the cherry mousse filling or a little less than 1¾ cups of each. Place the second 12-inch cake on top and gently press the layers together.

NOTE: These filled layer cakes are now called "tiers" in the language of wedding cakes.

Frosting the Tiers

1. Place a cake tier (still on its cardboard base) on a cake decorating turntable or lazy susan. Using a metal icing spatula, frost the sides and then the top of each tier with buttercream frosting. This is called the "crumb coat" and is supposed to seal the cake. Refrigerate until the frosting is firm, about 30 minutes.

2. Frost each tier again, more thickly this time. Apply the frosting so it is very smooth. Refrigerate the tiers for at least 30 minutes before assembling.

Stacking the Tiers

1. Put the 12-inch cake tier, still on its sturdy base, on a cake decorating turntable or lazy susan. Center a 9-inch cake pan on top and trace the outline with a toothpick. Cut 6 plastic straws to the same height as the cake tier. Insert the cut straws inside the traced circle, spacing them evenly. The straws will help support the tiers when they are stacked.

2. Place the 9-inch cake tier, still on its cardboard round, on top of the 12-inch tier.

3. Repeat the procedure to support the next tier. Center a 6-inch cake pan on top of the 9-inch cake tier and trace the outline with a toothpick. Cut 4 plastic straws to the height of the 9-inch tier and insert them inside the traced circle. Place the 6-inch cake tier, still on its cardboard round, on top of the 9-inch tier.

Decorating the Wedding Cake

1. Fit a pastry bag with a plastic coupler and leaf tip #69. Fill the bag two-thirds full with buttercream frosting (page 143). Pipe a ruffled border around the base of each tier.

2. Next, using leaf tip #66, pipe a ruffled border around the edges of each tier.

3. Last, using leaf tip #66, pipe evenly spaced swags on the sides of each tier. Where the swags join, pipe 2 buttercream leaves.

4. Decorate the wedding cake with fresh flowers at its final destination.

Transporting the Wedding Cake

If you have to transport the completed cake, a flat surface in the back of a station wagon or van is the best spot. Place the cake on a damp towel to prevent it from sliding.

Cutting the Wedding Cake

1. Begin cutting with the 6-inch tier, followed by the 9-inch tier, and finally the bottom 12-inch tier (see Note below). To slice the top tier, cut 8 pie-shaped wedges. Remove the cardboard round and pluck out the plastic straws.

2. To slice the middle tier, cut into 16 pie-shaped wedges. Again, remove the cardboard round and plastic straws.

3. To slice the bottom tier, cut a circle about 3 inches in from the edge of the cake. Cut the outer circle into 28 slices. Cut the inner circle into 8 pie-shaped wedges.

You should have 60 slices in all.

NOTE: Some couples like to follow an old wedding tradition and save the top tier of the cake for their first anniversary. If you do, just make sure to remove the tier, still on its cardboard round, wrap it well in plastic and foil, and freeze it as soon as possible after the rest of the cake is cut.

A slice of wedding cake, with fresh blackberries and peaches.

Autumn

Winter

Breakfast, Brunch, and Beyond

In our restaurant kitchen we sometimes play a word game that got started because we have a fellow named Bob who brings us bread from a bakery in the Bronx, and my baker's name is Becky. We started making up stories with as many "B" words as we could think of. Here's how one goes: "Bronx Baker Bob brings bread, baguettes, biscuits, and bagels by Becky's Brookside Bakery and Bistro. Brother Bill's beauteous blue-eyed bride Barbie babbles believingly before bakery buyers, bragging Becky bakes bread when she really is a pastry chef and bakes baklava, babas, Bundts, buckles, brown Bettys, brioche, and brownies." So far, we've made up at least 25 different biographies inspired by "B" words. So you see where the title of this chapter came from. But back to the buffet . . .

This was a leisurely Sunday brunch, starting at ten in the morning and continuing until two in the afternoon. Everyone helped themselves to the buffet while the Sunday papers were read and discussed at length. Some friends brought their children, who were ecstatic to find French toast and blood orange wedges on the buffet. Everything was set out in the kitchen—the food on the counters and the freshly squeezed juice, champagne (for mimosas), and coffees and teas on the kitchen island. This worked out well because we were able to keep the oven on low, and serve the sausage patties, French toast, and goat cheese tart hot. The coffees and teas were placed near the cooktop and a kettle of hot water was kept ready for refills. We offered large buffet plates and napkins rolled up with silverware, which guests carried to the large kitchen table or outside to tables on the deck.

For a smaller crowd, we could have split the menu and served half the number of

Coffees, teas, juices, champagne, and bagels were served from the kitchen island. The rest of the buffet was set up on the back counters.

dishes. For a larger crowd, we could have expanded it with the addition of fresh-baked bagels, which I like to serve with herbed cream cheese, fruit butter, fresh tomatoes, and thinly sliced onions. Regardless of the number of guests, I will often put out a platter of bagels for people to munch on as soon as they arrive.

Sunday brunch is a classic way to entertain friends and family, but I find that breakfasts and brunches are becoming popular for business occasions too. After a busy day at the office many business people want to get home to their families and not have to attend evening cocktail parties. For a business event I would make some adjustments to this menu, serving smaller portions, perhaps cutting the portobellos in half or quarters, and offering a fruit salad bowl instead of the larger melon crowns.

Coffees and teas have reached such a level of sophistication that the choices are mind-boggling. Like olive oil, coffee is a matter of personal taste. Some people are partial to beans from certain regions, others like blends or flavored coffees. There are many ways to brew a good, rich cup of coffee at home, but I prefer the French press. These heavy glass pots in metal holders have a fine filter plunger attached to the lid. All you do is put measured coffee and boiling water into the pot, close the lid, let the coffee brew for 5 to 8 minutes, then firmly push down on the plunger until the grains are pressed to the bottom of the pot. When the plunger is completely compressed, the coffee can be served. Coffee brewed this way is full bodied because the coffee oils are not filtered out the way they are when paper coffee filters are used.

Grinding coffee just before you brew it will give you a more aromatic and flavorful cup. Electric coffee grinders are relatively inexpensive. I have two in my kitchen, one just for coffee and another for grinding spices.

Tea drinking is a venerable custom, possibly dating back as far as 2737 B.C. in China. According to legend, a Chinese emperor was drinking hot water one day when some leaves from a nearby bush blew into his cup. The emperor took a sip of the beverage and declared it sent from heaven. All tea actually comes from the same tea plant, *Camellia sinensis*; different types of tea (green, black, and oolong) are made by picking and processing the leaves differently. Herbal and medicinal teas are made from flavorful infusions of flowers, herbs, and roots. These teas are energizing, healthful, soothing, and restorative. To brew any tea properly, you must start with fresh, cold, good-tasting, chemical-free water. Bring the water to a rolling boil, pour it over loose tea (contained in a tea ball if you prefer) or tea bags in a warm ceramic pot, and allow to steep for 3 to 5 minutes. Remove the tea bag or tea ball and serve immediately. If using loose leaves, pour the tea into a cup through a small fine strainer.

Remember to set out milk, sugar, honey, and lemon slices for the teas and coffees, and to offer decaffeinated alternatives for those who prefer not to get "java-ed out."

Breakfast, Brunch, and Beyond

for 12

Crunchy Nutted French Toast

Berry Berry Vanilla Syrup

Fresh Pork and Apple Sausage

Melon Crowns with Marinated Berries

———

Baked Goat Cheese and Hazelnut Tart

Dandelion Salad with Soft-Boiled Farm Eggs

Rhubarb Vinaigrette

Salmon and Two-Potato Hash on Portobello Mushrooms

———

Blood Orange Wedges

Fresh-Squeezed Orange Juice

Chilled Champagne

Brewed Coffees and Teas

Crunchy Nutted French Toast

This recipe is more of a concept than a set of step-by-step instructions. Feel free to use other cereals for the coating, or to make a savory crusted French toast using a mixture of cereals and nuts flavored with herbs.

My husband, Bernard, who is French, tells me he's never eaten our style of French toast in France! In the nineteenth century a dish called pain perdu, *which consists of stale bread dipped in egg and then fried, was a popular way to use up day-old loaves. This "lost bread" became part of Creole and Cajun cuisine in this country, and is still served in New Orleans, usually sprinkled with confectioners' sugar and cinnamon, with Louisiana cane syrup on the side.*

6 cups unsweetened corn, wheat, or
    oat flake cereals
2 cups unsalted nuts, such as pecans,
    macadamias, peanuts, almonds, or
    cashews
1 cup sugar (see Note)
26 pieces white or wheat bread for
    toasting, sliced ¾ to 1 inch thick

10 eggs
2 quarts milk
¼ teaspoon each ground nutmeg
    and cinnamon
2 cups clarified butter or oil, for
    cooking

1. In a food processor, quickly grind together the cereal and nuts. Add the sugar and mix. Transfer the mixture to a flat pan.

2. In a large bowl, beat the eggs with the milk and nutmeg and/or cinnamon.

3. Dip each slice of bread in the egg mixture, and let sit a minute or two to soak up the liquid. Remove the bread and dip it in the cereal-nut mixture.

4. Heat a small amount of the butter or oil in a large skillet over medium heat. Add a few slices of the coated bread and cook about 3 minutes, until golden and crunchy; turn over and cook another 3 minutes. Remove and keep warm in a very low (200° F) oven while you cook the rest of the bread.

Serves 12, as part of buffet.

NOTE: If you use a sugar-coated cereal, delete the sugar in the coating mix. Or if you don't like sugar at all, eliminate it from the ingredients.

PLANNING AHEAD: French toast can be made a few hours ahead and then reheated in a 250° F oven for about 10 minutes before serving.

COUNTERCLOCKWISE FROM BOTTOM: *Pork and apple sausages; melon crowns filled with marinated berries; nutted French toast; and Berry Berry Vanilla Syrup.*

Berry Berry Vanilla Syrup

Syrup for pancakes or French toast can be made from a variety of fruits. Here the berries are added to the hot syrup at the end of the recipe, then the syrup is cooled. Firmer fruits, like pears or apricots, should be added while the syrup is cooking to allow them to soften.

But if you don't want to cook you can always call on an old reliable: real maple syrup. Here in the Litchfield hills there are a number of farms that tap the spring maples and make wonderful, rich syrup in old-fashioned sugar boiling shacks. If you can't find a good local source for real maple syrup, try one of the many New England mail-order sources.

1 whole vanilla bean pod, split and   Juice of 2 lemons
    vanilla scraped out   1 pint fresh blackberries
3 cups light brown or white sugar   1 pint fresh raspberries
2½ cups water

1. In a 2-quart pot, combine the vanilla, sugar, water, and lemon juice. Bring to a boil over high heat, then reduce the heat to medium-low and simmer for 5 to 8 minutes, until the sugar has dissolved into a light syrup. Remove from the heat and pour into a bowl to cool.

2. Stir in the berries and let cool completely.

Makes 4 cups syrup.

PLANNING AHEAD: This syrup can be made 4 to 5 days ahead and kept in a covered container in the refrigerator.

Fresh Pork and Apple Sausage

It is as easy to make your own sausage patties as it is to make hamburgers; the only difference is a few extra flavorings.

3 egg whites, beaten

2 apples, peeled and finely diced

¼ cup chopped dried fruit, such as apricots, cherries, figs, prunes, or pineapple

10 cloves garlic, finely chopped

1 bunch scallions, thinly sliced, including green tops

Optional: 1 tablespoon green peppercorns

2 teaspoons coarse salt

⅛ teaspoon ground nutmeg

2¾ pounds fresh, lean ground pork

1. In a large mixing bowl, beat the egg whites until just frothy. Stir in the apples, dried fruit, garlic, scallions, green peppercorns, salt, and nutmeg.

2. Place the pork in another large bowl, make a well in the center, pour in the egg white mixture, and knead together until well combined. Pinch off a small amount of the meat mixture, cook in a heavy skillet over medium-high heat, and taste for seasoning. Correct as necessary. Form the rest of the mixture into 1-inch-thick patties about 2½ inches in diameter.

3. Cook the patties approximately 7 to 8 minutes on one side, until browned, then turn over and cook about 6 more minutes on the other side.

Makes fifteen 3-ounce patties.

PLANNING AHEAD: The patties can be formed up to 3 days ahead and stored in a covered container in the refrigerator. They can be cooked up to 4 hours ahead and reheated in a low (200° to 250° F) oven.

A tempting plate of pork and apple sausage, nutted French toast topped with Berry Berry Vanilla Syrup, and melon with marinated berries.

Melon Crowns with Marinated Berries

You don't need to fuss with cutting melon crowns if you don't want to; simply cut the melon in half, remove the seeds, and fill with fruit. Melons are not only great-tasting, they make natural serving bowls.

6 cantaloupes or other local sweet
  melons
1 pint strawberries, washed,
  stemmed, and quartered, plus 15
  large strawberries, washed,
  stemmed, and halved

2 kiwis, peeled and cut in half
6 sprigs fresh mint, leaves picked
  and finely shredded
1 pint blueberries, washed
1 pint cherries, washed, pitted, and
  quartered

1. With a paring knife cut a small slice from the end of each melon so they will stand up straight. Then cut the melons in half horizontally in a zigzag pattern. Break the halves apart and scoop out the seeds.

2. In a food processor or blender, puree the 30 strawberry halves with the kiwi until smooth. Add the mint, then pour the sauce into a bowl. Toss in the 1 pint of quartered strawberries, the blueberries, and cherries and mix well. Just before serving, spoon the fruit into the melon crowns.

Serves 12, as part of buffet.

PLANNING AHEAD: The sauce can be made, and the melon halves prepared and wrapped in plastic, 1 day ahead and kept in the refrigerator.

Baked Goat Cheese and Hazelnut Tart

This basic cheese tart can be embellished with many different ingredients, such as ripe cherries, pears, asparagus, beets, sun-dried tomatoes, or smoked meats. Let your imagination be your guide.

1 prebaked Hazelnut Tart Pastry
   Shell (recipe follows)
1 pound fresh goat cheese
1 tablespoon Dijon-style mustard
2 tablespoons chopped fresh chervil,
   chives, or tarragon (or any combination of these herbs)

4 eggs
1½ cups heavy cream
Freshly ground black pepper

1. Make the pastry shell and prebake.

2. With a rubber spatula, mash together the goat cheese, mustard, and herbs until soft and smooth.

3. Whisk the eggs and cream together with the pepper. Add the egg mixture to the goat cheese mixture and mix until smooth. Pour into the pastry shell.

4. Preheat the oven to 350° F. Bake the tart approximately 20 to 25 minutes, until the center of the filling is set and the tart shell is golden.

Makes one 10-inch tart.

PLANNING AHEAD: The tart can be baked up to 2 days ahead, kept in the refrigerator, and then warmed in a 250° F oven for about 10 to 15 minutes before serving.

Hazelnut Tart Pastry Shell

A savory nut crust that is so tender it cuts with just the touch of a knife.

1 cup ground hazelnuts
1 cup whole-wheat flour, sifted
1 teaspoon baking soda
1 teaspoon coarse salt

8 ounces (2 sticks) unsalted butter,
   cut into cubes
1 tablespoon cold water

(CONTINUED)

IN FOREGROUND: *Goat cheese and hazelnut tart.* BEHIND: *Dandelion salad and soft-boiled farm eggs garnished with Johnny jump-up flowers.*

1. In a food processor, mix together the hazelnuts, flour, baking soda, and salt. Add the butter and process until a coarse meal is formed. Add the water, a little at a time, to form a dry dough. Do not overwork.

2. Using your fingers, push and fit the dough into a 10-inch tart pan (because the dough is crumbly I find this is easier than trying to roll it). Place the lined tart pan in the refrigerator for at least 1 hour.

3. Preheat the oven to 350° F. Remove the tart pan from the refrigerator and prick the dough with the tines of a fork. Bake for approximately 8 to 10 minutes, until the crust is pale golden in color. Remove from the oven, and continue with the Baked Goat Cheese and Hazelnut Tart recipe on page 161.

Makes one 10-inch pastry shell.

PLANNING AHEAD: The lined tart pan can be wrapped in plastic and left for up to 3 days in the refrigerator before prebaking. It can also be frozen.

Dandelion Salad with Soft-Boiled Farm Eggs

This salad, one of my favorites, is very simple: Salad greens are topped with eggs that are cooked on the outside but have runny yolks—a stage the French call "oeufs mollets." The salad is dressed with a little vinegar and oil, and when the egg breaks the yolk becomes a tasty part of the dressing.

Many different lettuces can be used, of course. I like the more bitter greens, such as dandelion greens or chicory, but spinach or romaine can be substituted as well.

12 farm eggs (see Note)
1 tablespoon coarse salt
3 bunches dandelion greens, washed, dried, stems removed

Rhubarb Vinaigrette (recipe follows) or olive oil and good-quality balsamic, red wine, or sherry vinegar

1. Place the eggs in a large pot, add the salt, and cover with cold water. Bring to a boil over high heat. Set the timer, and cook the eggs for exactly 2 minutes from the point at which the water begins to boil. Remove the eggs immediately and cool in an ice bath or under cold running water. Peel, then store in cold water in the refrigerator until ready to use.

2. Place the dandelion greens in a large salad bowl and the eggs in another bowl.

Serve with Rhubarb Vinaigrette or oil and vinegar on the side, and let the guests toss their own salads.

Serves 12, as part of buffet.

NOTE: Farm eggs have a superior taste to commercially produced eggs, but be sure they are 3 to 4 days old when you boil them; otherwise they won't peel easily, if at all.

PLANNING AHEAD: The eggs can be boiled and peeled, and the greens washed and dried, up to 1 day ahead and kept in the refrigerator.

Rhubarb Vinaigrette

Rhubarb gives this dressing a fruity flavor and lovely light pink color. Drizzle it on the dandelion salad (page 163) or on stuffed portobello mushrooms (page 165).

10 large stalks rhubarb, washed and
    cut into ½-inch slices
2½ cups water
½ cup raspberry vinegar

4 tablespoons honey
1 cup vegetable oil
Coarse salt and freshly ground black
    pepper to taste

1. In a 2-quart saucepan, combine the rhubarb, water, vinegar, and honey. Bring to a boil over high heat, then reduce the heat and simmer for 15 minutes, until the rhubarb is mushy.

2. Place the rhubarb in a food processor or blender and puree, adding the oil in a steady stream until the dressing is emulsified. Season with salt and pepper. Strain through a fine-mesh strainer.

Makes 3 to 4 cups.

PLANNING AHEAD: This dressing can be made up to 6 days ahead and kept in the refrigerator in a covered container. It may separate a bit; just reblend when ready to use.

Salmon and Two-Potato Hash on Portobello Mushrooms

Portobello mushrooms make a rich, flavorful base for all sorts of toppings, from vegetables, cheeses, and tofu to poultry and seafood.

2 cups pure virgin olive oil
1 cup finely diced leeks
8 cloves garlic, chopped
10 sprigs fresh thyme, leaves picked
12 large portobello mushrooms,
    stems removed and brushed clean
Coarse salt and freshly ground black
    pepper

HASH:
4 large Yukon Gold or white
    potatoes, peeled and cut into
    1-inch dice

Coarse salt
3 large sweet potatoes, peeled and
    cut into 1-inch dice
Optional: 2 tablespoons truffle oil
    (see Note on page 175)

1 pound salmon fillets, skin removed
Rhubarb Vinaigrette, for serving
    (page 164)

1. Preheat the oven to 400° F. Pour ½ cup of the oil on a rimmed baking sheet. Sprinkle the leeks, garlic, thyme, salt, and pepper over the oil. Lay the mushrooms on top, gill side down, and sprinkle with the remaining oil. Roast in the oven until mushrooms darken and soften, approximately 10 minutes. Remove from the heat and let cool in the pan. Stack the mushrooms with their roasting liquid in a covered container and set aside until ready to use, or refrigerate.

2. To make the hash, place Yukon Gold or white potatoes in a large pot, sprinkle with salt, and cover with cold water. Bring to a boil over high heat. Three minutes after the water has begun to boil, add the sweet potatoes. Bring back to a boil, and continue cooking for about 10 minutes more, until the potatoes are tender. Drain in a colander and transfer to a flat pan to cool completely. Sprinkle with some of the portobello roasting juice and the truffle oil, if you are using it. Toss to incorporate.

3. Cook the salmon by grilling, broiling, smoking (page 228), or poaching. If you want to poach it, you can use the potato cooking liquid. Strain and pour it into a shallow pan, then add the salmon and simmer on low just to barely cook it, about 5 minutes. Remove from the liquid with a perforated spatula and let cool. Flake the salmon and combine with the potatoes to make a hash.

(CONTINUED)

IN FOREGROUND: *Roasted portobello mushrooms topped with salmon and potato hash.*

4. Preheat the oven to 350° F. Place the mushrooms on a baking sheet, gill side up, and heap a portion of hash on each one. Pack it with your fingers. Bake for 12 to 15 minutes to heat through. Serve with Rhubarb Vinaigrette on the side.

Serves 12, as part of buffet.

VARIATION: During the last 2 minutes of cooking, sprinkle the stuffed mushrooms with shredded hard cheese, such as Swiss. Or make the hash completely vegetarian by omitting the salmon.

PLANNING AHEAD: The mushrooms can be roasted, and the potatoes and salmon cooked, up to 3 days ahead and left covered in the refrigerator. The dish can be assembled and baked up to 3 hours before serving if you want to serve it at room temperature.

Fresh-Squeezed Orange Juice

Simple and pure—and Mother Nature's best source of vitamin C! When you're making juice, figure that it takes approximately 3 medium juice oranges to make one 8-ounce cup. For 12 cups of juice, you will need 36 oranges.

The method is simple: Wash the oranges and cut in half. Extract the juice with a hand-held or machine juicer, checking to be sure that all the seeds have been strained out. Pour into a pitcher, chill if you like, and serve.

Fresh-squeezed grapefruit juice is also delicious, especially if you use Ruby Reds, which are naturally sweet and have a lovely color.

Soups as a Meal

A soup buffet is one of the easiest, most versatile, and least expensive ways to entertain groups of friends, from four to forty. Particularly in winter months, soups are warm and welcoming. This is the perfect buffet, for instance, to set out following an afternoon of cross-country skiing or skating. The key to an interesting soup buffet is to offer a choice of several soups, along with an array of tasty accompaniments—garnishes for the soups, breads, salads, and vegetables. It is the combination of dishes that will determine how hearty or light the meal will be. I've provided recipes for six different soups and six accompaniments, but these can be mixed and matched as you like, depending on the size and tastes of your group. Because the buffet is casual and easily expandable, you don't have to worry if a few more friends decide to join the party. Just add another side dish, a quickly tossed salad, and a few more biscuits. When deciding on your menu, however, do try to balance thick soups with brothy ones, meat-based with seafood, and be sure to include a vegetarian alternative.

You will notice that most of these soup recipes call for water or juice as a base rather than stock. I was trained as a classical chef, and years ago I wouldn't have dreamed of making onion soup without beef or chicken stock and onions sautéed in generous amounts of butter. Now my onion soup is made with a base of apple cider, the flavor enhanced with oyster sauce and fresh rosemary. The result is a lighter, tastier soup that is also faster to prepare. For maximum flavor in seafood soups I do use fish stocks because they take very little time to make and don't mask the natural flavors of the other ingredients.

I rarely use cream, flour, or other traditional thickeners in soups. In my seafood chowder, for instance, I use Yukon Gold potatoes as a thickener, for flavorful soup

A rustic soup buffet set out on an antique farm worktable in my kitchen. BACK ROW: *Apple and onion soup; tomato and wild rice soup; and pumpkin mussel soup.* FRONT ROW: *Cheddar cheese biscuits; herb cheese balls; ribboned lamb skewers; endive, orange, and flat-leaf parsley salad.*

without all the fat and calories. I also use purees of rice, beans, winter squashes, or other vegetables to thicken soups.

I like to serve soup in cereal bowls or grapefruit bowls as well as traditional flat-rimmed soup bowls. I find that deeper, smaller-diameter bowls—which can be made of ceramic, glass, or other materials—fit neatly on a dinner-size plate, allowing room for accompaniments, and also have the advantage of keeping the soup warmer. Remember that the bowls don't all have to match. An eclectic mix can be much more interesting to look at on a table than twelve bowls that are identical. Asian markets are often a good source for inexpensive soup bowls in different patterns and shapes.

I often find piles of odd tablespoons and forks at thrift shops and tag sales, and make a habit of buying the ones that appeal to me when I see them. I'm particularly fond of old coin silver, which has a wonderful light feel, and have collected lots of it over the years. Whatever your preference, it's a good idea to have a generous supply of spoons, forks, plates, and bowls on hand when you're doing this soup buffet. Remember to multiply the number of guests by the number of soups you are serving to get the total number of bowls you will need. Although guests can usually keep the same dinner plate, they will need to pick up a fresh bowl to sample a different soup. Since this buffet is informal, they won't necessarily need a different spoon for each soup, but it's a good idea to have extras on the table.

To keep hot soups hot, there are several different options. Electric warming trays work well; so do crockpots and gas cassette stoves. I've also taken bricks and built my own little stove with Sterno fuel underneath. If you're having a really big crowd, you might consider renting warming devices from a catering supply company. Another option is to leave the soups over low heat on your kitchen range, and let guests serve themselves. Set out the garnishes and accompaniments on a nearby table or counter. Remember to use good-looking cooking pots—Le Creuset, Calphalon, copper, stainless, or heat-tempered glass—if you are serving directly from them.

If you want to add desserts to this buffet, I would suggest the pick-up variety so you won't wind up with a stack of extra dishes to wash. Cookies are a good choice, either store-bought or homemade. For those who like to bake, I've included a terrific chocolate chip cookie recipe at the end of this chapter.

Soup Buffet

for 10

M ENU I
Apple and Onion Soup
Cheddar Cheese Biscuits

Pumpkin Mussel Soup
Endive, Orange, and
Flat-Leaf Parsley Salad

Tomato and Wild Rice Soup
Herb Cheese Balls
Ribboned Lamb Skewers

M ENU II
Beet and Yucca Soup
Corn and Cilantro Fritters

A Terrific Fish Chowder
Lentil, Broccoli, and Bacon Salad

Flavored Asian Chicken Noodle Soup
Frizzled Sesame Green Beans

Chocolate Chocolate Chip Cookies

Apple and Onion Soup

I use apple cider instead of stock as the base for this very delicious and easy soup. Freshly pressed apple cider is readily available in the fall at farmstands and markets; if you buy more than you need, or want to enjoy this soup at another time of year, remember that apple cider can be successfully frozen.

Hard, tart apples—such as Granny Smith, Greenings, or Empires—will give you maxium flavor. Sprinkle each serving with a little freshly grated Swiss cheese, or float Cheddar Cheese Biscuits on top.

¼ cup vegetable oil

8 cups sliced yellow onions (about 4 large)

1 tablespoon chopped fresh rosemary

1 tablespoon chopped fresh thyme

½ cup oyster sauce (available in Asian markets and some grocery stores)

4 large tart apples, peeled, cored, and cut into ¼-inch-thick slices

3 quarts apple cider

Coarse salt and freshly ground black pepper to taste

Optional: Grated Swiss cheese or Cheddar

Cheese Biscuits (recipe follows), for serving

1. Heat the oil in an 8-quart pot over high heat. Add the onions, rosemary, and thyme and sauté for approximately 3 minutes, until the onions are soft but not browned.

2. Stir in the oyster sauce. Add the apple slices and cider, bring to a boil, and season with salt and pepper. Lower the heat and simmer for about 15 minutes. Serve with grated Swiss cheese or Cheddar Cheese Biscuits, if desired.

Makes 1 gallon; serves 10 or more, as part of buffet.

VARIATION: To deepen the flavor of this soup, add a pint of dark ale and decrease the quantity of apple cider to 2½ quarts.

PLANNING AHEAD: This soup can be prepared up to 1 week in advance, stored in the refrigerator, and reheated at serving time. It can also be frozen for up to 2 months.

Cheddar Cheese Biscuits

These light and tasty biscuits are always a favorite. Be sure to make enough; guests will probably pick up another one or two when they revisit the buffet to sample a different soup.

1½ pounds all-purpose flour	**2 ounces cheddar cheese, shredded**
1 tablespoon baking powder	**4 ounces (1 stick) unsalted butter,**
1 teaspoon baking soda	**solid vegetable shortening, or lard**
1 teaspoon coarse salt	**1½ to 2 cups buttermilk**

1. Sift together the flour, baking powder, baking soda, salt, and cheese. Using a pastry cutter or a food processor fitted with a metal blade, work in the butter, shortening, or lard, until the mixture resembles coarse crumbs. Remove to a bowl. Using your hands, mix in enough buttermilk so the dough is soft but not too sticky. It is important to form the dough quickly once the buttermilk is added to avoid overworking the dough. Let the dough rest for a few minutes.

2. Preheat the oven to 400° F. Turn the dough out onto a well-floured surface and roll into a rough circle about ½ inch thick. Cut into rounds with a 3-inch biscuit cutter and place ½ inch apart on lightly greased baking sheets. Bake for approximately 15 minutes, until the biscuits are puffed and golden.

Makes 36 biscuits.

VARIATION: To make herbed cheese biscuits, add 2 tablespoons coarsely chopped fresh herbs, such as dill, chives, tarragon, basil, or flat-leaf parsley, to the dough. Finely chopped lemon thyme or rosemary are also good choices, but use less (2 teaspoons) as these flavors are stronger.

PLANNING AHEAD: Biscuits are best made the same day they are served. Reheat in a 350° F oven for 6 to 8 minutes, wrapped in foil.

Pumpkin Mussel Soup

Everyone who tastes this soup falls in love with it. Many different kinds of squash—buttercup, butternut, or red kuri, for example—can be substituted for the pumpkin in this recipe. I like to roast pumpkin whole rather than boil or steam it because the pulp is less watery and the flavor is superior using this method. Save the pumpkin seeds; toasted, they are good as a snack, in salads, or as an additional garnish for the soup. If you prefer a creamier soup, you can whisk in a small amount of heavy cream at the very end of the cooking process.

4- to 5-pound pumpkin
½ cup vegetable oil
2 medium Spanish onions, peeled and cut into medium dice
10 cloves garlic, peeled and smashed
8 sprigs fresh thyme
¼ teaspoon freshly ground black pepper
4 pounds mussels, washed and beards removed

3 cups white wine
2 quarts Fish Stock (page 184)
½ teaspoon freshly grated nutmeg
Juice of 1 lemon

Optional Garnish: Truffle oil (see Note) and chopped fresh herbs (dill, chives, tarragon, or flat-leaf parsley)

1. Preheat the oven to 350° F.
2. Wash the pumpkin very well, leaving the stem on. Put in a roasting pan to fit snugly. Fill the pan with 4 to 5 inches of water and cover with foil. Bake for about 1½ hours, until the pumpkin is tender (test with the tip of a paring knife). Remove the pan from the oven, take off the foil, and drain off excess water. Let the pumpkin cool to room temperature. When cool, cut in half, remove the seeds and strings, and scrape out the pulp to use in the soup.
3. Heat the oil over high heat in an 8-quart stockpot. Add the onions, garlic, thyme, pepper, and mussels. Pour in the wine, cover the pot, and cook the mussels until they just begin to open, about 5 to 8 minutes. Be careful not to overcook them, as they will shrink. Discard any mussels that haven't opened. Remove the rest of the mussels from the pot, reserving the liquid. Let them cool, then pull them from their shells, trying not to break them, and set aside in a bowl.
4. In a food processor or blender, or using an immersion blender, puree half of the pumpkin pulp with a small amount of the mussel liquid until smooth. Repeat with the remaining pulp. Put the pumpkin puree in a 4- to 6-quart pot and whisk in the rest of the mussel liquid, the fish stock, and nutmeg. Bring to a boil over medium heat, then

reduce the heat and simmer for 5 minutes, stirring occasionally. The soup should have a creamy consistency, but should not be overly thick. Adjust seasoning, and finish with the lemon juice. Stir the mussels into the soup just before serving. Let the guests top their bowls with a few drops of truffle oil and a handful of fresh herbs.

Makes 1 gallon; serves 10 or more as part of buffet.

NOTE: Truffle oil—which can be found in many gourmet and specialty shops—is a wonderful infused oil made from fresh truffles; it gives you the taste of truffles without the expense. You need only a few drops, as it is very fragrant. Be sure to buy the best quality; the taste should be strong and pure. This oil also heightens the flavor of cooked pasta, risottos, chicken ragouts, fish, and many other dishes.

PLANNING AHEAD: The pumpkin can be roasted, and the pulp removed, up to 3 days ahead. Or you can do it even further ahead and freeze the pulp, in which case the pulp should be thawed before proceeding with the recipe.

The mussels can also be cooked up to 3 days ahead and stored in the refrigerator in their broth until ready to use.

The fish stock can be made well in advance and kept in the freezer until you need it.

Endive, Orange, and Flat-Leaf Parsley Salad

Parsley—particularly the flat-leaf Italian variety—is a great-tasting herb that has been overlooked as a salad ingredient. Here it is combined with endive to make a very delicious seasonal salad that is simple to prepare and can be embellished with other raw vegetables, such as shaved fennel or celery root.

5 oranges (navel or temple) or
   tangelos
½ cup nut oil or extra-virgin olive
   oil
2 bunches flat-leaf parsley

1 teaspoon coarse salt
½ teaspoon freshly ground black
   pepper
4 large Belgian endives

1. With a paring knife, cut off the top and bottom of 4 oranges and cut away the skin and white pith. Quarter them and then cut into thin slices. Place in a large salad serving bowl and squeeze the juice from the remaining orange over them. Add the oil and toss lightly.

2. Wash the parsley and shake or spin dry. Remove the leaves with a knife and coarsely chop. Add to the oranges in the bowl. Season with the salt and pepper.

3. Cut the endives in half, then into diagonal slices, and add to the salad. Toss again and serve.

Serves 10, as part of buffet.

PLANNING AHEAD: The oranges and parsley may be cut up to 1 day ahead and kept in covered containers in the refrigerator until ready to use. The endive should be cut and tossed into the salad right before serving to prevent discoloration.

Tomato and Wild Rice Soup

A sophisticated tomato soup that can be served year-round. It's fine made with canned plum tomatoes in winter, and delightful in summer with fresh garden tomatoes. The wild rice is cooked separately and combined with the tomatoes toward the end of the recipe, which results in a fresh-tasting soup with distinct flavors.

1 cup pure or virgin olive oil
1 large white or red onion or
    2 medium leeks (washed well),
    cut into medium dice
8 fresh thyme sprigs, leaves picked
8 ounces uncooked wild rice
3 quarts water
Coarse salt and freshly ground black
    pepper to taste
20 large ripe garden tomatoes or
    3 (28-ounce) cans plum tomatoes
    in their juice

8 cloves garlic, peeled and chopped
24 to 30 fresh basil leaves
¼ cup sherry vinegar
Herb Cheese Balls (recipe follows)
    or large shavings of your favorite
    hard cheese, such as Parmesan,
    cheddar, or morbier, for serving

1. Heat ½ cup of the oil in a 6-quart pot over high heat. Add the onion or leeks and thyme and sauté a couple of minutes until soft. Add the wild rice and stir to coat. Add 2 quarts of the water, stir, and season with salt and pepper. Cover, bring the mixture to a boil over high heat, then turn down and simmer for 45 minutes, until the liquid is absorbed and the rice is tender. Remove the pot from the heat and turn the rice out onto a sheet tray to cool.

(CONTINUED)

An herb cheese ball floats in a bowl of tomato and wild rice soup. Skewered lamb and cheddar cheese biscuits are the accompaniments.

2. Remove the core from the fresh tomatoes and cut them into eighths (no need to remove skin or seeds; they are strained out later). If you are using canned plum tomatoes, crush them in their juice.

3. Heat the remaining oil in a 6-quart pot. Set over high heat. Add the garlic and sauté quickly for 30 seconds. Add half of the basil leaves and the fresh tomatoes or the canned tomatoes and juice. Pour in the remaining 1 quart water. Season with salt and pepper and bring the mixture to a boil. Reduce the heat and let simmer, stirring occasionally, for 25 minutes for fresh tomatoes; 15 minutes for canned tomatoes. Remove the tomato mixture from the heat and pour through a coarse strainer held over a large bowl. Puree the pulp in a food processor or blender until smooth. Strain the pulp back into the bowl with the tomato liquid.

4. Shred the remaining basil leaves. Combine the basil, tomato mixture, and wild rice in a 4-quart pot and stir. Bring to a boil over medium heat, add the sherry vinegar, reduce the heat to low, and simmer for 20 minutes.

5. Serve with Herb Cheese Balls or large shavings of your favorite hard cheese.

Makes about 1 gallon; serves 10, as part of buffet.

PLANNING AHEAD: The wild rice-onion-thyme mixture can be cooked well in advance and frozen in sealable plastic bags until needed. The tomato mixture can be cooked up to 3 days ahead and kept covered in the refrigerator. Assemble the soup no more than a few hours before serving if possible. If you leave the rice in the soup any longer it will absorb too much liquid, become mushy, and make the soup too thick.

Herb Cheese Balls

Any soft cheese—such as blue cheese or Boursin—can be substituted for the goat cheese in this recipe. The herbs you use can vary too—fresh tarragon or cilantro work well.

8 ounces fresh goat cheese
2 bunches fresh dill, finely chopped
  (about 1 cup)

24 chive stalks, finely chopped

Roll the goat cheese into little balls about the diameter of a quarter. You should have about 16. Combine the chopped dill and chives and roll the balls in the herb mixture.

Makes 16 or more balls.

Ribboned Lamb Skewers

Excellent as an hors d'oeuvre or first course, these are known as satés *in Southeast Asian cooking. The lamb can be marinated in many different flavorings and served with a variety of mild to spicy dipping sauces.*

3 pounds boneless leg of lamb or 2
   lamb loins, about 10 ounces each
1 teaspoon ground turmeric
1 teaspoon chili powder
1 teaspoon ground fennel
½ teaspoon ground cinnamon
½ cup extra-virgin or pure olive oil
Juice and zest from 1 orange

4 cloves garlic, minced
½ teaspoon coarse salt and ½
   teaspoon freshly ground black
   pepper, mixed together

Garnish: 1 bunch scallions, finely
   sliced

1. Cut the lamb into 2 × 5-inch strips. You should have about 30. Prepare an equal number of 6-inch bamboo skewers by soaking them in water.

2. Combine the turmeric, chili powder, fennel, and cinnamon in a sauté pan. Heat over medium-low for 1 to 2 minutes, stirring with a wooden spoon, until the spices begin to "bloom" and smell fragrant; be careful not to burn. Remove the pan from the heat and put the spices in a bowl large enough to hold the lamb. Mix in the olive oil, orange juice and zest, garlic, and salt and pepper. Add the lamb strips, toss, cover, and let marinate in the refrigerator for 2 hours, or up to 2 days.

3. "Ribbon" or thread each lamb strip onto a separate bamboo skewer, and grill or broil for 1½ to 2 minutes per side. Top with sliced scallions and serve.

Serves 10, as part of buffet.

PLANNING AHEAD: This dish can be started up to 2 days ahead, the lamb left to marinate in the refrigerator.

Beet and Yucca Soup

Two root vegetables are combined here to make a spectacularly colored soup with a sublime flavor. Yucca is used extensively in Caribbean and South American cooking. Its richness and velvety texture are a wonderful complement to the earthy sweetness of beets.

4 pounds beets
4 pounds yucca root (cassava)
8 cloves garlic, peeled and chopped
2 chopped fresh jalapeño peppers
   or 2 teaspoons chili paste
1 cup Asian sesame oil
   (see Note, page 189)
1 cup red wine vinegar or balsamic
   vinegar

Coarse salt and freshly ground black
   pepper to taste
7 quarts water

Garnishes: **Coarsely chopped fresh**
   cilantro
Wedges of fresh lime

1. Cut the tops and stems off the beets and peel. Cut the yucca root in half crosswise, then lengthwise, and pare off the waxy tough brown skin with a sharp knife. Cut both vegetables into medium-sized pieces and place in a large soup pot.

2. Add the garlic, jalapeño or chili paste, oil, vinegar, salt, pepper, and water to the pot. Stir. Bring to a boil over high heat, then reduce to medium-low, cover, and simmer approximately 45 minutes, stirring occasionally, until the beets and yucca are soft and cooked through. Remove from the heat.

3. In a blender or food processor, puree the soup in batches until smooth. Or use an immersion blender to puree it right in the pot. Then pass the soup through a conical strainer or food mill (see Note) to make it completely smooth. Serve hot, with cilantro and a squeeze of fresh lime to heighten the flavor.

Makes 1½ gallons; serves 10 or more, as part of buffet.

NOTE: You can buy conical strainers at restaurant supply stores. I often find old ones at tag sales and flea markets. Originally used to make applesauce, these strainers have their own holder and can sit over a pot right on the kitchen counter. I find them very useful and efficient for straining soups and purees. China caps work well too, but not extra-fine mesh ones, which are for consommés and sauces.

PLANNING AHEAD: This soup will keep for up to 4 or 5 days in an airtight container in the refrigerator. It might thicken slightly, so if necessary add some liquid when reheating. This soup also freezes well.

Ingredients for the beet and yucca soup.

Corn and Cilantro Fritters

These puffy fritters are a tasty accompaniment to the Beet and Yucca Soup (page 180). The basic fritter batter can be varied by using small pieces of other vegetables, fruits, seafood, or cheeses.

2½ cups all-purpose flour
1 tablespoon baking powder
1 tablespoon sugar
1 teaspoon coarse salt
2 eggs, beaten
3 ounces unsalted butter, melted
¾ cup buttermilk

2 cups whole kernel corn, fresh or frozen
6 scallions, roots removed and thinly sliced
1 bunch cilantro, leaves washed and chopped (about 1 cup)
Vegetable oil, for frying

1. Sift together the flour, baking powder, sugar, and salt, and set aside. Whisk together the eggs, butter, and buttermilk until smooth. Fold in the corn, scallions, and cilantro followed by the flour mixture. Mix well to form a stiff batter that will drop from a spoon.

2. Heat ½ inch of oil in a frying pan or wok until very hot, about 350° F. Test by sprinkling a few droplets of water in the oil and watching to see if the water sputters. Or drop a small amount of batter in the oil and see if it starts to set up and fry right away. When the oil is at the right temperature, drop in the batter by the tablespoon and fry in batches, turning with a metal skimmer, until the fritters are golden on both sides, about 5 minutes. Remove the fritters to a wire mesh tray or paper towels to drain. Serve hot.

Makes approximately 36 golf ball–size fritters.

PLANNING AHEAD: The batter can be mixed a day ahead and kept in the refrigerator until needed. The fritters can be made up to a few hours before serving and reheated in a low (250° F) oven.

A Terrific Fish Chowder

The most important ingredient in this simple-to-make chowder is a good fish stock. Mashed potatoes thicken the soup and give it a creamy consistency without flour or cream.

7 large Yukon Gold potatoes
¼ cup vegetable oil or 2 ounces
    unsalted butter
2 cups chopped onions
    (about 2 large onions)
1 cup chopped leeks
12 sprigs fresh thyme, leaves picked
3 quarts Fish Stock (recipe follows)
1 teaspoon coarse salt

¼ teaspoon freshly ground black
    pepper
2 pounds cod, bass, or grouper fillet,
    cut into cubes

Garnish: ¼ cup finely chopped flat-
    leaf parsley or scallion greens

1. Peel and quarter 4 of the potatoes. Place in a saucepan filled with salted water, cover, and bring to a boil over high heat. Cook the potatoes until soft, about 15 minutes. Drain and mash until smooth. You should have about 2 cups. Set aside.

2. Peel the remaining raw potatoes and cut into medium dice. Set aside.

3. Heat the oil or butter in a heavy, 6-quart pot set over medium heat. When hot, add the onions and leeks and sauté until soft. Add the thyme and stock and bring to a boil. Whisk in the mashed potatoes, blending well. Bring the soup back to a boil, stir, then add the diced raw potatoes, salt, and pepper. Cover the pot, reduce the heat, and let simmer for 15 minutes. Stir in the fish and simmer for 5 minutes more. Pour the soup into a warm soup tureen and garnish with the parsley or scallion greens.

Makes 1 gallon; serves 10, as part of buffet.

VARIATION: If you prefer a soup that is lighter in color, add 1 cup light or heavy cream at the very end and heat through before serving.

PLANNING AHEAD: Make this soup a day or two ahead to improve its flavor. Heat slowly before serving, stirring occasionally.

Fish Stock

Fish stock makes a real difference in the flavor of seafood soups and chowders, so it is one of the few stock recipes I use. The cooking time is short, but the process of making fish stock does leave an odor in the kitchen, so don't make it on a day you are expecting guests.

Fish bones are available at most fish markets. If the heads have gills attached, cut them off with scissors because they will make the stock bitter. Shrimp shells can also be used to make stock, but a longer cooking time (1 hour) is needed for maximum flavor.

5 pounds whitefish bones and heads (from flounder, cod, snapper, grouper, halibut, or other non-oily fish)
6 stalks celery, coarsely chopped
2 large or 4 medium white onions, coarsely chopped
1 bunch flat-leaf parsley

12 sprigs fresh thyme
2 bay leaves
30 cracked black peppercorns
Optional: **2 cups dry white wine**

Optional extra vegetables: **fennel, celery root, parsnips, scallions, leeks, or mushrooms**

Wash the fish bones and heads under running water and break or chop them into pieces. Place in an 8- to 10-quart stockpot and cover with cold water. Add the celery, onions, parsley, thyme, bay leaves, peppercorns, and the white wine and extra vegetables (if using). Bring to a boil over high heat, skimming off the foam as it rises to the surface. Reduce the heat to medium and simmer for 30 minutes. Remove the stock from the heat, let cool, and strain.

Makes 2 gallons.

PLANNING AHEAD: Fish stock will keep in the refrigerator for 5 to 6 days; it can be frozen for up to 3 months in plastic bags or covered containers.

Lentil, Broccoli, and Bacon Salad

I prefer to use French du Puy lentils for this salad because they are smaller and, when cooked, have a nicer color and texture than other types of lentils. For the bacon, I use either pancetta, an Italian bacon, or a slab bacon.

¼ cup vegetable or pure olive oil
1 large onion or 3 leeks, cut into
   medium dice
6 cloves garlic, sliced
10 sprigs fresh thyme, leaves picked
12 ounces dried lentils, preferably
   du Puy
3 carrots, diced small
1½ quarts water

1 cup good-quality red wine vinegar
   or balsamic vinegar
Coarse salt and freshly ground black
   pepper
2 cups Fresh Tomato Vinaigrette
   (page 74)
2 pounds pancetta or slab bacon, cut
   into ½-inch cubes
2 bunches fresh broccoli, florets only

1. Heat the oil in a 4- to 6-quart pot. Add the onion or leeks, garlic, and thyme and sauté over high heat until the vegetables are soft. Stir in the lentils and carrots. Stir in the water, vinegar, salt, and pepper. Adjust seasoning if necessary. Cover the pot and bring the mixture to a boil. Stir, reduce the heat, and simmer until the lentils are tender and cooked, about 1¼ hours, checking from time to time to make sure that the liquid hasn't cooked out before the lentils are done; add more water if necessary. Cool the lentils.

2. While the lentils are cooking, prepare the pancetta or bacon. To blanch, place in a pot, cover with cold water, and bring to a boil. Drain in a colander. Heat a heavy skillet, then add the blanched bacon and sauté over high heat until brown and crisp. Drain the bacon in a colander and discard excess fat. Set aside.

3. Bring a pot of salted water to a boil. Add the broccoli florets and cook until just tender. Drain and immediately plunge into cold water to stop the cooking process. Drain again.

4. Place the cooked, cooled lentils and the bacon in a large bowl. Add the vinaigrette and toss. Add the broccoli just before serving (to keep its color bright) and toss again.

Serves 10 to 12, as part of buffet.

PLANNING AHEAD: The lentils can be cooked, tossed with the vinaigrette, and kept in the refrigerator for up to 1 week.

An elegant soup buffet served in the antique copper lustreware I love to collect. BACK ROW: *Beet and yucca soup; fish chowder; and Asian chicken noodle soup.* FRONT ROW: *Corn fritters; lentil, broccoli, and bacon salad; and frizzled sesame green beans.*

Flavored Asian Chicken Noodle Soup

This is one of my favorite, year-round "comfort" soups, with an Asian twist. It's light, healthy, delicious, and couldn't be easier because everything is cooked in the same pot.

Try to buy a high-quality, less-processed chicken. You won't believe the difference in flavor.

1 2½- to 3-pound whole chicken (innards removed), rinsed
Approximately 4 quarts water
¼ cup coarsely chopped fresh ginger (peeling not necessary)
8 cloves garlic, peeled and smashed
1 tablespoon hot chili paste (see Note)
16 sprigs fresh cilantro, leaves picked
16 sprigs fresh mint, leaves picked

½ pound fresh wonton noodles, cut into ½-inch strips
1 large head bok choy, coarsely cut on the diagonal
1 pound fresh shiitake mushrooms (or 4 ounces dried), stems removed and thinly sliced
1 bunch scallions, thinly sliced on the diagonal
Optional: Fresh Asian greens, such as tatsoi, napa cabbage, or mizuna

1. Place the chicken in an 8-quart stockpot and cover with at least 4 quarts water. Add the ginger, garlic, chili paste, and half of the cilantro and mint. Cover the pot, bring to a boil, then reduce the heat and simmer for about 40 minutes, until the chicken is cooked. Remove the chicken with a large cook's fork and set aside to cool.

2. When the chicken is cool enough to handle, remove and discard the skin, pull the chicken meat from the bones, and tear into large pieces. Strain the chicken broth into another pot and bring to a boil. Stir in the wonton noodles, bok choy, and shiitakes. Reduce the heat and simmer for approximately 8 minutes, until the noodles are soft. Stir in the scallions, remaining fresh herbs, and cooked chicken. Top with the Asian greens (if using).

Makes 1 gallon; serves 10 or more, as part of buffet.

NOTE: Because the chili paste is added at the very beginning of the recipe, this soup is flavorful but mild. If you think some of your guests might like their soup spicier, set a small bowl of chili paste on the buffet table.

PLANNING AHEAD: The cooked chicken and the strained broth can be stored together in an airtight container in the refrigerator for 3 days. Close to serving time, bring the broth to a boil and continue with recipe.

Frizzled Sesame Green Beans

As long as you have good green beans in your market, this dish has no season. Guests have a choice of adding the beans to their bowls of Flavored Asian Chicken Noodle Soup (page 187) or eating them on a separate plate.

These versatile beans can also enliven plain grilled chicken, meat, or fish, and can work as part of a main course for a vegetarian buffet.

2 pounds green beans, ends snapped
1 cup Asian sesame oil (see Note)
8 cloves garlic, peeled and sliced
4 tablespoons soy sauce

2 tablespoons sesame seeds,
   preferably unhulled (see Note)
Optional: **Sliced scallions**

1. Blanch the green beans in boiling water until al dente. Drain in a colander.

2. In a wok or large cast-iron skillet, heat ½ cup of the oil over high heat until smoking. Toss in half of the beans and spread them out evenly. Cook for approximately 2 minutes to sear, color, and "frizzle" the skin of the beans. Add half of the garlic and stir-fry for 2 minutes more. Sprinkle with half of the soy sauce and half of the sesame seeds and turn out onto a platter.

3. Remove the pan from the heat and wipe out with a paper towel. Repeat the stir-fry process with the remaining beans. If you like, sprinkle the finished dish with sliced scallions.

Serves 10, as part of buffet.

VARIATION: If you are not fond of the taste of sesame oil, you can substitute a vegetable, nut, or olive oil and top the dish with nuts or sunflower seeds instead of sesame seeds. Slivers of sweet red pepper and grated fresh ginger also make a tasty addition to this salad.

NOTE: For this dish it is best to use a pure Asian sesame oil, not to be confused with sesame-flavored vegetable oil. There are many varieties available. The highest-quality oils are from Japan, and they should be used for dressings. The Chinese oils are fine for cooked dishes such as this one.

Unhulled sesame seeds, generally found in health-food stores, do not have their outer shell removed. They are larger and tastier, and look as if they have been toasted. If you use hulled sesame seeds, toast them first in a skillet or oven.

Chocolate Chocolate Chip Cookies

Whenever I serve these double chocolate cookies they always disappear quickly.

2¼ cups all-purpose flour

½ cup unsweetened cocoa powder

1 teaspoon baking soda

1 teaspoon coarse salt

6 ounces (1½ sticks) unsalted butter, softened

¾ cup granulated sugar

¾ cup light brown sugar

2 eggs

1 teaspoon vanilla extract

1 cup chocolate chips

1. Preheat the oven to 350° F. Grease 2 baking sheets or line with parchment paper.

2. Sift together the flour, cocoa, baking soda, and salt. Using an electric mixer, cream the butter with the granulated and light brown sugars until light and fluffy. Slowly add the dry ingredients, eggs, and vanilla, beating after each addition. Fold in the chocolate chips.

3. Spoon batter by tablespoons onto the baking sheets, leaving about 1 inch between cookies. Bake approximately 15 to 18 minutes, until cookies are dry around the edges. Remove from the oven while the centers are still slightly soft. Let cool on baking sheets.

Makes about 20 medium-sized (2½-inch) cookies.

PLANNING AHEAD: These cookies will keep well for up to 3 weeks in a tightly covered container.

Harvest Moonfest

Vibrant colors and golden hues, crisp dry air, the smell of apples and whiffs of fires, clear nights exploding with stars, and the eerie presence of ghouls and goblins—this is autumn in New England, my favorite season of the year. Litchfield County, in particular, is almost too picturesque for words, its rolling hills ablaze with brilliant foliage.

Autumn is special because the robust colors and textures of the season are all around us. In addition to the visual delight of the changing leaves, for me there is the thrill of finding chanterelle mushrooms under fallen leaves; of visiting farms and buying huge bushel baskets of sweet, just-picked fruit; of harvesting multicolored squashes from the vine at their peak of flavor before the first frost—Hubbard, red kuri, cheese pumpkins, sugar dumplings, and, of course, pumpkins. Farmers are bringing in late-harvest tomatoes, large green pole beans, fresh speckled cranberry beans, Brussels sprouts on their stalks, shallots, and potatoes still covered with dirt.

One of my favorite orchards is Averil Farms in Washington, Connecticut. This 100-acre farm celebrated its two hundred fiftieth anniversary in 1996, a tribute to years of hard work and dedication. Wonderful varieties of apples are grown on the farm: Quinte, Jersey Macs, Ida Reds, Macoons, Delicious, Modern Mitsu; heirloom apples like Northern Spys, Rhode Island Greenings, and Pearl Crabapples; and disease-resistant Liberty apples. Averil Farms also grows Seckel, Bartlett, and Bosc pears, and has the largest quince orchard in Connecticut. And, of course, they make their own cider!

This bounty of vegetables and fruits may sound a little hard to believe, but it's true if you live around here. So how could we not create a harvest buffet menu?

We held this party in early October close to a full moon. (This menu could have worked for a Thanksgiving celebration, too.) Everyone was invited for an invigorating late-afternoon walk in the hills, then back to the house for the hearty buffet. To celebrate the season we asked guests to bring hand-carved jack-o'-lanterns, which we grouped together in the sitting room, then lit with candles in the evening.

The house where we held the party is an authentic eighteenth-century parsonage, with fireplaces in each of the original rooms. A spacious great room was added on to the house for entertaining by the current owner, a friend of mine. Both chilled and hot mulled cider were offered near the large cooking hearth in the sitting room (the original parsonage kitchen), then guests moved on to the great room for the buffet. Starting off the buffet was a dish of seasonal chanterelle mushrooms, Brussels sprouts, and bay scallops, followed by a simple roasted pork loin and a choice of five different vegetable dishes. To complement the harvest theme the table was covered with a pear-pattern cloth, and we used whole squashes, pumpkins, fruits, and gourds as table decorations. Seating was informal, on couches, chairs, and benches around the room.

When it was time for dessert, we returned to the sitting room for two seasonal sweets—a luscious pear and hazelnut strudel and a cranberry and apple torte—accompanied by *real* hot chocolate with whipped cream.

New-style "micro brew" beers, wines, and waters were the spirits chosen for the party. Later in the season, after the second week of November, a Beaujolais Nouveau would have complemented the menu perfectly.

BEER TASTING

Many people today are enjoying brewing beers at home, and a beer-tasting/buffet party—planned around Oktoberfest perhaps—is a nice way to get friends together. Beer has been around since ancient times, probably 4000 B.C., and was brought to America by the Pilgrims. Until recently in Europe there were beer purity laws that prohibited European brewers from adding corn, rice, sugar, or any other grains to beer. To insure the highest quality only four ingredients could be used besides yeast: water, hops, malted barley, and wheat. American brewers, on the other hand, were not bound by these laws and started mass-producing lighter beers. In this country brewing has returned to its roots, and small regional breweries, brew pubs, and home-brewing have become immensely popular once again. Many unique and delicious styles of beer are being produced: beers to which maple syrup, sorghum, honey, chocolate, and even pumpkin have been added; fruit beers made with cherries, raspberries, lemons, oranges, blueberries, boysenberries, and loganberries; beers brewed with herbs like marjoram, caraway, coriander, and juniper, or spices like cinnamon, cloves, anise, nutmeg, and ginger; even smoked beers.

Beer aficionados love to sample different styles and varieties of beer. For a beer-tasting party, offer a dozen or so brands of bottled beer or your own and your friends' home brews. There are hundreds of beers to choose from, but here are the basic categories.

GERMAN ALES—Alt and Kolsch

GERMAN MALTED WHEAT ALES—Weizen, Berliner Weisse, Hefe-weizen, and Dunkel Weizen, Weizenbock

BELGIAN UNMALTED WHEAT ALES—Wit, Lambic

BELGIAN ALES—Pale, Trappist Ales, Saison, Belgian Red, Hander Brown Ales, Belgian Strong Golden Ales, Belgian Dark Strong Ales, Bière de Grande

PALE ALES—Bitter, Scottish Ales, English Pale Ale, American Pale Ale, India Pale Ale

BROWN ALES—Mild, English Brown, American Brown

PORTER—Robust and Brown

STOUT—Dry, Foreign, Sweet, Oatmeal, and Imperial

STRONG ALE—English Old, Scottish, and Barley Wine

LAGERS—American Lite, Standard and Premium, Dry, Dark, Bock, and Malt Liquor

CLASSIC PILSNERS—Bohemian and German

DORTMUNDER OR EXPORT

VIENNA—Marzen or Oktoberfest

MUNICH—Helles, Munich Dunkel, Schwarzbier, and Rauchbier

BOCK—Helles, Dopplebock, Eisbock

HYBRID STYLES—California Common Bear, Cream Ale

"MICRO BEERS"

A selection of "micro brew" beers, kept icy cold in an old ironstone bowl.

Harvest Moonfest
for 12 to 15

BUFFET DINNER

Chanterelle Mushrooms, Scallops,
Brussels Sprouts, and Shallots

Roasted Pork Loin with Ginger Mustard Rub

Baked Quince Topped with Spinach and Nuts

Sugar Dumpling Squash Filled with
Cranberry Beans, Quinoa, and Corn

Autumn Slivered Root and Vegetable Salad

Harvest Layered Potato Cake

Stewed Green Pole Beans and Tomatoes

SWEETS

Cranberry-Apple Torte

Pear and Hazelnut Strudel

Mulled Cider

Hot Chocolate with Whipped Cream

Chanterelle Mushrooms, Scallops, Brussels Sprouts, and Shallots

Golden chanterelles, with their trumpet shape and earthy aroma, are an eagerly awaited autumn delicacy. With scallops, Brussels sprouts, and shallots, they make a colorful, well-balanced dish.

3 pints Brussels sprouts (about 40 pieces), outer stems and leaves removed

½ cup olive or vegetable oil

10 medium shallots, peeled and thinly sliced

10 cloves garlic, peeled and chopped

1½ pounds chanterelle mushrooms, trimmed and brushed cleaned

3 pounds bay or sea scallops, cleaned

1 cup Fish Stock (page 184) or white wine

Coarse salt and freshly ground black pepper to taste

¼ cup fresh lemon juice

½ cup coarsely chopped flat-leaf parsley

1. Bring a pot of salted water to a boil over high heat, add the Brussels sprouts, and blanch about 3 minutes, until al dente. Strain through a colander, then plunge into an ice bath to stop the cooking process. Drain again and set aside.

2. Heat the oil in a large skillet over high heat. Add the shallots and garlic and sauté over high heat until softened. Add the chanterelles and cook approximately 3 minutes. Toss in the scallops, then the stock or wine, and cook 2 minutes more. Taste for seasoning, and add salt and pepper. Toss in the Brussels sprouts and cook 2 to 3 minutes just to reheat them. Add the lemon juice and toss. Transfer to a serving platter, sprinkle with the parsley, and serve.

Serves 12 to 15, as part of buffet.

PLANNING AHEAD: The Brussels sprouts can be blanched up to 2 days ahead and stored in a covered container in the refrigerator. With the garlic and shallots sliced, and the parsley chopped, this dish can be assembled very quickly before the guests arrive. Keep warm in a low (200° to 250° F) oven.

Roasted Pork Loin with Ginger Mustard Rub

This spice rub can be used on other meats, including lamb, venison, chicken, and rabbit. It is particularly useful for enhancing the flavor of meats that are trimmed of all excess fat before roasting, such as the pork in this recipe.

2 (4-inch) pieces ginger, peeled and
    cut into pieces
1½ cups Dijon-style mustard
4 sprigs fresh rosemary, leaves
    picked and finely chopped
6 sprigs fresh oregano, leaves picked
    and finely chopped

2 (4- to 5-pound) boneless pork
    loins, fat trimmed
Vegetable oil, for coating the
    roasting pan
Optional: ½ cup Madeira
4 cups chicken stock

1. Place the ginger pieces in a food processor and finely chop. Add the mustard, rosemary, and oregano and process until you have a paste.

2. Rub the pork on all sides with the mustard paste. Cover with plastic wrap and refrigerate at least 8 hours.

3. Preheat the oven to 375° F. Coat the bottom of a roasting pan with vegetable oil and put in the oven to heat. When hot, add the pork loins and roast approximately 1 hour 15 minutes, until the pork is cooked through and the juices run clear when pierced with a skewer. Remove to a platter, and let rest for 20 minutes before slicing.

4. If you want to make a pan sauce, skim the excess fat from the roasting juices, add Madeira (if using) and chicken stock, and bring to a boil over medium-high heat, scraping and stirring to deglaze the pan. Lower the heat and simmer about 3 to 4 minutes to reduce sauce by half. Pour through a fine-mesh strainer into a saucepan and set aside. Reheat when ready to serve the pork.

Serves 12 to 15, as part of buffet.

PLANNING AHEAD: The pork can marinate in the mustard rub for up to 3 days in the refrigerator before roasting.

Baked Quince Topped with Spinach and Nuts

Quinces are an old-style fruit that are starting to make a comeback with modern chefs. Yellow and pear-shaped, quinces are covered with a fuzz similar to peaches. Although their smell is sweet and fragrant, their taste is so tart and astringent that they cannot be eaten raw. Because they contain a lot of pectin, quinces are often used for jellies. Here I have baked and stuffed them to make a savory fruit-and-vegetable accompaniment to the pork.

7 large quinces
Juice of 3 lemons
Coarse salt and freshly ground black
   pepper to taste
14 tablespoons honey
2 tablespoons vegetable oil

4 pounds fresh spinach leaves,
   washed, dried, and chopped
2 cups nuts (pine nuts, pecans,
   almonds, or walnuts), coarsely
   chopped
4 cloves garlic, finely chopped

1. Preheat the oven to 425° F. Cut off the ends of the quinces, then cut in half. Remove the cores with a melon baller or teaspoon. Place the quinces, brushed with oil, in a baking dish large enough to hold them in 1 layer. Sprinkle with lemon juice, salt, and pepper, and drizzle each with a tablespoon of honey. Bake for 20 to 25 minutes, until soft. Remove from the oven and set aside.

2. Measure the oil into a wok or large skillet set over high heat. When very hot, add a fourth of the spinach and cook until wilted. Add another fourth of the spinach, sprinkle with the nuts and garlic, toss, and cook another minute. Add the remaining spinach and cook until wilted. Remove the spinach to a colander and let drain. When cool enough to handle, divide among the quince halves.

3. When ready to serve, heat in a 425° F oven for 10 minutes.

Serves 14, as part of buffet.

PLANNING AHEAD: The quinces can be baked up to 2 days ahead, but should not be stuffed and heated until close to serving time. The spinach stuffing can also be made 2 days ahead and kept covered in the refrigerator.

Sugar Dumpling Squash Filled with Cranberry Beans, Quinoa, and Corn

Sugar dumplings are pretty, roly-poly-shaped, mottled squash with deep orange-colored flesh. Their flavor is similar to that of acorn squash.

Fresh cranberry beans are shell beans that are picked with the late harvest. Their skin is creamy beige with cranberry speckles. When these beans are cooked, most of the color disappears and the texture becomes soft and creamy.

15 sugar dumpling squash, washed
¼ cup vegetable oil
2 small onions, peeled and cut into medium dice
12 cloves garlic, chopped
4 sprigs fresh savory or thyme, leaves picked and chopped
3 cups fresh cranberry beans (see Note)

Coarse salt and freshly ground black pepper to taste
2 quarts water or chicken or veal stock
4 cups cooked quinoa (recipe follows)
4 cups fresh corn kernels, blanched or pan-seared

1. Preheat the oven to 350° F. Cut the tops off the squash and save them, to serve as lids. Scoop out the seeds. Place the squash in a roasting pan large enough to hold them snugly. Pour hot water around the squash until it comes a fourth of the way up the sides. Cover the pan with foil and bake for about 25 minutes, until the flesh is tender to the touch.

2. While the squash are cooking, heat the oil in a 3-quart saucepan set over high heat. Add the onions, garlic, and savory or thyme, and cook for about 2 minutes just to soften. Add the cranberry beans, stir to coat, and season with salt and pepper. Add the water or stock, bring to a boil, then reduce the heat to medium and cook for approximately 25 minutes, until the beans are tender. Remove from the heat and let cool.

3. Preheat the oven to 350° F. In a large bowl, toss together the cooked beans, quinoa, and corn. Stuff some of the mixture into each squash and cover with the lids. Bake for about 15 to 20 minutes just to heat.

Serves 15, as part of buffet.

NOTE: Cranberry beans are also available dried. If you are using dried beans, either presoak them overnight to soften them or double the amount of water or stock and let them cook longer, until tender.

PLANNING AHEAD: The squash can be cooked, and the filling prepared, up to 3 days ahead and stored in covered containers in the refrigerator.

Quinoa

Quinoa is a small, crunchy "supergrain" that is very high in protein and other nutrients. It has a slightly grassy flavor and is either natural or black in color. The quinoa plant is native to the South American Andes, and probably dates back in history to the Inca civilization.

1½ cups quinoa, washed and drained	**3 cups water or chicken or veal stock**

1. Place the quinoa in a fine-mesh strainer over a sink or bowl and rinse with cold water, stirring. Change the water when it becomes cloudy, drain, and continue rising until the water is clear.
2. Bring the salted water or stock to a boil over high heat. Add the quinoa, bring back to a boil, then reduce the heat to low and simmer for approximately 15 minutes, until the liquid is absorbed. Remove from the heat, cover, and let sit for 5 minutes to finish cooking. Transfer to a bowl to cool.

Makes 4 cups.

PLANNING AHEAD: Quinoa can be cooked up to 3 days ahead and stored in a covered container in the refrigerator.

Autumn Slivered Root and Vegetable Salad

Root vegetables make tasty, crunchy salads that hold up well when dressed and tossed ahead and set out on a buffet.

2 knobs celery root, peeled
2 bulbs fennel, stalks removed, washed
1 medium head red cabbage
2 Belgian endives
2 bunches arugula, washed and dried
Juice of 2 lemons

CREAMY CUMIN DRESSING:
2 tablespoons ground cumin
1 cup plain yogurt
1 cup sour cream
Juice of 1 lemon
Coarse salt and freshly ground black pepper to taste

1. Prepare the vegetables: Cut the celery root, fennel, and red cabbage into slivers with a sharp knife or using a mandoline. Cut the endives into diagonal pieces. Chop the arugula into 1-inch pieces. Sprinkle the celery root, fennel, and endive with the lemon juice to prevent discoloration.

2. Combine all of the vegetables in a salad bowl.

3. To make the dressing, place the cumin in a skillet and heat over medium-low heat for 1 to 2 minutes, stirring with a wooden spoon, until it begins to "bloom" and smell fragrant. Combine with the yogurt, sour cream, lemon juice, and salt and pepper in a food processor or medium bowl and process or whisk until well combined. Pour the dressing over the vegetables and toss.

Serves 12 to 15, as part of buffet.

PLANNING AHEAD: This salad can be prepared and tossed with the dressing up to 8 hours before serving.

The dinner buffet. COUNTERCLOCKWISE FROM LEFT: *Slivered root and vegetable salad; chanterelle mushrooms, scallops, Brussels sprouts, and shallots; layered potato cake; stewed green pole beans and tomatoes; roasted pork loin with ginger mustard rub; baked quince with spinach and nuts; sugar dumpling squash filled with cranberry beans, quinoa, and corn.*

Harvest Layered Potato Cake

A slow-roasted, layered potato cake with lots of color and subtle flavor.

½ cup virgin or pure olive oil
6 pounds Yukon Gold potatoes,
    peeled and thinly sliced
20 sprigs fresh thyme, leaves picked
    and chopped
Coarse salt and freshly ground black
    pepper to taste

6 large bell peppers (red, yellow, or
    green), roasted, with skins and
    seeds removed (see Note), cut into
    large pieces

1. Line a 9 × 12-inch heavy, enamel-coated roasting pan with parchment paper. Sprinkle with 2 tablespoons of the oil. Pat the potatoes dry, then arrange them in a double layer in the bottom of the pan. Sprinkle with some of the thyme, salt, pepper, and the remaining oil. Add a layer of roasted peppers. Repeat the layering process until you have a total of 3 layers of potatoes and 2 layers of peppers. The top layer should be potatoes, salt, and pepper. Cover the pan with parchment paper and top with aluminum foil.

2. Preheat the oven to 350° F. Bake the potato cake approximately 1 hour 15 minutes, until the potatoes offer little or no resistance when pierced with a skewer or knife tip. Uncover the pan (save the parchment and foil), turn up the heat to 400° F, and roast for 20 minutes more.

3. Remove the pan from the oven and let rest at least 1 hour, then cover with the reserved parchment and foil, weigh down with a heavy lid or cans and let rest an additional 20 minutes. Turn out onto a serving dish and cut into portions.

Serves 12 to 15, as part of buffet.

NOTE: See technique on page 102 for oven roasting peppers.

PLANNING AHEAD: The peppers can be roasted up to 3 days ahead and kept in the refrigerator. The potatoes can be peeled and kept in water in the refrigerator for up to 2 days. If you like, the whole dish can be baked up to 1 day ahead and reheated, covered, in a 350° F oven; if the dish is cold, this can take up to 45 minutes; 25 minutes if it is at room temperature. You can also cut up portions and heat them, covered with foil, on a baking sheet, which will take less time.

Stewed Green Pole Beans and Tomatoes

Green pole beans, Italian flat beans, and Kentucky Wonders are one and the same: wide, flat fresh green beans. They are delicious stewed with juicy end-of-summer garden tomatoes.

1 tablespoon vegetable oil

3 leeks, washed, or 2 small onions, peeled, cut in medium dice

10 cloves garlic, peeled and crushed

1 bunch fresh basil, leaves picked (about 1 cup)

1 bunch fresh dill and/or oregano, chopped (about 1 cup)

4 pounds tomatoes, peeled, seeded, and coarsely chopped, with juice

3 pounds fresh pole beans, ends trimmed, cut into 1½-inch pieces

2 teaspoons freshly ground black pepper

Coarse salt to taste

Heat the oil in a skillet over medium-high heat. Add the leeks or onions, garlic, basil, and dill or oregano, and cook 1 or 2 minutes to soften. Add the tomato pulp and juice and bring to a boil over high heat. Add the beans, pepper, and salt, reduce the heat, and simmer for approximately 25 to 30 minutes, until the beans are cooked through and tender (not al dente).

Serves 12 to 15, as part of buffet.

PLANNING AHEAD: This dish can be prepared up to 3 days ahead, stored in the refrigerator, and reheated over medium heat.

Cranberry-Apple Torte

I like to use Northern Spy or Baldwin apples for this dessert, but the more common Granny Smiths can be substituted. The combination of tartness and sweetness in the filling and the tender, buttery pastry will convince you to make this torte many times. But don't be limited to this combination of fruits; many others are possible.

BATTER:
6 eggs
1¾ cups light brown sugar
14 ounces (3½ sticks) unsalted
  butter, melted and cooled
4 cups all-purpose flour
1 teaspoon baking powder
¼ cup apple cider
1 teaspoon vanilla extract

FILLING:
6 apples, peeled, cored, and cut into
  medium slices
2 teaspoons fresh lemon juice
2 cups fresh cranberries
½ cup light brown sugar
1 teaspoon ground cinnamon

1. Using an electric mixer lightly beat together the eggs and sugar. Combine the melted butter, flour, and baking powder and add to the egg-sugar mixture in 3 parts, mixing well after each addition. Mix in the cider and vanilla. Let the batter rest for 15 minutes.

2. To make the filling, toss the apples with the lemon juice in a large bowl. Add the cranberries, sugar, and cinnamon and toss again.

3. Line two 9- or 10-inch round cake pans with parchment paper, or grease and flour them. Preheat the oven to 400° F.

4. Pour the batter evenly into the 2 pans. Divide the apple mixture and spoon on top of the batter in each pan, pressing down lightly. Bake about 40 minutes, until the cake is golden and the fruit is tender. Let cool in the pans 1 hour before removing. Run a knife around the edges and turn out onto 2 serving plates.

Makes two 9- or 10-inch round tortes.

PLANNING AHEAD: This torte can be baked up to 2 days ahead, wrapped in plastic, and kept in the refrigerator. Warm slowly in a 250° F oven before serving.

A dessert plate holds a slice of cranberry-apple torte, accompanied by a mug of hot chocolate with whipped cream.

Pear and Hazelnut Strudel

I made strudel for the first time with pastry chef Albert Kumin, who, with his large, amazing hands, showed me how to carefully stretch the dough until paper-thin over a long pastry table. Fortunately, we don't have to make strudel dough that way anymore; instead, we can use frozen phyllo dough. Here, I layer the fruits, nuts, and sugars between the layers of dough, which makes the strudel crispy.

2 cups coarsely ground hazelnuts
2 cups sugar
8 cups shredded pear (use a mando-
    line or grater and about 8 pears)
½ teaspoon freshly grated nutmeg

Juice of 1 lemon
1 box phyllo sheets
12 ounces (3 sticks) unsalted butter,
    melted

1. Combine the nuts and sugar in a medium bowl. In a separate bowl, combine the pears, nutmeg, and lemon juice.

2. Open the phyllo package and lay the stack of sheets out flat on a dry surface. Cover with a layer of parchment paper, then top with a clean, slightly damp cotton towel.

3. To make the first strudel, brush 2 phyllo sheets with melted butter, then place 2 more sheets on top. Brush again with butter. Sprinkle with a little of the nut-sugar mix, then some of the pears. Layer 2 more phyllo sheets on top, brush with butter, and top with the nut-sugar mixture and pears. Repeat this process one more time. Do the same for the second strudel, making 3 layers filled with the nut-sugar mixture and the pears.

4. Roll up each phyllo into a tight jelly roll, starting at one of the long ends. Brush with butter. Carefully pick up and place the rolls, seam side down, on a parchment-lined baking sheet. Using a serrated knife, score the top of each into 8 or 9 slices. Chill in the refrigerator for at least 1 hour.

5. Preheat the oven to 300° F. Bake the strudels for 50 to 60 minutes, until golden and cooked through. Let rest at least 20 minutes before cutting into pieces, using the score lines as guides.

Makes two 12-inch strudels.

PLANNING AHEAD: The strudels can be assembled and left to rest in the refrigerator for up to 24 hours before baking.

Desserts were set out in an old cupboard in the sitting room. FROM LEFT TO RIGHT: *Pear and hazelnut strudel; whipped cream; cranberry-apple torte; and real hot chocolate.*

Mulled cider was served in an old pressed glass pitcher in the sitting room.

Mulled Cider

Like the changing colors of the leaves, the smell of cider mulling is a sure sign that autumn is upon us.

1 gallon fresh cider
3 cinnamon sticks

⅛ teaspoon ground cloves
⅛ teaspoon allspice

1. Combine the cider, cinnamon, cloves, and allspice in a large pot and bring almost to a boil over low heat. Remove from the heat, strain, and serve warm.

Makes 16 cups.

PLANNING AHEAD: Cider can be mulled up to 8 days ahead and reheated over low heat on the stove.

Hot Chocolate

The best way to make real hot chocolate is to start with a basic chocolate sauce and then stir it into hot milk or cream.

CHOCOLATE SAUCE:
1 pound semisweet chocolate
1 cup boiling water
2 ounces unsalted butter, softened
6 quarts whole milk or cream

Optional: **Whipped cream or cocoa powder**

1. To make the chocolate sauce, chop the chocolate into chunks by hand or in a food processor. Place in a medium pot and stir in the boiling water. Continue stirring over the low heat until the chocolate is completely melted. Add the butter and stir until the sauce is smooth.

2. In a separate, large pot, scald the milk over high heat. Remove from the heat and whisk in the chocolate sauce until completely blended. Serve with dollops of whipped cream and a sprinkling of cocoa powder if you like.

Makes 24 cups.

PLANNING AHEAD: The chocolate sauce can be made up to 2 weeks ahead and kept in a covered container in the refrigerator. Reheat in the top of a double boiler over gently simmering water before blending with the hot milk.

The Tasting Table:
An Hors D'Oeuvres Buffet

Many people find the idea of offering small tastes of an array of different foods appealing. The menu can be more flexible and interesting, and guests have more choices. This kind of buffet works especially well for cocktail parties, afternoon gatherings, and post-concert events, when a lighter meal with more variety is preferred.

This was an informal cocktail party held in the late afternoon at a friend's studio/guesthouse, which was built in a vintage apple orchard on her property in Middlebury, Connecticut. The slate floors, fireplace, and contemporary design make the studio a perfect setting for parties. It was such a beautiful day that we decided to set up the bar outside under the shade of some beautifully gnarled old apple trees. The bar was self-serve, but for a larger crowd we could have hired a bartender. Sun-dried tomato and olive palmiers and a bowl of marinated olives were set out on a rustic bench on the patio for relaxed nibbling with drinks. The rest of the hor d'oeuvres were arranged on the hostess's long primitive table inside the main room of the studio. When setting up this kind of buffet I like to use tiered platters to give the table a lot of texture and depth. I can also fit more dishes on the table by taking advantage of vertical space. I use a variety of objects—wooden molds, pedestal dishes, interestingly shaped vases or buckets, and stands—to hold platters, choosing them according to their stability and dimensions. I also like to use items that are not necessarily made for food service—a candlestick to hold toothpicks for the lemon chicken meatballs or a model-size carved Indian cart to serve the sesame soy dipping sauce for the sushi. Use your creativity and think up unique ways to present food on the table; try not to get

Eleven different savory hors d'oeuvres were arranged on the hostess's 14-foot-long primitive table.

locked into thinking that you can only use objects for the purposes for which they were originally intended.

The platters were decorated very simply, using edible herbs and flowers, as well as ingredients used in the preparation of the hors d'oeuvres—for example, a cleaned lobster body and claws for the lobster avocado tortilla crisps. The table itself was decorated with simple flower bouquets and ornamental carved figures. We wrote out the menu so the guests would know what was on the table in order of placement; this also gave our party the festive feeling of a real "tasting" event. Guests didn't have to sample the hors d'oeuvres in any particular order, however; the buffet was intended to be casual, with guests returning to the table as many times as they liked to pick up more food. Because the hors d'oeuvres were bite-sized, only napkins and small plates were needed. I always put out several stacks of both at various points on the buffet table so guests can reach them easily.

Friends had the choice of dropping by for half an hour for a drink and one or two hors d'euvres, or staying for the entire three-hour party. For those who stayed, there was plenty of food to make up a complete meal. We also offered a few sweets, as well as coffee, toward the end of the party; I find this gesture is always appreciated by guests. Just make sure to keep the desserts small, easy to eat, and not overly sweet.

Remember that you can also add simple items, such as smoked salmon slices, roasted beef tenderloin with French bread slices, a cheese tray, or a raw vegetable basket, to an hors d'oeuvres buffet. I've offered you many alternatives on this menu; feel free to use as many of the dishes as you like. And don't forget that there are many other appetizer and snack recipes in this book that you might want to try.

When you are planning an hors d'oeuvres party keep these general questions in mind.

—How many types of hors d'oeuvres do you want, and will they precede a meal or be served alone? NOTE: For an hors d'oeuvres party, plan on 2 to 2½ of each hors d'oeuvre per person, except for shrimp or crab; allow 3 to 4 per person of these always-popular hors d'oeuvres. If the hors d'oeuvres will precede a full meal, allow 1½ per person.

—Is there a balance of vegetable, meat, and seafood hors d'oeuvres? Have you avoided including too many dough-based, fried, or cheesy dishes?

—Will the hors d'oeuvres be served hot, cold, or at room temperature?

—What serving pieces will you need? How will you keep the food at the right temperature?

—Are the hors d'oeuvres the "pick-up" variety, requiring just a cocktail napkin, or will there be more substantial hors d'oeuvres, needing a small plate? Do any of the hors d'oeuvres require a skewer, toothpick, or fork?

—Will the hors d'oeuvres be assembled before serving, or do you want guests to make their own, complete with garnishes and condiments?

—Do you want all of the hors d'oeuvres to be set out on tables, or do you want some to be passed on trays?

—Will you need to ask friends or hire staff to help pass trays, replenish the buffet table, or tend the bar?

Over the years I have made literally thousands of hors d'oeuvres, and have always enjoyed the fun and challenge of creating new ones. It was difficult for me to choose which hors d'oeuvres to put on this menu, and I think you will find yourself in the same quandry once you begin to develop your own repertoire.

The Tasting Table:
An Hors d'Oeuvres Buffet

for 25–30

Sun-Dried Tomato and Olive Palmiers

Wonton Cups with Corn Mango Duck Salad

Vegetarian Ginger Sushi with Sesame Soy Sauce

Black Bean Pancakes with Pico de Gallo

Dilled Beet and Beef Zarzukis

Zucchini, Tomato, and Basil Bruschetta

Portobello Mushroom Herb Croustade

Wild Rice Pancakes with Smoked Salmon Salad

Lemon Chicken Meatballs

Bayou Rock Shrimp Balls with Spicy Sherry Sauce

Lobster Avocado Tortilla Crisps

SWEETS

Bittersweet Chocolate Cupcakes

Sweet Ricotta Chocolate Chip Fruit Phyllos

Peaches with Cinnamon Goat Cheese

Sun-Dried Tomato and Olive Palmiers

These tasty puff pastries look great, are simple to make, and are easy to eat.

8 sun-dried tomatoes, soaked in
    warm oil or water
20 imported black olives, pitted
¾ cup shredded provolone cheese
2 tablespoons fresh chopped chives,
    thyme, or rosemary leaves

2 tablespoons chopped garlic
2 puff pastry sheets, each measuring
    5 × 6 × ¼-inch

1. Finely chop the sun-dried tomatoes and olives. Place in a medium bowl with the provolone, chives, thyme, or rosemary and garlic. Set aside.

2. On a floured surface, roll out the puff pastry sheets into two ⅛-inch-thick rectangles about 9 × 12 inches. Brush off the excess flour. Sprinkle each sheet with half of the tomato-cheese mixture. Starting from a long end, tightly roll each sheet in toward the center to form a scroll. Place the rolls in the refrigerator between layers of parchment paper or plastic wrap, and chill for at least 1 hour.

3. When ready to bake, preheat the oven to 425° F. Remove the rolls from the refrigerator and cut into ½-inch-thick slices. Bake on parchment-lined baking sheets for about 9 minutes, until puffed and golden. Let cool on the baking sheets.

Makes about 50 hors d'oeuvres.

PLANNING AHEAD: Unbaked palmiers, cut or uncut, can be kept in the freezer in a covered container for at least 1 month. Once baked, palmiers will keep for up to 3 days in an airtight container. Warm in the oven to recrisp them and enhance their flavor.

Wonton Cups with Corn Mango Duck Salad

These crunchy wonton cups are baked, not fried, and can hold any array of chopped salads, savory or sweet. The presentation is fun, simple, and appreciated by guests. Be sure to finely chop the salad ingredients; long pieces will make this hors d'oeuvre messy to eat.

WONTON CUPS:

2 packages (about 60) small, in thin wonton wrappers, about 3 inches square

CORN MANGO DUCK SALAD:

2½ pounds roasted duck meat (see Note)

2 cups fresh bean sprouts

2 cups fresh corn kernels

2 cups finely chopped carrots

2 cups finely chopped jicama

2 cups finely chopped scallions

2 cups finely chopped mangoes

1 cup chopped fresh cilantro

1 cup fresh basil leaves, finely shredded

Optional: 1 cup tatsoi greens, finely shredded

5 tablespoons Asian oyster sauce

1. Preheat the oven to 375° F. Brush mini-muffin tins with a small amount of vegetable oil or spray with vegetable cooking spray. Place 1 wonton sheet in each opening, pushing down in the center to form a cup. Bake about 5 minutes, just until the cups are golden. Remove the pan from the oven and tip out the cups. Repeat the process (you don't need to re-oil the tins) until you have approximately 50 wonton cups (you'll need extras in case some break or get eaten). Set aside.

2. To make the salad, remove the fat from the duck and cut the meat into slivers, then finely dice. Place in a large bowl. Chop the bean sprouts into fine pieces and add to the bowl.

3. Sear the corn kernels in a wok or skillet over high heat. Let cool before adding to the bowl.

4. Add the carrots, jicama, scallions, mango, cilantro, basil, tatsoi greens (if using), and the oyster sauce. Toss well, let sit about 10 minutes, then taste for seasoning. Add more oyster sauce if needed.

5. Spoon the salad into the wonton cups.

Makes 45 hors d'oeuvres.

NOTE: One whole roasted 5½-pound duck will yield about 2½ pounds of duck meat. Or you can roast or barbecue 5 or 6 duck legs (see page 41) instead.

(CONTINUED)

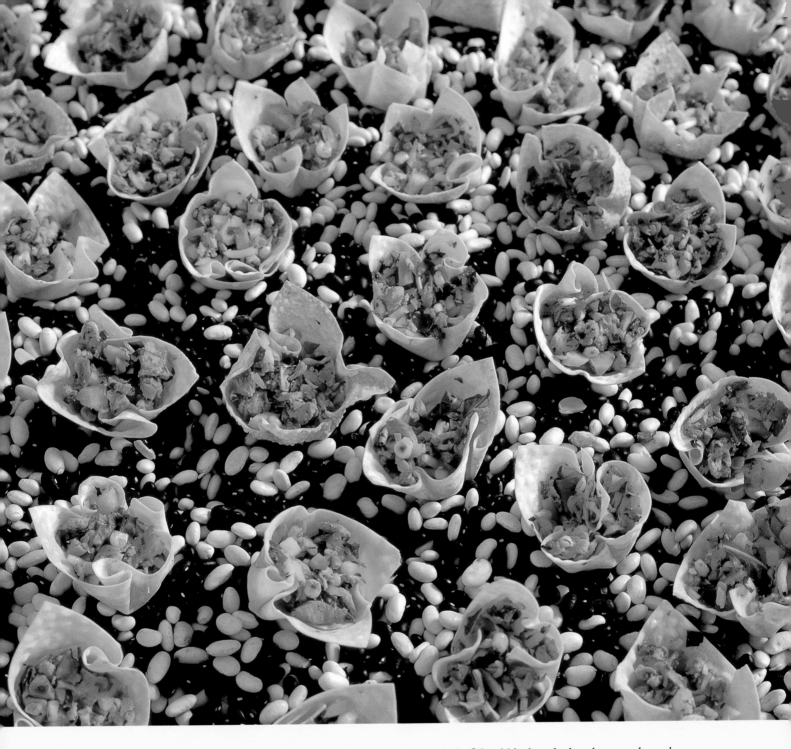

Wonton cups filled with corn mango duck salad were arranged on a bed of dried black and white beans to keep them upright.

PLANNING AHEAD: The wonton cups can be baked a week ahead and stored at room temperature in a covered container. The salad can be prepared 1 day ahead and stored in the refrigerator in a covered container.

Vegetarian Ginger Sushi with Sesame Soy Sauce

These are really nori-maki, *the Japanese term for rolled sushi made with nori, dried seaweed that is packaged in thin sheets. Filled with sticky jasmine rice and vegetables, these make light, beautiful hors d'oeuvres.*

To roll the sushi properly you will need a flexible bamboo mat (maki-su), which can be found at Asian markets. It is not difficult to make the rolls, but it does take a bit of practice to learn to pack them firmly enough. Make sure that all the filling is in the middle of the sheet of nori to get a proper roll. If you have difficulty rolling sushi, I suggest you visit a Japanese sushi bar, sit at the counter, and watch the chefs. You'll get the hang of it in no time.

STICKY RICE:

4 tablespoons rice vinegar
4 tablespoons sugar
1 tablespoon coarse salt
3½ cups raw jasmine rice

6 nori (dried seaweed) sheets
   (see Note 1)
Approximately 42 pickled ginger
   slices, cut into thin julienne strips

NORI FILLING:

1 medium beet, peeled
1 medium jicama or daikon
   (Asian radish) or 10 red radishes
1 medium cucumber, peeled
2 medium carrots, peeled
1 ripe avocado
1 package or bunch daikon, bean
   sprouts, or pea sprouts
1 bunch mizuna, tatsoi, or
   watercress

Optional: 14 large shiitake mushrooms, stems removed, julienned
   and sautéed

SESAME SOY SAUCE:

1 cup light soy sauce
3 scallions, thinly sliced
2 teaspoons sesame seeds, toasted
1 tablespoon sesame oil

Optional: Wasabi (see Note 2)

1. In a small bowl, combine the rice vinegar, sugar, and salt, stirring to dissolve. Set aside.

2. Place the rice in a very fine strainer over the sink or a bowl. Rinse with water, stirring with a wooden spatula, until the water is clear. Drain well. Transfer to a heavy-

bottomed, 3- to 4-quart pot, add 4 cups cold water, and stir. Bring to a boil over high heat, stir, cover tightly, and reduce heat to medium. Cook the rice for 6 minutes, then reduce the heat to low and cook 15 minutes more. Remove the rice from the heat and let stand, covered, for 10 minutes. The rice should be cooked through and sticky, but each grain should be separate. You can also cook the rice in an Asian rice cooker according to the manufacturer's instructions.

3. As soon as the rice is ready, turn it out onto a shallow pan. Using a wooden spatula, spread the rice out and sprinkle with the rice vinegar mixture. Turn the rice over lightly, fanning it as you turn; this will break apart the rice grains and help it cool.

4. To prepare the vegetables for rolling, using an Asian cutter or mandoline, finely shred the beet, jicama, cucumber, and carrots. Peel the avocado, remove the pit, and cut into 14 slices (sprinkle with some of the pickled ginger liquid to prevent discoloration). Wash and dry the greens and remove the large stems. Line up all of the ingredients, including the optional shiitakes, in neat bunches on a platter or put them in separate containers.

5. Traditionally, nori is prepared for rolling by toasting the shiny side over an open flame, which keeps the nori drier and more flavorful. However, this step is not essential.

6. To keep the rice from sticking to your hands as you work, prepare a "hand vinegar" (in Japanese this is called *tezu*) by combining ¾ cup water with 1 tablespoon rice vinegar.

7. Begin rolling using this method:

   a. Place a sheet of nori, shiny side down, on a flexible bamboo mat. Moisten your hands with the "hand vinegar."

   b. Using your fingers, evenly spread a thin (¼-inch) layer of rice over three-quarters of the nori sheet. You will need to use about 1 cup rice for this step. Leave the area farthest away from you uncovered.

   c. Lay a thin layer of vegetables and pickled ginger across the center of the rice, spreading evenly. Use a sixth of the total amount of vegetables and 7 pickled ginger slices for each nori roll.

   d. Hold the line of ingredients firmly in place with your fingertips and, with your thumbs, start rolling the edge of the nori nearest you and lift it up and over to meet the far edge of the sheet. Press the mat firmly around the roll to shape it, pinwheel-style.

   e. Remove the nori roll from the bamboo mat. Using a wet knife, cut the roll in half crosswise, then cut each half into 4 pieces. Clean the knife each time you make another slice. Cut straight through; don't saw.

8. Repeat the rolling and cutting process with 5 more sheets of nori and the rest of the fillling ingredients.

9. To make the sesame soy sauce, combine the soy sauce, scallions, sesame seeds, and sesame oil in a small bowl and mix with a fork or chopsticks. Serve with the nori rolls.

Makes 48 hors d'oeuvres.

NOTE 1: Nori are sold in packages, usually of 10, in Asian markets. They measure 6½ × 8 inches and have a shiny and a rough side. When making rolls, the shiny side should be on the outside (for appearances' sake), the rough side next to the filling.

NOTE 2: In addition to the sesame soy sauce, you may wish to serve the sushi with wasabi, a strong spice unique to the Japanese islands. Bright green in color, wasabi is comparable in flavor to horseradish, but more fragrant and less sharp-tasting. Fresh Japanese wasabi is difficult to find, but powdered wasabi or wasabi paste is readily available. The powdered kind can be reconstituted by mixing it with a small amount of tepid water until smooth, and letting it sit for 10 minutes to "bloom."

PLANNING AHEAD: The rice is better cooked the day you plan to use it. The vegetables can be cut up and stored in a covered container in the refrigerator overnight. The nori rolls can be made up to 4 hours ahead, cut into pieces, lined up on a nonmetallic platter, covered with plastic wrap, and kept in the refrigerator until serving time. The sesame soy sauce can be mixed up to 2 days ahead.

Black Bean Pancakes with Pico de Gallo

The cooked black beans in this recipe can be used in many other ways—in a rice and beans dish, rolled up in a flour tortilla, or as a delicious dip.

4 quarts cold water

1 pound dried black beans

¼ cup vegetable oil

1 medium onion, peeled and roughly chopped

8 cloves garlic, peeled and stems removed

1 tablespoon cumin

½ teaspoon cayenne pepper or 2 fresh chilies or jalapeños, coarsely chopped

1 teaspoon chili powder

Coarse salt to taste

1 cup plus 2 tablespoons all-purpose flour or rice flour

¾ cup chopped scallions

Vegetable oil, for frying

2 cups Pico de Gallo (recipe follows)

Optional: Sour cream

1. Pour 2 quarts of the cold water over the dried beans and let them soak for 4 to 12 hours to soften them. They will absorb all of the water.

2. Heat the oil in a 3-quart pot. Add the onion and sauté over high heat until soft, about 1 minute. Add the garlic, cumin, cayenne pepper or fresh peppers, and chili powder, and sauté for 3 minutes more. Add the beans and remaining 2 quarts water to the pot, stir, and season with salt. Bring the beans to a boil, reduce the heat to a simmer, and cook, covered, for approximately 1 hour fifteen minutes, stirring occasionally. If the liquid cooks out too quickly, add a little water. At the end of the cooking process the beans should be tender and slightly liquidy. Remove from the heat and let cool. Drain well.

3. Place 3 cups of the cooked black beans in a food processor. With the motor running, add the flour down the feed tube and process until completely mixed. Turn out into a mixing bowl, then fold in the rest of the black beans and the scallions. Form the bean mixture into pancakes about ⅓ inch thick and 1½ inches in diameter.

4. Coat a heavy-bottomed skillet with oil and heat over high heat. When the skillet is hot, add a batch of pancakes, reduce the heat to medium, and cook until the pancakes turn dark and crispy, about 2½ minutes. Turn over and cook another 2½ minutes on the other side. Remove to paper towels to drain and repeat with the remaining pancakes, adding a small amount of oil to the pan for each batch.

5. Serve with sour cream, if you like, and Pico de Gallo.

Makes 40 hors d'oeuvres.

PLANNING AHEAD: The black bean mixture can be made up to 3 days ahead. The pancakes can be cooked up to 8 hours ahead and served at room temperature. If you prefer them hot, store them in a covered container in the refrigerator and reheat in a warm skillet or on a baking sheet in a 300° F oven.

Pico de Gallo

This chunky tomato salsa is extremely popular as a dip or topping. Make a lot—it always disappears fast.

12 to 14 medium to large ripe tomatoes	**2 fresh jalapeño peppers or 3 serrano chilies (or substitute ¼ teaspoon cayenne pepper)**
2 medium red or white onions (or 1 large onion)	**½ cup fresh lime juice**
1 bunch cilantro, leaves picked (about 1 cup)	**Coarse salt to taste**

Wash the tomatoes, core, and cut into ¼-inch dice. Place in a large bowl. Peel the onions, cut into ¼-inch dice, and add to the tomatoes. Chop the cilantro leaves and add to the bowl. Finely chop the chilies (be careful to protect your hands with rubber gloves) and add them to the bowl. Add the lime juice and toss all the ingredients together. Taste for seasoning and add salt if necessary.

Makes 4 cups.

PLANNING AHEAD: This salsa can be made up to 3 days ahead and stored in a covered container in the refrigerator.

Dilled Beet and Beef Zarzukis

Zarzukis are little Russian hors d'oeuvres, a variation of the turnover pies that are popular in many different world cuisines. The sour cream makes the dough soft to the bite yet still sturdy enough for a pick-up hors d'oeuvre.

If you like, you can make the dough sweeter by eliminating the horseradish and adding sugar, citrus zest, or crystallized ginger. You can also substitute poultry, lamb, or seafood for the beef in the filling, or eliminate the meat and use only vegetables.

SOUR CREAM DOUGH:

5 cups all-purpose flour

1 teaspoon baking powder

2 teaspoons coarse salt

10 ounces (2½ sticks) unsalted
  butter, cut into small cubes

2 tablespoons prepared horseradish,
  slightly pressed

2 cups sour cream or plain yogurt,
  or 1½ cups buttermilk

FILLING:

1 tablespoon vegetable oil

1 large onion, peeled and finely
  chopped

1 pound boneless beef steak, fat
  removed, finely chopped

7 small to medium beets, peeled and
  finely chopped

1 bunch fresh dill, finely chopped
  (about 1 cup)

1 cup sour cream or plain yogurt,
  drained

Coarse salt and freshly ground black
  pepper to taste

EGG WASH:

1 egg mixed with 2 tablespoons
  water

1. To make the dough, sift together the flour, baking powder, and salt into a large bowl. Cut in the butter until a coarse meal is formed. Add the horseradish and sour cream or yogurt and knead into a smooth, pliable dough. Form the dough into 2 balls, flatten, and let rest in the refrigerator at least 1 hour, wrapped in plastic.

2. To make the filling, heat the oil in a medium sauté pan over high heat. Add the onion and cook over high heat until just softened. Add the beef and brown. Remove the onion and beef to a bowl, add the beets, dill, and sour cream or yogurt, and mix. Correct the seasoning with salt and pepper. Let cool.

3. Remove the dough balls from the refrigerator and roll out on a floured surface to a thickness of ⅛ inch. Use a 3-inch round biscuit cutter to cut out circles. Spoon some of the filling into the center of each circle of dough, then pull the dough over the filling to make a half-moon shape. Press the edges together with your fingers or a fork. Arrange on baking sheets and chill in the refrigerator at least 1 hour, wrapped in plastic.

4. When ready to bake, preheat the oven to 400° F. Brush the dough with the egg wash and bake for approximately 15 minutes, until golden yellow in color.

Makes approximately 50 hors d'oeuvres.

PLANNING AHEAD: Zarzukis can be stuffed and stored in the refrigerator for up to 2 days before baking, or they can be frozen for up to 1 month (if frozen, bake 2 to 3 minutes more). Baked zarzukis are good at room temperature, but if you want to reheat them, put them in a 250° F oven for about 8 minutes.

Zucchini, Tomato, and Basil Bruschetta

Traditionally bruschetta are made by rubbing slices of peasant bread with garlic, sprinkling them with olive oil and salt, and grilling over a fire. Here I've added a layer of roasted zucchini and tomatoes to make an excellent vegetable hors d'oeuvre. Try topping the bread with pesto, tapenade, or cheese.

1 cup pure or virgin olive oil
3 to 4 medium zucchini, sliced
　　straight or on the diagonal into
　　¼-inch-thick slices
2 tablespoons chopped garlic
2 tablespoons chopped fresh thyme,
　　oregano, or marjoram
Coarse salt and freshly ground black
　　pepper to taste

20 fresh plum tomatoes, cut in half
　　lengthwise
40 pieces country bread, ½ inch
　　thick
½ cup extra-virgin olive oil

Garnish: 40 fresh basil leaves, washed
　　and dried

1. Preheat the oven to 300° F. Spread ¼ cup of the olive oil on a rimmed baking sheet and lay the zucchini slices on top. Sprinkle with 1 tablespoon each of the garlic and fresh herbs, the salt and pepper, and another ¼ cup oil. Roast in the oven for about 30 minutes, until the zucchini is soft. Remove from the oven and let cool on the baking sheet.

2. Repeat this same process with the tomatoes, laying the tomato halves cut side down. Roast 45 minutes to 1 hour, until soft. Let cool on the baking sheet. When cool enough to handle, peel off the skin.

3. While the vegetables are roasting, grill or toast the peasant bread. Lay out on a baking sheet and drizzle with extra-virgin olive oil.

4. Place 1 slice of zucchini and half a tomato with a little of the cooking juices on top of each slice of bread. Garnish with basil leaves.

Makes 40 hors d'oeuvres.

PLANNING AHEAD: The zucchini and tomatoes can be roasted up to 4 days ahead and stored in covered containers in the refrigerator. You can slice the peasant bread up to 2 days ahead, but don't grill it until the day you make the bruschetta. Assemble the hors d'oeuvres no more than 2 hours before you plan to serve them. Bruschetta is fine at room temperature, but it can be reheated over a grill or in a low (250° F) oven, if desired.

Portobello Mushroom Herb Croustade

Every time I serve these I know for certain I am going to be asked for the recipe. Try them and you will see why.

½ cup pure or virgin olive oil
4 large or 6 medium portobello
   mushrooms, stems removed and
   brushed clean
Coarse salt and freshly ground black
   pepper to taste
3 teaspoons chopped garlic

2 cups Homemade Mayonnaise
   (page 64)
4 ounces Parmesan or Romano
   cheese, grated
½ cup chopped flat-leaf parsley
½ cup shredded basil leaves
40 slices Croustade (recipe follows)

1. Preheat the oven to 400° F. Pour ¼ cup of the oil onto a rimmed baking sheet. Lay the mushrooms on top, gill side down, and sprinkle with salt, pepper, 2 teaspoons of the garlic, and the remaining ¼ cup oil. Roast in the oven approximately 10 to 12 minutes. Remove from the heat and let cool in the pan. Cut the mushrooms into small dice and set aside.

2. Place the mayonnaise in a food processor. With the motor running, add the remaining garlic, then the cheese, parsley, and basil through the feed tube and process just until mixed. Remove to a medium bowl, then fold in the mushrooms.

3. Preheat the oven to 350° F. Spread some of the mushroom mixture on each slice and arrange on a baking sheet. Warm in the oven for 5 to 8 minutes.

Makes 40 hors d'oeuvres.

PLANNING AHEAD: The mushroom mixture can be made up to 1 week ahead and kept in a covered container in the refrigerator. The mushroom-topped croustades can be baked up to 2 hours ahead and reheated in a low oven.

Croustade

These are also called crostini, or croutons, and can be used as a base for many canapés or other hors d'oeuvres. Croustades can be brushed with butter or oil before baking if you like, but I generally prefer to toast the bread dry to keep it crisp.

1 thin 20-inch baguette

Optional: **Melted unsalted butter, or virgin or pure olive oil**

1. Preheat the oven to 400° F. Cut the baguette into about 40 ½-inch-thick slices, straight across or on the diagonal depending on the size of the hors d'oeuvres you are making.

2. Arrange the bread on a baking sheet and brush with butter or oil if you wish. Heat in the oven for approximately 8 to 10 minutes, until golden.

3. Remove from the oven, let cool on the baking sheet, and store in covered containers or plastic bags at room temperature.

Makes 40 croustades.

PLANNING AHEAD: Croustade will keep for up to 2 weeks in an airtight container.

Wild Rice Pancakes with Smoked Salmon Salad

I served these pancakes at the restaurant for a year and a half, and when I finally took them off the menu, our customers demanded I put them back on! They make delicious hors d'oeuvres, but I have also used them as breakfast pancakes or as an accompaniment to poultry, liver, or game dishes.

6 cups cooked and cooled wild rice

6 scallions, chopped

3 egg whites, lightly beaten

1¼ cups all-purpose, whole-wheat, or rice flour

Juice and zest of 1 lemon

½ cup dried cherries, coarsely chopped

Coarse salt and freshly ground black pepper to taste

2 cups vegetable oil

Smoked Salmon Salad (recipe follows) or other salad of your choice

1. In the bowl of an electric mixer fitted with a paddle attachment, combine the rice, scallions, and egg whites. Mix well. Add the flour, lemon juice, and zest and mix to form a sticky pancake batter. If the mixture seems too dry to form into pancakes, add a little water; if too wet, add some flour. Mix in the cherries, then taste for seasoning. Add salt and pepper to taste.

2. Form the batter into 40 pancakes about 2½ inches in diameter. Keep a small bowl of water nearby to dip your hands in during this process. If not cooking the pancakes immediately, arrange them in layers with parchment or plastic in between and refrigerate.

3. When ready to cook, cover the bottom of a heavy-bottomed skillet with a thin layer of oil and heat. Add a batch of pancakes and cook over medium heat for about 2½ minutes, then turn over and cook another 2½ minutes on the other side, until crispy. Remove to absorbent towels to drain. Repeat with the remaining pancakes, adding a little oil to the pan for each batch.

4. Serve the pancakes topped with Smoked Salmon Salad or other toppings of your choice.

Makes 40 hors d'oeuvres.

PLANNING AHEAD: The wild rice can be cooked up to 5 days ahead and stored in plastic bags in the refrigerator; it can also be frozen up to 3 months.

The pancakes can be formed up to 2 days ahead and kept in the refrigerator. Cooked, they will keep 2 days. If you want to serve them hot, reheat in a 300 ° F oven for about 5 minutes.

Smoked Salmon Salad

Home-smokers are simple and fun to use. Try using different herbs and curing mixtures to vary the flavor of smoked fish, meats, and vegetables.

1 orange

1 lemon

1 lime

1 cup brown sugar

1 cup coarse salt

1 (2- to 2½-pound) salmon fillet, skin on

2 cups plain yogurt or sour cream, drained

1 tablespoon whole-grain mustard

Juice of 1 lemon

1 medium red onion, peeled and finely diced

1 bunch fresh dill, tarragon, or chervil, chopped (about 1 cup)

Wild Rice Pancakes (page 227) or crisp crackers, for serving

1. Cut the orange, lemon, and lime in half, then quarters, and then eighths. Place in a food processor with the sugar and salt and chop.

2. Wipe or wash the salmon, dry, place in a dish to hold, and pack the citrus mixture on top. Cover with plastic and let cure in the refrigerator for at least 6 hours and up to 24 hours.

3. Start the smoker, and add wood chips. Remove the salmon from the refrigerator, wipe off the curing mixture, and place on a rack in the smoker. Smoke about 4 hours, until cooked. You can also remove the salmon from the smoker before it is completely cooked in the center and finish in a 300° F oven for about 15 minutes. Do not overcook the fish.

4. Let the salmon cool. When cool, pull the flesh from the skin and break into pieces over a bowl. Keep covered in the refrigerator until ready to assemble the salad.

5. In a mixing bowl, whisk together the yogurt or sour cream, mustard, and lemon juice. Stir in the onion and herbs. Fold in the salmon. If the salmon seems too dry, add more yogurt.

6. Serve on top of Wild Rice Pancakes or crisp crackers.

Makes 4 to 5 cups salad.

PLANNING AHEAD: The salmon can be left to cure in the refrigerator for up to 24 hours. Smoke it up to 2 days ahead. The mixed salad can be prepared up to 3 days ahead and left, covered, in the refrigerator until ready to use.

Lemon Chicken Meatballs

These light and lemony meatballs make a special hors d'oeuvre. They are also good as an entrée with pasta, rice, or vegetables.

3 pounds boneless, skinless chicken breasts

10 to 12 slices white sandwich bread, crusts removed, cut into cubes

3 cups heavy cream

6 egg whites

9 anchovy fillets, in oil

Juice and chopped zest of 2 lemons

1 cup chopped flat-leaf parsley

½ cup capers, drained

1 teaspoon freshly ground black pepper

1 teaspoon ground nutmeg

Coarse salt to taste

2 quarts chicken stock or water

3 tablespoons cornstarch or arrow-root diluted in ½ cup water

Garnish: Chopped chives or flat-leaf parsley

1. Remove the excess fat and tendons from the chicken and cut into 2-inch cubes. Set aside.

2. Put the bread cubes in a large bowl, pour the cream over them, and let soak about 30 minutes.

3. In 3 batches, in a food processor, coarsely grind the chicken with the egg whites. Remove to a large mixing bowl. Add the anchovies, lemon zest, parsley, capers, pepper, nutmeg, and salt to the food processor (no need to clean it) and pulse briefly to mix. Pour over the soaked bread and knead. Add the bread mixture to the ground chicken and mix quickly but thoroughly with your hands or a large spoon. Form into meatballs 1½ inches in diameter. You should have about 50.

4. Heat the stock to boiling in a large-surface open pot that is about 3 to 4 inches deep, such as a poaching pan or sauteuse. Drop in 1 or 2 test meatballs and cook approximately 2 to 3 minutes, until they are light in color and float to the surface. Taste for seasoning, correct if necessary, and adjust the cooking time. Cook the rest of the meatballs in batches, lifting the finished ones out with a skimmer and placing in an ice bath to cool quickly. Drain. Reserve the poaching liquid.

5. When all of the meatballs are cooked, strain the poaching liquid through a fine-mesh strainer into a 2-quart pot. To thicken the sauce, whisk in the cornstarch (or arrowroot) and water mixture. Simmer, stirring occasionally, for about 20 minutes, until the sauce is thickened and smooth. Remove from the heat and strain. Stir in the lemon juice, then add the meatballs to reheat them. Serve warm in

Bayou rock shrimp balls were accompanied by a spicy dipping sauce.

the sauce, sprinkled with chives or parsley, on small plates with toothpicks or hors d'oeuvre forks.

Makes about 50 hors d'oeuvres.

PLANNING AHEAD: The cooked meatballs can be left in stock or water to cover in the refrigerator for up to 3 days. Reheat them in stock or the lemon sauce, then place in a chafing dish on the buffet to keep warm.

Bayou Rock Shrimp Balls with Spicy Sherry Sauce

These shrimp puffs are always a hit at any party, so plan on serving at least 2 or 3 per person. I guarantee there won't be any left.

1 large red bell pepper, stem, seeds, and ribs removed
1 large green bell pepper, stems, seeds, and ribs removed
1 fresh jalapeño pepper, stem and seeds removed, or 1 teaspoon cayenne pepper
10 scallions, roots removed, coarsely chopped
Chopped zest of 2 limes

1 bunch cilantro, leaves picked (about 1 cup)
3 pounds rock or tiny shrimp, peeled and cleaned
6 egg whites
1 cup cornstarch
4 cups vegetable oil, for frying
Spicy Sherry Sauce, for serving (recipe follows)

1. In a food processor, combine the bell peppers and jalapeño or cayenne pepper and pulse briefly. Add the scallions, lime zest, and cilantro and process until finely chopped. Remove to a large mixing bowl. Without cleaning the processor bowl, add the shrimp and egg whites in 3 batches and coarsely chop. Remove to the bowl with the peppers and fold in. Add the cornstarch and mix. Cover the bowl and refrigerate at least 1 hour.

2. In a wok or large skillet, heat the oil to 350° F. Using a spoon or small scoop, form the shrimp mixture into balls about 1½ inches in diameter. Drop the shrimp balls into the oil in batches and fry for about 3 minutes, until golden brown. Remove

to a wire rack or absorbent paper towels to drain. Serve with toothpicks, accompanied by Spicy Sherry Sauce.

Makes 40 to 50 hors d'oeuvres.

PLANNING AHEAD: The shrimp mixture can be prepared and kept in the refrigerator in a covered bowl for up to 3 days. The balls can be fried up to 6 hours ahead and re-heated in a 275° to 300° F oven for about 5 minutes. These are best served warm.

Spicy Sherry Sauce

1 cup mayonnaise, preferably
    homemade (page 64)
½ cup Dijon-style mustard
¼ cup spicy ketchup, preferably
    homemade (page 69)
¼ cup dry sherry
3 anchovy fillets, chopped
Juice of 1 lemon

Garnishes: 12 small sour gherkins,
    chopped
2 tablespoons fresh chopped
    tarragon or chervil

1. Combine the mayonnaise, mustard, ketchup, sherry, anchovies, and lemon juice in a small bowl or food processor. Mix together until well combined.
2. Garnish the sauce with the chopped gherkins and herbs.

Makes 2 cups.

PLANNING AHEAD: The sauce can be prepared up to 5 days ahead and kept in a covered container in the refrigerator until ready to use.

Lobster Avocado Tortilla Crisps

If you don't want to make the tortilla crisps you can, of course, buy them premade. Just choose a firm chip with lots of flavor.

Having cleaned thousands of lobsters in my cooking career, I don't put lobster on my menus much anymore; cleaning them is messy work. But I don't mind cleaning a couple to enjoy as an hors d'oeuvre.

10 small corn tortillas
Vegetable oil, for frying
Coarse salt
3 ripe avocados
2 cups sour cream or plain yogurt, drained
1 teaspoon chopped garlic
¼ teaspoon cayenne pepper
Juice of 1 lemon

Juice of 1 lime
1 bunch cilantro, leaves picked and chopped (about 1 cup)
2 (1½-pound) lobsters, cooked, cooled, and meat removed (about 2 cups lobster meat); see method on page 280

Garnish: **20 fresh chives**

1. Cut each tortilla into 4 triangles. Heat the oil to 350° F in a wok or large skillet. Have ready 2 metal ladles that will fit inside each other.

2. Place a tortilla triangle on one of the ladles and dip into the oil. Use the other ladle to press it into the cup. Once the crisp is formed you can release it and let it continue to cook while you start on another tortilla. Cook about 1 minute, then remove the crisps to a rack or absorbent towels to drain. Sprinkle lightly with salt.

3. Cut the avocados in half lengthwise, break open, and remove the pit. Run a spoon lightly between the skin and flesh, and the whole half should come out easily. Cut the flesh into 1-inch pieces and put in a bowl. Using a spoon or mortar, mash the avocado with the sour cream or yogurt, garlic, cayenne pepper, lemon and lime juice, and cilantro to make a chunky spread. You can also do this in a food processor if you are careful not to puree the ingredients. Set aside.

4. Slice the lobster tail meat and set aside. Cut the rest of the lobster into small dice and add to the avocado mixture.

5. To assemble, spread each tortilla crisp with some of the avocado mixture, top with sliced lobster meat, and garnish with the chives.

Makes 40 hors d'oeuvres.

(CONTINUED)

Lobster avocado tortilla crisps.

PLANNING AHEAD: The tortilla crisps will keep for up to 5 days in an airtight container. The lobster can be cooked and cleaned up to 3 days ahead. The avocado spread can be made up to 1 day ahead and stored, covered, in the refrigerator. Assemble the hors d'ouvres no more than 2 hours ahead.

Bittersweet Chocolate Cupcakes

In my restaurant I place a dollop of whipped cream on these cupcakes and serve them on a little plate surrounded by chocolate sauce. As one fan commented, "You look at this little cupcake and think, isn't it a bit small? Then you bite into it, and you can't believe the chocolate intensity!"

The recipe can be doubled or tripled to make more or larger cupcakes.

2 pounds 3 ounces good-quality bittersweet chocolate	**CHOCOLATE GLAZE (OPTIONAL):** **1 cup heavy cream**
10 whole eggs	**16 ounces semisweet chocolate chips**
5 egg yolks	**4 ounces (1 stick) unsalted butter,**
2 cups sugar	**cut into pieces**

1. Melt the chocolate in the top of a double boiler over barely simmering water.

2. While the chocolate is melting, combine the whole eggs, yolks, and sugar in the bowl of an electric mixer. Using the balloon whisk attachment, beat on high speed until pale yellow in color and tripled in volume. With the machine running, add the melted chocolate and mix quickly. Turn off the machine and use a rubber spatula to scrape down the chocolate from the sides of the bowl. Fold in until the chocolate is evenly distributed.

3. Preheat the oven to 375° F. Spray mini-muffin tins with nonstick vegetable cooking spray or grease with oil. Spoon in the batter so the tins are three-fourths full. Bake for about 12 minutes, until the cupcakes have risen and the tops are cooked and cracking. Let cool to room temperature in the tins.

4. Remove the cupcakes carefully, tapping the tin on a counter to loosen them. Most of the cupcakes should lift out; use a paring knife or small metal spatula to nudge out any difficult ones.

5. To make the chocolate glaze, scald the cream in a 1-quart saucepan. Put the chocolate chips in a food processor and, with the motor running, pour the hot cream through the feed tube and mix until smooth. Add the butter, bit by bit, and blend in.

(CONTINUED)

Bite-size desserts—ricotta fruit phyllos and chocolate cupcakes—were set out on a large wicker tray garnished with strawberries. In the rear are peach slices stuffed with cinnamon goat cheese.

The mixing process should be completed in only a couple of minutes. Remove the glaze to a small container and let cool. Hold each cupcake by its base and dip into the glaze in one motion.

Makes 40 mini-cupcakes or 24 medium-size cupcakes.

PLANNING AHEAD: The cupcakes can be baked up to 2 days ahead and stored in a covered container in a cool place.

Sweet Ricotta Chocolate Chip Fruit Phyllos

These crispy little bundles can be made without the chocolate, and other fruits and nuts of your choice can be substituted. Working with phyllo takes a little practice, but once you get the hang of it you'll be wrapping everything in it.

FILLING:
5 cups ricotta cheese (the drier the better)
½ cup semisweet chocolate chips
½ cup chopped dried cherries
2 tablespoons chopped crystallized ginger
1 tablespoon sugar

Optional: ¼ cup chopped hazelnuts, pecans, almonds, or Brazil nuts

WRAPPING:
1 box phyllo, defrosted
8 ounces (2 sticks) unsalted butter, melted

1. To make the filling, place the ricotta cheese, chocolate chips, dried cherries, crystallized ginger, sugar, and nuts (if using) in a large bowl and fold together. Set aside in the refrigerator until ready to use.

2. Spread the phyllo sheets out flat on a dry surface, cover with parchment paper or plastic wrap, then lay a clean, damp cotton towel on top. Carefully lift 2 sheets of phyllo off the pile and onto a dry surface. Brush completely with melted butter. Add 2 more sheets on top. Using a pizza wheel or thin-bladed knife, cut the stack in half lengthwise, then in quarters crosswise so that you have 8 pieces total. Put a tablespoon of filling in the middle of each piece, draw up the corners, and twist to form a bundle or purse. Place the bundles on parchment-lined baking sheets, brush with more melted butter, and chill in the refrigerator for at least 1 hour. Repeat the process with the remaining phyllo sheets and filling.

3. Preheat the oven to 425° F. Bake the phyllo bundles for approximately 20 to 25 minutes, until golden, switching the position of the baking sheets in the oven halfway through the baking time so the phyllo will color evenly.

Makes 40 to 48 small bundles.

PLANNING AHEAD: Unbaked phyllo bundles will keep in the refrigerator for 1 day and in the freezer for 1 month.

You can bake the bundles a day ahead and reheat them in a 250° to 275° F oven for about 5 to 6 minutes just to warm before serving.

Peaches with Cinnamon Goat Cheese

Goat cheese blends well with many ripe fruits for an hors d'oeuvre, snack, or dessert. I've used peaches here, but apricots, fresh figs, and tart apples are also delicious. Different herbs, spices, ground nuts, or seeds can be substituted.

5 ripe medium peaches
4 ounces fresh goat cheese
2 tablespoons honey
2 tablespoons ground cinnamon

Optional: **2 tablespoons Cointreau**
3 tablespoons finely ground pecans

1. Wash the peaches, cut in half, remove the pit, and cut into eighths.
2. Place the goat cheese in a bowl and mash in the honey, cinnamon, and Cointreau (if using). Place a small piece of cheese on top of each peach slice and press lightly to fill the hollow.
3. Lay out the nuts on a small plate. Holding each peach wedge upside down, press into the nuts.

Makes 40 hors d'oeuvres.

PLANNING AHEAD: The peach slices can be stuffed up to 8 hours ahead of serving and stored, well-covered, on a tray in the refrigerator.

All-Through-
the-House Buffet

The holidays are definitely *the* time to get together with family and friends. An open house works particularly well during this rush-rush season because the timing is relaxed and flexible. Guests can be invited to stop by anytime during a four-to-five-hour period, with the option of staying for the whole party or, depending on their schedules, for drinks and hors d'oeuvres, dinner, or dessert.

We prepared this buffet at the charming home of Monique Shay, a dear friend who is a passionate collector and dealer in eighteenth- and nineteenth-century Canadian antiques. Her nineteenth-century farmhouse has many cozy rooms, making it a perfect setting for an all-through-the-house party. Three different buffets were set out: the hors d'oeuvres in the country living room off the kitchen, which features the house's original cooking hearth; the dinner buffet in the formal dining room; and the dessert buffet on a coffee table near the fire in the main living room.

One of the many advantages of serving different foods in different areas of your home is that it invariably makes the party more lively. When guests move around, conversation just flows. Think about the size and configuration of your rooms as you plan this buffet, and try to imagine the traffic patterns. To avoid congestion, arrange the buffets in settings that make sense. If you have a large open kitchen you might want to serve drinks and hors d'oeuvres there; a dining room or living room is the natural place for dinner; a study or library might work well for desserts and coffee. If you are expecting a lot of children, you might consider setting up a table in a playroom or family room with a separate buffet of kid-friendly foods, such as a baked macaroni casserole, chicken kebobs, tea-size peanut butter-and-jelly sandwiches, and cherry punch.

The appetizer buffet looks festive on a red-and-white check jacquard cloth. The hostess's collection of primitive wood and iron figures decorates the table. COUNTERCLOCKWISE FROM THE LOWER LEFT: *Homemade crispbreads and crackers; venison loin tartare; marinated artichokes; marinated olives; vegetable platter antipasto; and, in the chafing dish, fresh crabmeat gratin.*

At most open houses guests will find their own seating. But when you are setting up for the party be sure to give some thought to how much and what kind of seating you will need in each room. For example, since most people are accustomed to standing at a cocktail party, you will probably need less seating in the room where you have set out hors d'oeuvres and drinks.

For dinner, seating is definitely required, and it should be easy to find and not too far from the buffet. Remember to arrange chairs and other seating in convivial groupings to keep the party festive.

Everything on this buffet can be prepared ahead, so with a little planning you should be able to relax and enjoy your own party. The cookies and crackers can be made at least three weeks in advance; the antipasto platter and salad (without dressing) can be assembled the morning of the party and kept in the refrigerator; eggnog can be made hours ahead and kept in the fridge too. The salmon en croûte can be started three or four days ahead and baked the day of the party. The crabmeat gratin and chickens can also be prepared ahead and served at room temperature or briefly reheated. If you prefer to serve the main course hot, simply make an announcement about 1½ hours into the party that dinner is ready, and ask everyone who is staying for dinner to serve themselves from the buffet. To keep these dishes hot, use chafing dishes over warming candles, Sterno, or electric warming trays.

Keep in mind that there are a lot of options with this menu and that you don't have to make every dish. For instance, if you are pressed for time, a smoked ham or roast turkey—prepared by you or the local market—could be sliced and served in place of the chickens.

As for drinks, most guests are perfectly happy serving themselves from a bar that you have set up, but make sure that everything needed is in plain sight. You don't want guests rummaging through kitchen drawers looking for a corkscrew or bottle opener. A wine bar is simplest—given the season, you might also consider serving a hot mulled wine punch—but if you prefer an open bar, read the suggestions on pages xii–xiii. And don't forget sodas, sparkling waters, and other nonalcoholic beverages.

Although this party is not difficult to manage alone because so much can be done ahead, a kitchen helper is useful for a very large crowd. He or she can clear dishes, glasses, and flatware, stack them in the dishwasher, and replenish food at the buffet tables.

All-Through-the-House Buffet
for 20

APPETIZERS
Fresh Crabmeat Gratin

Vegetable Platter Antipasto

White Bean and Roasted Garlic Dip

Venison Loin Tartare

Rolled Oat Crispbread

Salted Sesame Shortbread

DINNER
Roasted Salmon, Trio of Mushrooms,
and Dilled Grains en Croûte

Young Chickens with Sun-Dried Tomato and Ginger Pesto

'Tis the Season Blood Orange, Watercress, and Fennel Salad

HOLIDAY SWEETS
Pinwheel Cookies ✦ Sesame Oatmeal Bars

Date Crescents ✦ Chocolate, Fruit, and Nut Chunkies

Meringue and Prune Tartlets ✦ Gingersnaps

Sugar Bow Ties ✦ Holiday Fruit Bowl

A True Creamy Eggnog

Fresh Crabmeat Gratin

For this dish it's best to use fresh, real crabmeat—from Maryland blue crabs, Maine Jonah crabs, or West Coast Dungeness crabs.

3 pounds fresh crabmeat, shells removed

3 cups homemade mayonnaise (page 64)

1 pound Swiss or provolone cheese, shredded

3 tablespoons whole-grain mustard

2 medium zucchini, stems removed, diced

3 ripe pears, peeled and diced

1 large bunch (about 12 stems) fresh tarragon or basil, leaves picked and coarsely chopped

Coarse salt and freshly ground black pepper to taste

Crackers, flatbreads (pages 250 and 251), or vegetables, for serving

1. Drain the crabmeat in a colander to remove the excess water. In a large mixing bowl, fold together the crabmeat, mayonnaise, half of the cheese, the mustard, zucchini, pears, tarragon or basil, salt, and pepper.

2. Preheat the oven to 400° F. Spread the crabmeat mixture in a large, flat 3- to 4-quart baking dish and cover with the remaining shredded cheese. Bake for 25 to 30 minutes, until browned on top. Remove from the oven and keep warm over a warming candle or Sterno on the buffet table. Serve with crackers, flatbreads, or vegetables.

Serves 20, as part of buffet.

PLANNING AHEAD: The mayonnaise can be made up to 1 week ahead and kept covered in the refrigerator. The crabmeat mixture can be prepared a day ahead and kept in the refrigerator; when ready to serve, turn into a casserole dish, top with the remaining cheese, and bake as directed.

Vegetable Platter Antipasto

A colorful platter of roasted, steamed, and marinated vegetables is a tasty addition to the buffet table, especially for guests who are just stopping by for a short while and want something light. The following recipes will make more than enough for 20 people.

Steamed Asparagus

2 pounds asparagus

White Bean and Roasted Garlic Dip (page 248)

1. Peel the asparagus stalks if jumbo size and steam in a covered steamer basket over boiling water until just barely tender. Remove to a flat pan lined with paper towels to drain.

2. Serve with White Bean and Roasted Garlic Dip.

NOTE: Cooked asparagus soak up water and become soggy easily, so it is important to slightly undercook them and drain immediately.

Marinated Beets

2 pounds beets
2 tablespoons honey
1 tablespoon Dijon-style mustard

½ cup orange juice
½ cup balsamic vinegar
1 cup nut oil or extra-virgin olive oil

1. Remove the stems and roots of the beets. Cook by either boiling or roasting.

To boil: Wash the beets well and place in a large pot with water to cover. Cover the pot, bring to a boil, and cook the beets until tender, about 40 minutes. Check the pot from time to time to make sure the water hasn't boiled out. Drain, let cool, and slip the beet skins off.

To roast: Put the beets in a roasting pan, sprinkle with salt, pepper, and vegetable oil, and roast in a 300° F oven until tender, approximately 2 hours. Slip skins off.

2. To make the marinade, whisk together the honey and mustard. Pour in the orange juice, vinegar, and oil in a steady stream and whisk until thickened and emulsified.

3. Cut the beets into wedges and toss in a bowl with the marinade. Let marinate in the refrigerator at least 2 hours and up to 1 week.

Marinated Roasted Carrots and Parsnips

1 pound carrots
1 pound parsnips
2 cups vegetable oil
1 cup white wine vinegar

8 cloves garlic, peeled and chopped
1 tablespoon ground cumin
Coarse salt and freshly ground black
    pepper to taste

1. Preheat the oven to 425° F. Peel the carrots and parsnips, then cut into ¼-inch diagonal slices.

2. In a mixing bowl, whisk together the oil, vinegar, garlic, cumin, salt, and pepper. Add the carrots and parsnips and toss to coat evenly, then lift them out of the marinade with a slotted spoon and arrange in 1 layer on a baking sheet. Roast the vegetables until just tender, approximately 15 minutes. Remove from the oven, let cool, and store in a covered container in the refrigerator with the reserved marinade for at least 2 hours and up to 1 week.

Marinated Artichokes

24 baby artichokes (or 8 to 10
    medium artichokes)
1 lemon, cut in half
2 cups extra-virgin olive oil
1½ cups balsamic vinegar
12 cloves garlic, peeled and chopped

Zest of 1 lemon
½ cup coarsely chopped flat-leafed
    parsley
15 fresh basil leaves, cut into slivers
1 small red chili pepper, cut into
    slivers

1. Cut off the artichoke stems and tops about a third of the way down; the inside choke should be visible. With a paring knife, cut off all the tough outer green leaves, leaving the smooth tender heart. Rub the artichokes with the lemon halves to prevent discoloration. Put the artichokes and lemon in a pot with salted water to cover, and cover with a clean tea towel or thick paper towels (this helps the artichokes cook evenly). Bring to a boil over high heat, then reduce the heat to medium and cook until the artichokes are tender in the center when poked with a knife tip, about 20 minutes. Drain and let cool.

2. If you are using medium or large artichokes, pull out the choke and discard. Using a melon baller or teaspoon, remove the fine hairs at the bottom of the choke. Cut the artichokes into quarters or sixths, depending on their size. Baby artichokes can be left whole.

3. Make a vinaigrette by whisking together the oil, vinegar, garlic, lemon zest, parsley, basil, and chili pepper. Pour over the artichokes, cover, and let marinate in the refrigerator for at least 2 hours and up to 1 week.

Marinated Cipollinis

These delicious sweet, flat, Italian onions come into season in late autumn. They are a tad difficult to peel, but the taste is worth the effort.

30 cipollinis
2 cups champagne vinegar
1 cup sugar
8 sprigs fresh thyme, leaves picked, chopped
4 sprigs fresh rosemary, leaves picked, chopped

1 teaspoon saffron (about 20 threads)
1 bay leaf
½ cup raisins

1. Peel the onions and put in a medium saucepan.

2. Whisk together the vinegar, sugar, thyme, rosemary, and saffron. Pour over the onions in the pan, stirring to coat completely. Add the bay leaf. Bring to a boil over high heat, then reduce to a simmer, and cook the onions until tender, about 15 minutes. Remove from the heat, add the raisins, and let the onions cool in the marinade. Remove the bay leaf before serving.

Marinated Olives

Imported olives can be marinated in a small amount of extra-virgin olive oil flavored with your favorite combination of herbs, citrus zest, garlic, and spicy peppers. When marinated, olives will keep indefinitely in the refrigerator. Always buy good-quality olives. If possible, sample them and choose according to your taste and the flavor of the marinade you plan to use.

Roasted Potatoes

**2 pounds small red or new white
   potatoes**
1 cup vegetable oil
**3 sprigs fresh rosemary, leaves
   picked, chopped**

**Coarse salt and freshly ground black
   pepper to taste**
**White Bean and Roasted Garlic Dip
   (page 248)**

1. Scrub the potatoes. Pour the oil into a large roasting pan and heat in a 400° F oven until the oil is smoking. Add the potatoes in 1 layer and sprinkle with the rosemary, salt, and pepper. Shake the pan to coat the potatoes with the hot oil. Roast for 10 minutes, then turn the potatoes with tongs and roast about 20 minutes more, until tender and evenly colored.

2. Serve with White Bean and Roasted Garlic Dip.

PLANNING AHEAD: These potatoes may be roasted 1 day ahead, but they will need to be reheated in the oven before serving. Reheating brings back the color and adds crispness.

White Bean and Roasted Garlic Dip

8 ounces dried white beans (about 1½ cups)

½ cup pure olive oil

1 large onion, peeled and chopped, or 2 medium leeks, chopped and washed

1 tablespoon fennel seed

1 large sprig fresh rosemary, leaves picked and chopped

2 sprigs fresh oregano, leaves picked and chopped

1 quart water or vegetable or chicken stock

Coarse salt and freshly ground black pepper to taste

4 bulbs roasted garlic (see method on page 103)

½ cup fresh lemon juice

1 cup grated Parmesan cheese

Optional: 2 tablespoons finely chopped anchovy fillets

Optional: 1 cup fresh chopped herbs—basil, thyme, oregano, parsley, or chives

1. Soak the beans in cold water to cover for at least 8 hours, or overnight. Drain and set aside.

2. In a heavy-bottomed 3- to 4-quart pot, heat the olive oil over high heat. Add the onion or leeks and sauté until soft and transparent, about 2 minutes. Add the fennel, rosemary, and oregano, and cook 1 minute more. Add the beans, stir, and cook 2 minutes. Pour in the water or stock, stir, and taste for seasoning. Bring to a boil over high heat, then reduce the heat and simmer on low for approximately 30 to 40 minutes, until the beans are tender. Remove from the heat and let cool in the liquid.

3. When cool, drain any excess liquid and place the beans in a food processor. Cut the roasted garlic bulbs in half and squeeze the cloves into the workbowl with the beans. Puree to desired consistency, from chunky to smooth. Mix in the lemon juice, Parmesan cheese, and optional anchovies. Fold in fresh herbs for color if you like.

Makes 3½ to 4 cups.

PLANNING AHEAD: The beans can be cooked up to 5 days ahead and kept in a covered container in the refrigerator until ready to make the dip.

Venison Loin Tartare

Venison's popularity has soared in the last few years. It is the leanest of all red meats, is not gamy in flavor, and doesn't require a lot of cooking. Venison's taste and texture are perfect for tartare.

1½ pounds finely chopped or ground fresh venison (loin preferred)

3 egg yolks

4 tablespoons chopped chives or shallots

1 tablespoon Dijon-style mustard

Coarse salt and freshly ground black pepper to taste

Optional: 2 tablespoons brandy or cognac

Optional: 1 tablespoon green peppercorns, lightly smashed

Garnish: Chopped chives, anchovy fillets, or caviar

Crackers, dark pumpernickel bread, or Croustade (page 226), for serving

1. Mix the meat with the egg yolks, chives or shallots, mustard, salt, and pepper. Add the optional brandy or cognac and the green peppercorns, if using. Mound the mixture on a plate, score with a knife, and garnish.

2. Serve with crackers, dark pumpernickel bread, or Croustade.

Makes 4 cups.

Rolled Oat Crispbread

Of course, you don't have to make your own crackers. But it is satisfying to do, and guests are always amazed. In reality the dough is simple to make, just six basic ingredients. It does take a bit of muscle, however, to roll out the dough.

3 cups rolled oats
3 cups all-purpose flour
1 teaspoon baking soda
1 teaspoon coarse salt

6 ounces (1½ sticks) unsalted butter,
** melted**
1½ cups buttermilk

   1. In a food processor, grind the oats until they are of a fine consistency. Remove to a large bowl and mix in the flour, baking soda, and salt. Pour in the butter and buttermilk and mix to form a stiff but moist dough. Let the dough rest for 10 minutes to make it less sticky and easier to work with.

   2. Preheat the oven to 375° F. Lightly grease 4 cookie sheets.

   3. Divide the dough into 4 parts. Roll out each portion of dough to a thickness of ⅛ inch directly onto a cookie sheet, being sure to cover the sheet completely. Use a sharp knife to trim the edges and score the dough into rectangle or square shapes. Using either a rolling docker or a fork, prick the dough all over a number of times. Bake in the oven for 15 to 20 minutes, until the crackers are crisp and golden brown. When cool, break apart along the score lines. Serve with Fresh Crabmeat Gratin (page 243), Venison Loin Tartare (page 249), and other appetizers.

Makes 36 to 40 crackers.

PLANNING AHEAD: These crackers will keep well for a month or more in a tightly covered container.

Salted Sesame Shortbread

These savory shortbread crackers are very easy to make and great to have on hand to serve with appetizers or snacks.

2 cups all-purpose flour

2 teaspoons coarse salt

¼ teaspoons cayenne pepper

4 ounces (1 stick) unsalted butter, cut into small pieces

4 tablespoons solid vegetable shortening or lard

1 large egg beaten with 2 tablespoons water

1 cup sesame seeds, preferably unhulled

Coarse salt, for sprinkling

1. Combine the flour, salt, and cayenne in a food processor. With the motor running, add the butter and shortening through the feed tube and process until the mixture resembles coarse meal. Add the egg-water mixture and sesame seeds and mix briefly. If the dough looks too dry (it should just stick together), add a few tablespoons ice water. Form the dough into a log with a 2-inch diameter. Wrap in plastic. Flatten the sides to make a long square. Refrigerate the dough for 3 to 4 hours.

2. Preheat the oven to 350° F. Cut the shortbreads into ¼-inch-wide slices and place close together on an ungreased baking sheet. Bake for 15 to 18 minutes, until cooked through but not browned. Remove immediately from the oven and sprinkle with coarse salt. Let cool.

Makes 30 crackers.

PLANNING AHEAD: Packed in an airtight container, these crackers will stay fresh for up to 2 months.

Roasted Salmon, Trio of Mushrooms, and Dilled Grains en Croûte

This is a long recipe, but it can be done in stages (see PLANNING AHEAD). Once the dish is baked, it can be set aside until you are ready to serve; it's good hot or at room temperature. For a smaller party, you might want to serve this festive, all-in-one dish accompanied by a simple salad.

The recipe can be varied by substituting other grains, such as wild rice, for the kasha and barley. The salmon can be replaced with another firm-textured fish, pieces of cooked fowl, or meat tenderloins. Another option: Eliminate the fish or meat and make a totally vegetarian dish using just vegetables and grains. Once you try this recipe I feel sure you will want to make it again and again. The presentation is impressive, and it is neat and easy to serve.

One salmon will feed 8 to 10 people; this is a double recipe, which will serve 16 to 20.

GRAIN AND MUSHROOM FILLING:

8 ounces kasha (see Note 1)

1 egg or 2 egg whites

3 quarts salted water (see Note 2)

½ pound hulled barley, soaked overnight in cold water and drained

4 quarts salted water

1 tablespoon chopped fresh thyme and 10 sprigs fresh thyme, leaves picked

1 bay leaf

1 pound white mushrooms

1½ pounds shiitake mushrooms

1½ pounds portobello mushrooms

¾ cup vegetable oil

6 medium onions, cut into medium dice

1 cup finely chopped dill

12 cloves garlic, peeled and chopped

Coarse salt and freshly ground black pepper to taste

PASTRY CRUST:

4½ cups all-purpose flour

2 teaspoons salt

12 ounces (3 sticks) unsalted butter, cut into small pieces, or same amount solid vegetable shortening or lard

3 eggs

Juice of 2 lemons

2 (3½- to 4-pound) salmon fillets, skin and bones removed

1 egg beaten with 1 teaspoon water, for egg wash

TO MAKE THE FILLING:

1. In a heavy-bottomed, 4-quart saucepan, combine the kasha and egg or egg whites. Cook, stirring, over medium heat, until the kasha is dry and separated into single kernels.

2. Meanwhile, bring 3 quarts salted water to a boil over high heat. Pour a third of the water over the kasha, stir well, and bring back to a boil. Cook 2 to 3 minutes (the kasha will absorb the water quickly), stir in the remaining boiling water, reduce the heat to medium, and let the kasha simmer for about 10 minutes, stirring occasionally, until the water is absorbed and the kasha is tender.

3. In a heavy-bottomed, 6-quart pot, combine the barley, 4 quarts salted water, the 1 tablespoon chopped thyme, and the bay leaf, and bring to a boil over high heat. Stir, cover, reduce the heat, and simmer until the barley is tender and the liquid is absorbed, about 45 minutes. Remove the bay leaf.

4. Remove the stems from the mushrooms, brush or wipe clean, and dice into ¼-inch pieces. Heat ½ cup of the oil in a wok or large sauté pan set over medium heat. Add the onions and cook about 10 minutes until soft and transparent. Remove to a bowl and stir in the dill. Wipe out the sauté pan and return to the heat. Add the remaining ¼ cup oil. When hot, add the mushrooms and sauté for 2 minutes. Sprinkle with the thyme leaves, garlic, salt, and pepper, and toss. Continue cooking until the mushrooms are tender, about 5 minutes. Remove to a colander to drain.

5. In a large bowl, mix together the cooked kasha and barley, onions, and mushrooms. Set the filling aside until ready to assemble the dish.

TO MAKE THE PASTRY DOUGH:

1. In a food processor or mixer, combine the flour and salt. Add the butter or shortening or lard, and process until the texture is like coarse meal. Add the eggs and lemon juice, mixing just long enough to incorporate well.

2. Remove the dough to a floured board and knead briefly. Divide in half and shape into 2 balls. Wrap in plastic and refrigerate for at least 1 hour and up to 5 days.

TO ASSEMBLE AND BAKE:

1. Working on a floured surface, roll out one of the pastry dough balls into a large rectangle longer than the salmon (approximately 20 inches × 12 inches). Starting at the center of the dough, lay out a fourth of the filling to the length and width of one of the salmon fillets. Place the salmon on top and cover with another fourth of the filling, working as neatly as possible and brushing the grains back into the salmon with a pastry brush if they fall off. Brush the dough around the salmon with some of the egg wash. Fold the upper part of the dough over to seal, then cut off any excess dough,

leaving 2 to 3 inches to seal with a rolling tuck. Gently brush off any excess flour that may have adhered to the dough and brush with the egg wash. If desired, cut decorations from the dough scraps, brush lightly with the beaten egg, and place on top of the pastry crust. Cut 2 small steam holes on top.

2. Carefully move the salmon to a parchment-lined baking sheet. Place in the refrigerator for at least 3 hours and up to 24 hours to let the dough rest and become firm. Repeat the process with the second salmon fillet.

3. Preheat the oven to 425° F. Bake the salmons for about 30 minutes, until the dough is cooked and golden. Remove from the oven, let cool for 15 minutes, then place on serving platters.

Serves 16 to 20, as part of buffet.

NOTE 1: For better flavor and cooking results, use organic grains from a health-food store. These grains will usually be fresher than those commonly found on grocery-store shelves.

NOTE 2: I always season with salt the water or stock in which I am cooking grains, legumes, potatoes, pastas, and rices. These starches are almost impossible to season after they are cooked; the flavor simply does not penetrate. Another advantage to seasoning the cooking liquid first is that you will need to use less salt than if you season later. Always taste the seasoned liquid to be sure that it is to your taste, then proceed with the cooking.

PLANNING AHEAD: Cook this recipe in stages so that all you have to do the day of the party is bake the salmon. The following schedule works well.

Up to 5 days ahead:
—Make the pastry dough and refrigerate it. The dough can also be frozen.

Up to 3 or 4 days ahead:
—Soak the barley.
—Cook the kasha and barley, and put them in plastic bags or covered containers in the refrigerator.
—Sauté the onions and mushrooms and assemble the filling. Refrigerate.

1 day before the party :
—Roll out the pastry, fill with the salmon and mushroom-grain mixture, and transfer to baking sheets. Refrigerate for up to 24 hours.

Day of the party:
—Bake salmon and serve.

The dinner buffet served in the dining room. FROM LEFT TO RIGHT: *Blood orange, watercress, and fennel salad; roasted salmon en croûte; and young chickens with sun-dried tomato and ginger pesto. Antique Christmas balls from the hostess's collection sparkle on the table.*

Young Chickens with Sun-Dried Tomato and Ginger Pesto

I prefer the taste of poussins, very young chickens weighing a pound or more, over Cornish hens, but see for yourself. This pesto really spices up a simple roast chicken, and is also wonderful in pasta dishes, risottos, and vegetable tarts.

PESTO:

3 cups sun-dried tomatoes

4-inch piece fresh ginger, peeled and
  cut into ½-inch slices

1½ cups pecans

12 cloves garlic, peeled

2 sprigs fresh rosemary, leaves
  picked and chopped

Zest of 1 orange

10 (1- to 1½-pound) young chickens
  (poussins) or Cornish hens

1. Place the sun-dried tomatoes in a bowl and pour boiling water over to cover. Soak for 30 minutes to rehydrate. Drain, reserving the soaking liquid.

2. In a food processor, chop the ginger. Add the sun-dried tomatoes, pecans, garlic, rosemary, and orange zest, and puree to a thick paste. Add a small amount of the tomato soaking liquid if the mixture is too thick. Transfer to a covered container and store in the refrigerator.

3. Wash and dry the chickens. Spoon some of the pesto mixture into a pastry bag. Run your finger between the skin and flesh around the leg joint and breast, and squeeze the pesto into the pockets you have created. You can also use a small spoon. Spread the pesto as evenly as possible.

4. Lightly oil a roasting pan and place in a 375° F oven to heat. Place the chickens, backbone down, in the hot pan and cover with foil. Roast for 25 minutes, remove the foil, and roast 10 minutes more until the juices run clear when a knife tip or skewer is inserted. Remove from the oven and let cool. Cut out the backbone and quarter each chicken, removing breast and rib bones.

Serves 20, as part of buffet.

PLANNING AHEAD: The pesto can be made up to 6 weeks ahead and kept in the refrigerator. The chickens can be roasted and cut up a day ahead, covered with foil, stored in the refrigerator, then reheated in a 350° F oven for about 15 minutes before setting out on the buffet.

'Tis the Season Blood Orange, Watercress, and Fennel Salad

Blood oranges come into season in the winter. With their reddish orange pulp and sweet-tart taste, they are a good complement to the watercress and fennel in this salad.

DRESSING:
Juice of 10 juice oranges
½ vanilla bean, split lengthwise,
    seeds scraped out, or 1 tablespoon
    vanilla extract
1 tablespoon mustard
½ cup olive or vegetable oil

SALAD:
7 to 8 blood oranges
3 bulbs fresh fennel
3 bunches watercress

1. To make the dressing, combine the orange juice with the vanilla in a medium saucepan. Simmer until the liquid is reduced by half. Let cool, then transfer to a food processor. With the motor running, add the mustard and oil in a thin stream until the mixture is thickened and emulsified. Alternatively, you can use an immersion blender.

2. Peel the blood oranges, removing all the white pith. Cut in half crosswise and then into ¼-inch slices. Place in a large salad bowl and pour the vinaigrette over them.

3. Remove the stems from the fennel and wash. Thinly shred the bulb with a mandoline or sharp knife. Place in a bowl and toss with the oranges and dressing.

4. Cut off and discard the lower stems from the watercress, sprinkle the watercress over the salad, and toss with the other ingredients and dressing.

Serves 20, as part of buffet.

PLANNING AHEAD: The dressing can be made 1 week ahead, the salad ingredients prepared, and everything kept covered in the refrigerator, but don't add the watercress until close to serving time.

Pinwheel Cookies

Every November when I was growing up my mother would make all kinds of Christmas cookies, pack them in tins, and store them in the attic to give as gifts at holiday time. Her pinwheel cookies were especially popular with the kids in our family. Whenever we thought no one was watching we would climb the attic stairs and raid the tins. I even devised a certain way of eating these classic cookies, one colored ring at a time.

12 ounces (3 sticks) unsalted butter, softened

1 cup sugar

6 cups all-purpose flour, sifted

Pinch of salt

Juice of ½ lemon mixed with 1 tablespoon cold water

¼ cup unsweetened cocoa powder

1. Cream the butter in an electric mixer set on medium speed. Add the sugar, a little at a time, and beat until the mixture is fluffy and pale yellow. Add the flour, salt, and lemon juice-water mixture and mix together to make a stiff dough. Divide the dough into 2 equal parts. Return 1 part to the mixing bowl, add the cocoa, and mix to incorporate completely. Form each piece of dough into 2 logs; you should have 4 logs: 2 chocolate and 2 plain sugar. Wrap in plastic and chill in the refrigerator for at least 2 hours.

2. When ready to assemble cookies, on a floured surface roll out one plain and one chocolate log into 9 x 12 x ⅛-inch-thick rectangles. Lay the chocolate dough on top of the plain dough, cut off any excess, and roll up, starting at a long side, to make a pinwheel log. Repeat with the remaining logs so that you have 2 pinwheels. Wrap in plastic wrap and chill in the refrigerator for at least 2 more hours.

3. When ready to bake, preheat the oven to 350° F and lightly grease 3 cookie sheets or line with parchment paper. Cut the dough into ¼-inch-thick slices and lay them on the baking sheets about 1½ inches apart. Bake for 10 to 12 minutes, until the plain dough looks golden. Let the cookies cool on the baking sheets.

Makes approximately 5 dozen cookies.

PLANNING AHEAD: These cookies will keep for up to 2 months in a tightly covered container or tin.

The dessert buffet set out on a coffee table in front of the fire. ON THE TRAY, FROM FRONT TO BACK: *Meringue and prune tartlets; pinwheel cookies; sesame oatmeal bars; date crescents; sugar bow ties; and gingersnaps.* ON THE PEDESTAL PLATE: *Chocolate, fruit, and nut chunkies.*

Sesame Oatmeal Bars

A good year-round cookie that is soft and chewy, with lots of honey and sesame flavor.

4 ounces (1 stick) unsalted butter
3 tablespoons honey
⅓ cup light brown sugar
1¼ cups rolled oats
½ cup chopped almonds
⅓ cup shredded unsweetened
  coconut (found in health-food
  stores)

⅓ cup sesame seeds

For chocolate-dipped cookies:
4 ounces semisweet chocolate
1 teaspoon vegetable oil

1. In a medium pot over medium heat, melt together the butter, honey, and sugar, stirring. Remove from the heat. Add the oats, almonds, coconut, and sesame seeds, and mix to combine.

2. Preheat the oven to 350° F and grease or line with parchment paper an 11 × 7 × 2-inch baking pan. Using a metal spatula or the back of a spoon, press the cookie mixture evenly into the pan. Bake for 15 to 18 minutes, until golden. Cool for 10 minutes, then score into 18 bars. Let the cookies cool completely, then cut along score lines and remove from the pan.

3. If you'd like the bars dipped in chocolate, melt the chocolate with the oil in a double boiler over simmering water. Remove the top of the boiler from the heat, dip the bars diagonally into the chocolate, and place on a rack until the chocolate is set.

Makes 18 cookies.

PLANNING AHEAD: These cookies will keep for 2 weeks in a tightly covered container or tin. The recipe can easily be doubled.

Date Crescents

These moist and delectable cookies are a holiday favorite in Eastern European and Mediterranean countries. Fresh medjool dates are usually available around Christmas, but dried dates also work in this recipe.

Fresh dates can be filled with soft cheeses or savory mousses to make a tasty wintertime hors d'oeuvre.

DOUGH:
16 ounces cream cheese, softened
8 ounces (2 sticks) unsalted butter, softened
4 cups all-purpose flour, sifted
2 teaspoons vanilla extract

FILLING:
2 tablespoons sugar
½ cup hot water
Juice and zest of 1 lemon
1 cup finely chopped dates

1 egg, beaten, for glaze

1. In an electric mixer, cream the cream cheese and butter. A little at a time, add the flour and vanilla, and mix to form a soft dough. Form the dough into a ball, flatten, and wrap in plastic. Chill in the refrigerator for at least 2 hours and up to 2 days.

2. To prepare the filling, combine the sugar with the hot water in a small saucepan and stir to dissolve. Add the lemon juice, zest, and dates and simmer over medium heat, stirring often, until the mixture thickens. Remove from the heat and allow to cool.

3. Preheat the oven to 425° F and lightly grease 2 baking sheets or line with parchment paper. Remove the dough from the refrigerator and divide into thirds. On a floured surface, roll out 1 piece of dough to a thickness of ⅛ inch. Cut out circles with a 2½- to 3-inch round cutter. Spoon a small amount of filling into the center of each circle and fold over to create half-moon shapes, sealing the edges with your fingers. Repeat with the rest of the dough. Arrange the cookies ½ inch apart on the prepared baking sheets and brush with the egg glaze for color. Bake for 12 to 15 minutes, until the cookies are golden brown. Let cool on the baking sheets.

Makes approximately 40 cookies.

PLANNING AHEAD: Stored in an airtight container, these cookies will keep well for 3 weeks.

Chocolate, Fruit, and Nut Chunkies

Surprise children and grown-ups alike with these rich, melt-in-your-mouth, no-bake chunkies, a home-style version of the famous candy bar. Kids love to help make these. You can use any combination of dried fruits and nuts. Let the season capture your creative spirit.

2½ cups sugar

¾ cup water

18 ounces bittersweet or semisweet chocolate

18 ounces (4½ sticks) unsalted butter, softened

3 cups unsweetened cocoa powder

3 whole eggs plus 6 egg yolks, beaten together

2¼ cups shelled hazelnuts, coarsely chopped

1 cup raisins or currants

1 cup dried cherries

1 cup dried apricots, diced

14 ounces (about 1½ cups) coarsely chopped chunks white chocolate

1. Combine the sugar and water in a medium saucepan, bring to a boil, and cook 5 minutes, until the sugar has dissolved into a syrup. Set aside.

2. Melt the bittersweet or semisweet chocolate in the top of a double boiler set over simmering water. Set aside to cool.

3. Using an electric mixer, cream together the butter and cocoa. Slowly add the sugar syrup, melted chocolate, and eggs, mixing well after each addition.

4. Combine the nuts, raisins or currants, cherries, apricots, and white chocolate, then fold into the cooled chocolate mixture. Pour into a 10 × 13-inch pan. Cover with plastic wrap and chill overnight in the refrigerator. Cut into squares.

Makes about 30 chunkies.

PLANNING AHEAD: These chunkies can be stored in a covered container in the refrigerator for up to 3 weeks, if they are around that long.

Meringue and Prune Tartlets

Prunes are really a misunderstood fruit. A lot of people say they don't like them, but they really haven't given them a try, especially baked into a delectable tart filling.

PASTRY DOUGH:
5¼ cups all-purpose flour, sifted
1 tablespoon sugar
1 teaspoon baking powder
6 ounces (1½ sticks) unsalted butter,
   cut into cubes
3 eggs, beaten
2 cups sour cream

FILLING:
8 cups pitted prunes, chopped
2½ cups light brown sugar
2 cups fresh orange juice

1 cup brewed Earl Grey tea
¼ teaspoon ground cinnamon
⅛ teaspoon ground nutmeg
⅛ teaspoon allspice
Zest of 1 orange

MERINGUE:
1 cup egg whites (about 6 to 8)
1 cup plus 2 tablespoons granulated
   sugar
1½ cups confectioners' sugar
3 tablespoons all-purpose flour

1. To make the dough, combine the flour, sugar, and baking powder in a large bowl. With a pastry cutter or your hands, work in the butter until the mixture resembles coarse meal. In a small bowl, beat together the eggs and sour cream. Make a well in the center of the flour-butter mixture and pour in the eggs and sour cream. Mix with your hands until the dough is smooth and well combined. Knead on a floured board until the dough is pliable, about 1 to 2 minutes. Divide the dough in half and form into 2 balls. Lightly coat the balls with flour and chill in the refrigerator for at least 30 minutes, wrapped in plastic.

2. To make the filling, combine the prunes, sugar, orange juice, tea, cinnamon, nutmeg, allspice, and zest in a 4-quart saucepan. Cook over low heat about 1 hour, until the prunes are soft, the liquid is reduced, and the mixture resembles a thick paste. Remove from the heat and let the mixture cool.

3. Remove the dough balls from the refrigerator. Roll out one of the balls to a thickness of ⅛ inch on a floured surface. Cut into circles with a 4-inch cutter. Repeat with the remaining dough ball. Fit the circles into approximately 30 3-inch tartlet pans, prick the dough with a fork, and cool in the refrigerator for at least 30 minutes.

4. Preheat the oven to 375° F. Bake the tartlets for 8 to 10 minutes, until light

A closer look at the holiday cookies. FROM LEFT TO RIGHT: *Pinwheel cookies, gingersnaps, sesame oatmeal bars, date crescents, more pinwheels, and sugar bow ties.*

golden in color. Remove from the oven and reduce the oven temperature to 250° F. Cool the tartlets slightly, then fill with the prune filling.

5. To make the meringue, whip the egg whites with an electric mixer until stiff peaks form. Add the granulated sugar and whip 20 seconds just to mix. Sift together the confectioners' sugar and flour and fold quickly into the whites. Spoon the mixture on top of the tartlets, or put into a pastry bag and pipe on top.

6. Bake the tartlets in the 250° F oven for approximately 20 minutes, until the meringue is lightly browned.

Makes approximately thirty 3-inch tartlets.

PLANNING AHEAD: The pastry dough and the prune filling can be made up to 1 week ahead and kept in the refrigerator. The tartlets can be filled (but not topped with meringue) up to 2 days ahead. Once these tartlets are meringued and baked, they should be served within 2 days.

Gingersnaps

Gingersnap aficionados love this recipe. After you taste them, you will agree they are the snappiest ginger cookies ever. One year a friend asked me to make up holiday gift boxes filled with these cookies for her clients. During a marathon baking session I made fourteen hundred gingersnaps in my home kitchen, and by the time I was finished we were all addicted to them, including Cleo, our Saint Bernard. Every time a batch came out of the oven she stood right there and nosed me until I gave her a sample. Try them, and you'll see!

½ cup light brown sugar

½ cup molasses

4 ounces (1 stick) unsalted butter

2 cups all-purpose flour

3 tablespoons ground ginger

1 teaspoon ground cinnamon

1 teaspoon baking soda

½ teaspoon coarse salt

1. In a medium saucepan over high heat, melt the sugar, molasses, and butter. Into a large bowl, sift the flour, ginger, cinnamon, baking soda, and salt. Add the melted sugar mixture and, using a wooden spoon, mix to form a stiff dough. Divide the dough into 3 pieces and wrap each in plastic. Chill at least 2 hours.

2. Preheat the oven to 375° F and lightly grease a baking sheet. On a floured surface, roll out a piece of dough to a thickness of ⅛ inch. Cut into shapes with a cookie

cutter and arrange on the baking sheet ½ inch apart. Repeat with the other 2 pieces of dough. Bake the cookies for approximately 8 minutes, until crispy around the edges. Remove from the oven and cool.

Makes 3 dozen cookies.

PLANNING AHEAD: The dough can be made up to 1 week ahead and kept in the refrigerator. Baked, these cookies will keep up to 6 months in sealed tins.

Sugar Bow Ties

Another childhood favorite of mine, these cookies are delicately flavored and very pretty. Once you get the knack of twisting the dough, they are simple to make.

5 whole eggs	*Optional:* **2 tablespoons brandy, for**
3 egg yolks	**added flavor**
2 tablespoons sugar	**4 cups all-purpose flour, sifted**
2 tablespoons heavy cream	**4 to 6 cups vegetable oil, for frying**
½ teaspoon coarse salt	**Confectioners' sugar, for sprinkling**

1. In a large bowl, beat together the eggs and yolks until light and lemon-colored. Beat in the sugar, cream, salt, and brandy (if using). Stir in the flour and mix with your hands to form a soft dough. Knead lightly. Cover and let rest for 10 minutes.

2. On a floured surface, roll out the dough to a thickness of ⅛ inch. With a pastry cutter or pizza wheel, cut the dough into rectangles about 3 × 1½ inches. (Work with small amounts of dough at a time and keep the rest of it covered, as the dough dries out easily.) With a sharp knife, slit each piece in the center and pull one end of the dough through to form a loose loop. Cover the shaped cookies with a damp tea towel while you heat the oil.

3. Heat the oil in a deep skillet until it reaches 375° F. Drop the dough in batches into the oil and cook until the cookies are delicately browned. Drain on absorbent paper and sprinkle with confectioners' sugar.

Makes 30 cookies.

PLANNING AHEAD: These cookies will keep for 2 weeks in a tightly sealed container.

Holiday Fruit Bowl

I find that guests always appreciate a bowl of cut fruit along with a variety of desserts on a buffet. Around holiday time I might choose a combination of blood oranges, pomegranates, mandarin oranges, kiwis, grapes, pineapple, bananas, and berries. You can hardly go wrong if you pick colorful fruits at their peak of ripeness. Everything (except the bananas, which will darken) can be cut up the morning of the party and kept in a bowl in the refrigerator. Add the bananas right before serving.

A True Creamy Eggnog

A lot of people tell me they hate eggnog, but once they taste this creamy, freshly made version they become true converts.

6 whole eggs	1½ cups dark rum
3 eggs, separated	⅛ teaspoon ground nutmeg
1½ cups sugar	⅛ teaspoon ground cinnamon
2 cups heavy cream	⅛ teaspoon ground cardamom
1 teaspoon vanilla extract	Extra ground nutmeg, for sprinkling
3 cups milk	on top

1. In a large bowl, using an electric mixer set on high speed, beat the whole eggs, yolks, and sugar until frothy and light, about 5 minutes. Add the heavy cream and vanilla and beat until thick, another 5 minutes. Beat in the milk. Set aside.

2. In a medium bowl, using an electric mixer or whisk, beat the egg whites until stiff. Stir the nutmeg, cinnamon, and cardamom into the rum. Pour the spiced rum into the egg-cream mixture, stir, then fold in half the egg whites. Pour the mixture into a large serving bowl. Dollop the remaining beaten egg white on top and sprinkle with extra nutmeg.

Serves 10.

PLANNING AHEAD: The eggnog can be started up to 1 day ahead, but don't whip the egg whites and add them until close to serving time.

VARIATIONS: Other liquors, cognac for instance, can be substituted for the rum in this recipe. Or you can eliminate the rum entirely and make a nonalcoholic chocolate eggnog by substituting 4½ cups chocolate milk for the milk and rum in the recipe. Another idea: mocha eggnog, made with chocolate milk and cold sweetened espresso.

COOKED VARIATION: If you or your guests are uncomfortable about eating raw egg yolks, you can make the eggnog this way instead. The result will be equally delicious but not as light in texture:

In a medium saucepan set over medium-high heat, scald the milk and vanilla. In a large bowl, whisk the whole eggs, yolks, and sugar until frothy and lemon-colored. Add the hot milk to the eggs, whisk to incorporate, then return the mixture to the saucepan. Stirring constantly with a rubber spatula, cook over medium heat until the mixture thickens, about 3 to 4 minutes. Do not boil. It should resemble a thin custard. Remove from the heat and strain through a mesh strainer into a mixing bowl. Set aside to cool. Add the heavy cream and beat until thick, about 5 minutes. Continue with the recipe, stirring in the beaten egg whites and spiced rum.

Starlight Supper

This supremely elegant supper is designed for those occasions when you want to pull out all the stops and entertain friends in style. With caviar and champagne, oysters, lobster, and foie gras, this is a "splurge" menu for a very special late-night occasion, such as New Year's Eve, a theater opening, or a big birthday. At times like this a certain degree of formality can be fun and makes everyone feel special. A printed menu or one that has been penned by a calligrapher, place cards, lustrous silver, and striking flowers can set the stage for a grand and memorable evening.

Many people think a formal meal has to be sit-down and plated, but in truth, a buffet is ideal for formal occasions. Although it's best for the host or hostess to have *some* help to feel truly relaxed at a posh party, all the helper needs to do is set out the buffets at the proper times, clear dishes, and perform a few minor kitchen tasks. As with most buffets, many of these dishes can be prepared either partially or completely ahead. No one needs to stand in the kitchen composing plates, and there is no need for formal table service.

For this New Year's Eve party, guests were invited for 8:30 P.M. The dining room table was set for dinner, candles were lit, and the luxurious hors d'oeuvres were set out on the buffet table. As guests arrived, they were offered a glass of champagne or iced vodka and directed to the buffet. They picked up small plates and forks and linen cocktail napkins, helped themselves, and ambled into the living room. Because the hors d'oeuvres were so substantial, the cocktail hour was extended a bit to allow guests time to savor each dish. At about ten, the helper cleared the hors d'oeuvres and set out the dinner buffet in the dining room. Dinner was announced, guests served themselves, and then took their pre-assigned places at the table. Both red and white

The scene is set for an elegant late-night supper. The hostess's handsome star plates were used as chargers.

wines were offered during dinner. Dinner ended about 11:30, and everyone was invited into the library to ring in the New Year with champagne. After the clock struck twelve, desserts were carried in on a big tray, along with the coffee service. Guests could have gone back into the dining room for dessert (the helper had cleared the dinner dishes during the countdown to midnight), but at this late hour, after such a formal dinner, the library seemed a more comfortable place for the party to continue and New Year's resolutions to be exchanged.

Starlight Supper
for 10

APPETIZERS
Black Sevruga and Salmon Caviar with Crème Fraîche
Baked New Potatoes with Chives
Shredded Beets
Artichokes with Curry Cauliflower and Currants
Oyster and Scallion Pancakes
Terrine of Foie Gras with Crisp Baguette Toasts

DINNER
Baked Penne Pasta and Lobster
Spiced Rack of Lamb
Tomato, Pear, and Cipollini Relish
Savoy Cabbage and Mushroom Packets
Wilted Broccoli Rabe Salad

DESSERTS
Frozen Espresso Sabayon with Fresh Berries
Hazelnut Meringue Drops
Cocoa Zinnsbar Sables

Black Sevruga and Salmon Caviar
with Crème Fraîche

How could anyone turn down caviar? I love it, and have been fortunate enough over the years to sample many kinds. Black sevruga caviar, from Caspian Sea sturgeon, is one of my personal favorites. The eggs are small and dark gray to black in color with a sweet mild taste. The best caviar should have the pleasant aroma of the sea, like the freshest fish, but not smell at all "fishy."

I am also fond of salmon caviar, which is much less expensive than Russian caviar. The eggs are large and salmon-red in color, the taste mild.

Whatever caviar you choose, imported or domestic, be sure to buy it from a reliable source with lots of turnover. Caviar is perishable. Fresh caviar should be refrigerated and consumed within one week of purchase; vacuum-packed caviar should be kept in a cool place for no more than 6 months. Once opened, caviar should be eaten within 2 or 3 days, but you probably won't have any left anyway!

Always serve caviar chilled, preferably over ice, with wedges of fresh lemon to enhance the flavor. Traditionally, silver and aluminum are not used to serve caviar because they can impart a metallic taste; bone or mother-of-pearl spoons are preferred.

For 10 people, plan on buying 4 to 8 ounces of caviar, depending on how many guests are caviar lovers.

Crème Fraîche

Crème fraîche is quite simple to make and very versatile. A natural accompaniment to caviar, it is also useful to have on hand to add to mashed potatoes and as a garnish for soups. Whipped and sweetened, crème fraîche is a luscious topping for fruit and desserts.

The only trick is to use pasteurized (not ultra-pasteurized) heavy cream; otherwise the crème fraîche does not thicken well.

1 quart pasteurized heavy cream   **2 tablespoons buttermilk**

1. In an upright non-aluminum metal container or a glass jar, combine the cream with the buttermilk. Stir, cover, and set aside in a warm (90° to 100° F) place, such as over a pilot light in a gas oven. Alternatively, you could set the container on top of the refrigerator toward the back of the unit, where the warm air given off by the appliance

will provide the right temperature. Let stand overnight, about 12 hours, until thickened to the consistency of sour cream on top.

2. Stir the crème fraîche and place in the refrigerator for about 6 hours to allow all of the mixture to thicken up.

Makes 4 cups.

PLANNING AHEAD: Thickened crème fraîche will keep for about 2 weeks in the refrigerator.

Baked New Potatoes with Chives

For this hors d'oeuvre I prefer small Yukon Gold potatoes or tasty white new potatoes. Topped with caviar or Shredded Beets (recipe follows), they are delicious.

20 potatoes (about 1½ pounds)　　**Coarse salt to taste**
¼ cup vegetable oil　　**15 stalks fresh chives, snipped**
2 cups Crème Fraîche (page 273)

1. Preheat the oven to 400° F. Put a large baking pan in the oven to heat up.
2. Wash and scrub the potatoes and rub with the oil. Remove the baking pan from the oven and arrange the potatoes in 1 layer. Put the pan back in the oven and roast the potatoes for about 25 minutes, until tender. Let the potatoes cool until they can be handled easily.
3. Cut the potatoes in half lengthwise and scoop out most of the pulp into a bowl (leave a little pulp in each potato to support the shell). Mash the pulp with a small amount of crème fraîche, salt, and chives, and spoon back into the potato shells.

Makes 20 hors d'oeuvres.

PLANNING AHEAD: The potatoes can be prepared earlier in the day and served at room temperature. They can also be reheated in a 250° F oven 30 minutes before serving.

The hors d'oeuvres table. COUNTERCLOCKWISE FROM LOWER LEFT: *Terrine of foie gras; baked new potatoes; bowls of chopped chives, shredded beets, and crème fraîche; artichokes with curry cauliflower and currants; salmon caviar; Sevruga caviar; oyster and scallion pancakes; baguette toasts.*

Shredded Beets

Vividly colored and quick to make, this relish is a tasty accompaniment to roasted meats, poultry, and fish. The recipe can be varied by using a combination of beets and apples or pears.

You can use a food processor to shred beets, but for an elegant look, try slicing them with an Asian mandoline. A mandoline is essential in my kitchen for fast and easy slicing and julienning. Be careful with this cutter, however, because it is extremely sharp.

2 medium beets, tops and stems removed, peeled
1 tablespoon sugar

2 tablespoons raspberry vinegar
Coarse salt and freshly ground black pepper to taste

Shred the beets using the grater attachment of a food processor or a sharp cutter. Mix in a bowl with the sugar and vinegar, and season to taste with salt and pepper. Cover and refrigerate until ready to use.

Makes 2 cups.

PLANNING AHEAD: This relish will keep for about 2 weeks in a covered container in the refrigerator.

Artichokes with Curry Cauliflower
and Currants

Artichokes are great-tasting natural serving vessels. Here I've filled them with an East Indian combination of curried cauliflower and currants, but all kinds of variations are possible.

10 whole artichokes
2 lemons, cut in half

FILLING:
1 cup vegetable oil
1 head cauliflower, cut into short
   florets
1 tablespoon coarse salt
1 cup dried currants

2 tablespoons good-quality curry
   powder
2 tablespoons red or white wine
   vinegar

Garnish: ½ cup coarsely chopped
   flat-leaf parsley

1. Cut off the stems and rough outer leaves of the artichokes. Remove the chokes. Rub the artichokes with the lemon halves to prevent discoloration. Place the artichokes and lemon halves in a pot with salted water to cover. Cover with a clean kitchen towel (the towel holds the artichokes down, and they cook evenly) and bring to a boil over high heat. Reduce the heat to medium and cook about 20 minutes, until the artichokes are tender in the center when poked with a knife tip. Drain, reserving the cooking liquid, and plunge the artichokes into a quick ice bath. Drain again, then store the artichokes in their cooking liquid in the refrigerator until ready to fill.

2. To make the filling, heat the oil in a large skillet or wok. Add the cauliflower, sprinkle with salt, and stir-fry over high heat approximately 2 minutes. Add the currants and curry powder and cook 1 minute more, until the cauliflower is crisp-tender. Add the vinegar, stir, and cook 1 more minute. Remove the mixture from the heat and let cool.

3. Remove the artichokes from the refrigerator and stuff with the filling. Garnish with parsley.

Serves 10 as an appetizer.

PLANNING AHEAD: The cooked artichokes can be stored in their liquid for up to 1 week in the refrigerator. Once they are filled, the artichokes should be served within a few hours. They are fine at room temperature, but if you prefer them warm, place the artichokes in a baking dish, cover with foil, and heat in a 200° F oven for about 30 minutes before serving.

Oyster and Scallion Pancakes

This is a very simple and delicious Korean-style pancake that can be made in a larger size and served as an entrée. The basic recipe can be varied by substituting other ingredients for the oysters and scallions, such as shrimp, scallops, mushrooms, corn, water chestnuts, even pears.

2¼ cups all-purpose flour
2¼ cups brown rice flour
4 cups water
1 tablespoon pure Asian sesame oil
   (see Note, page 188)
2 teaspoons soy sauce

3 large eggs, beaten
¾ cup vegetable oil, for frying
9 scallions, halved lengthwise and
   cut into 2-inch diagonal pieces
40 fresh shucked oysters

1. Combine the all-purpose and rice flours in a large bowl. Slowly pour in the water, mixing to make a smooth-flowing batter. If batter seems too thick, add a little extra water. Add the sesame oil and soy sauce, then the beaten egg. Set the batter aside to rest for 30 minutes.

2. In a flat-bottomed iron or nonstick skillet set over medium-low heat, heat 1 tablespoon of the vegetable oil for about 2 minutes. Sprinkle a little of the scallion over the bottom of the skillet. Pour in about 1 tablespoon of batter for each 2-inch pancake. Place 2 oysters on top of each and cook for about 3 minutes. Flip the pancakes over and cook 2 to 3 minutes more. Pancakes should be cooked through and golden. Remove to a warming tray.

3. Repeat the process with the remaining batter, scallions, and oysters, adding fresh oil to the skillet each time.

Makes twenty-four 2-inch pancakes.

PLANNING AHEAD: These pancakes are simple to make just before the party, but if you prefer to cook them earlier, place the cooked pancakes in a baking dish, cover with foil, and reheat in a low (200° to 250° F) oven just before serving.

You can also prepare the batter 4 to 5 days ahead and hold it in the refrigerator until ready to use.

Terrine of Foie Gras with
Crisp Baguette Toasts

Foie gras is expensive, but worth indulging in for an ultra-festive occasion. You can buy prepared foie gras terrine, but I like to make it myself. Once you remove the veins from the liver, the rest of the process is simple.

1½ pounds fresh duck foie gras (liver)
2 teaspoons coarse salt
1 teaspoon sugar
¼ teaspoon ground white pepper
4 tablespoons sauterne wine or Pineau Charentes

3 tablespoons duck or goose fat, melted

BAGUETTE TOASTS:
1 French bread baguette

1. Remove the liver from the refrigerator about an hour before cleaning it to allow it to come to room temperature and become pliable. Separate the two parts; one lobe is larger than the other. Place the larger piece, smooth side down, on a cutting board. With a small paring knife, cut down the center about ½ inch from either end and approximately ¾ inch deep. Open the incision, loosen the large vein, and remove it carefully with the point of a knife. Remove the smaller veins as well, but be careful not to break the lobe into small pieces; the veins are being removed to improve the appearance of the terrine. Remove any bits of blood with the point of the knife. Repeat with the other lobe.

2. Season both pieces of liver with a mixture of salt, sugar, and white pepper. Place the larger lobe into a 2-quart terrine, pressing lightly so it conforms to the terrine's shape. Add the other lobe and press down so the livers fill the terrine. Cover with the wine and melted duck or goose fat.

3. Preheat the oven to 250° F. Place the uncovered terrine in a large pan and pour in boiling water until it reaches halfway up the sides of the terrine. Carefully place the pan in the center of the oven and cook the terrine for approximately 25 to 30 minutes, until an instant-read thermometer inserted into the center of the terrine reads 110° F; be sure the oven temperature is kept low so that the foie gras does not overcook and melt. Remove the terrine from the oven and cool by placing in an ice bath; be sure to keep the terrine level. When cool, cover the terrine and refrigerate until ready to serve.

4. To make the baguette toasts, cut the bread with a sharp serrated knife into

¼-inch-thick slices, arrange on a baking sheet, and toast in a 350° F oven until lightly colored and crisp.

Serves 10 to 15 as an appetizer.

PLANNING AHEAD: The liver can be prepared and the terrine assembled 3 or 4 days ahead and refrigerated. Once cooked, the foie gras will keep up to 12 days in the refrigerator.

Baked Penne Pasta and Lobster

Think of this as grown-up macaroni and cheese. The basic pasta recipe can be varied by adding or substituting your favorite vegetables and cheeses.

8 sprigs fresh thyme
8 sprigs fresh flat-leaf parsley
12 black peppercorns
1 bay leaf
2 lemons, cut in half
4 1½-pound live lobsters, preferably from Maine
Handful of coarse salt
2½ pounds dried penne
3 tablespoons vegetable or olive oil
2 cups freshly grated Parmesan cheese

2 cups provolone cheese (imported, grated)
1 pound fresh spinach, washed, dried, and chopped
3 cups heavy cream
1 tablespoon truffle oil (see Note, page 175)
Coarse salt and freshly ground black pepper to taste
Optional: 1 to 2 medium truffles (black or white), slivered

1. To cook the lobster, fill an 8- to 10-quart pot three-fourths full with water. Add the thyme, parsley, peppercorns, and bay leaf. Squeeze in the juice of the lemons, then drop them in the pot. Cover and bring to a rolling boil over high heat. Add the lobsters and cook 12 to 15 minutes. Drain the lobsters in a colander, cover with ice, and let cool.

2. When the lobster is cool enough to handle, pull the tail from the body and remove the claws. Discard the body, or reserve for use in a sauce or stock. Cut the shell from the tail using a knife or scissors and remove the meat. With the blunt end of a knife chop off the tips of the claws as close to the ends as possible (this will help release

A close-up of the baked penne pasta and lobster, or what I like to call "adult baked macaroni."

the meat from the claws). Crack the claws in the center, break open, and carefully re-move the claw meat without breaking apart. Meat from the larger claws will have a piece of cartilage in it; this can be pulled out from the area where the claw fingers meet. Cut the tail meat into ½-inch slices. Leave the claws whole to use as a garnish. Set the lobster meat aside until ready to assemble the pasta dish.

3. To cook the pasta, fill a 6- to 8-quart pot with water, add salt, cover, and bring to a boil over high heat. Add the penne and stir. Cook the pasta for approximately 8 to 10 minutes, until al dente. Pour into a colander to drain. Do not rinse the pasta; just toss it to remove any excess water. Sprinkle the oil over the pasta and toss with a large chef's fork. Pour the pasta onto a sheet tray or shallow dish to cool (if it looks too sticky, sprinkle some more oil on at this point). Let the pasta cool to room tempera-ture. (See Note.)

4. When the pasta is cool, preheat the oven to 425° F.

5. Toss the cooled pasta in a bowl with the Parmesan and provolone cheese, spinach, heavy cream, and lobster meat (except claws). Season with salt and pepper. Transfer to a large round, oval, or oblong baking dish and bake for approximately 25 minutes, until bubbling hot. Garnish with the lobster claws and truffle slivers (if using).

Serves 10, as part of buffet.

NOTE: Pasta that has been cooked until al dente, coated with oil, and cooled can be kept in a covered plastic container in the refrigerator for up to 3 days without becom-ing mushy. Reheated, the pasta will be very close to freshly cooked pasta. I use this technique often; it is a terrific time-saver for busy cooks.

PLANNING AHEAD: This dish, without the heavy cream, can be assembled 8 hours ahead. Thirty minutes before serving pour in the heavy cream and bake as above.

Spiced Rack of Lamb

Rack of lamb is always popular at dinner parties. Once the meat is seasoned, it is simple to cook, cut, and serve. Allow 3 chops per person.

6 half racks of lamb
½ cup blanched almonds or pine
   nuts
1 tablespoon chopped fresh ginger
1 tablespoon black peppercorns
1 tablespoon coriander seeds

1 teaspoon juniper berries
6 whole cloves
⅛ teaspoon cayenne pepper
1 teaspoon coarse salt
Vegetable oil, for coating the
   roasting pan

1. Prepare the lamb by removing the top fat layer and all the silver skin with a sharp knife. Cut out the excess fat between the bones and scrape them clean of fat and sinew. If you don't want the work of cleaning a rack, let the butcher do this for you.

2. Combine the nuts, ginger, black peppercorns, coriander seeds, juniper berries, whole cloves, and cayenne pepper in a spice grinder or mortar and grind coarsely. Add the salt. Coat the racks with this seasoning mixture and let rest in the refrigerator for at least 1 hour to allow the flavors to permeate the meat.

3. When ready to cook, sprinkle a roasting pan with vegetable oil and heat it in a 450° F oven. Wrap the lamb bones in aluminum foil to prevent burning and place, bone side down, in the hot pan. Roast 15 minutes, turn over, and roast another 10 minutes for rare to medium-rare meat. Remove from the oven and let rest. Cut between each bone and place the chops on a serving platter.

Serves 10 to 15, as part of buffet.

NOTE: To make a sauce from the pan drippings, deglaze the pan with ½ cup cognac and whisk in 3 cups stock (meat or vegetable). Simmer until the sauce is reduced by half.

PLANNING AHEAD: The spice mix can be made up to a week ahead and stored in an airtight container at room temperature. Once it is patted on the lamb, the meat can be left in the refrigerator for up to 8 hours before roasting. The lamb is delicious served at room temperature, but if you prefer, undercook the chops by 5 minutes. Can be reheated in a 450° F oven 5 minutes before serving.

Tomato, Pear, and Cipollini Relish

Italian cipollinis are becoming increasingly popular and are generally available in markets during winter months. Small and flat, these onions have an appealing sweet taste. They make a delicious addition to relishes, chutneys, and vegetable dishes.

When cipollinis are in season I make up batches of this relish to give to friends; it makes a welcome gift.

2 cups vegetable oil
12 fresh plum tomatoes
4 cloves garlic, peeled and chopped
Coarse salt and freshly ground black
**   pepper to taste**
3 pears, peeled, cored, and cut into
**   ¼-inch slices**

Juice of 1 lemon
30 cipollinis
½ cup balsamic vinegar, preferably
**   aged 2 years or more**
1 tablespoon red chili paste

1. Preheat the oven to 300° F. Generously coat a roasting pan with ¼ cup of the oil. Core the tomatoes and cut in half. Lay the tomatoes in the pan pulp side down. Sprinkle with the garlic, salt and pepper, and ¼ cup of the oil.

2. Sprinkle the pear slices with the lemon juice. Coat another roasting pan with ½ cup oil and lay the pear slices in it.

3. Coat a third roasting pan with ½ cup oil and add the cipollinis. Sprinkle the cipollinis with the remaining ½ cup oil and salt and pepper.

4. Place all three pans in the oven. Cook the pears and onions about 1½ hours, until tender. Leave the tomatoes in the oven 30 minutes longer, approximately 2 hours total, until they are tender and cooked in their own juices. Remove the pans from the oven and let cool.

5. Pour off the excess cooking oil and juices and reserve. Pull off the tomato skin and discard. Peel the onions—their skins will come right off—and pare off the stems if necessary.

6. In a 3- to 4-quart mixing bowl, whisk together the vinegar, chili paste, and reserved cooking oil and juices. Add the tomatoes, pears, and onions and toss together. Correct the seasoning.

Makes 2 quarts.

Planning Ahead: This relish will keep for at least 2 weeks in the refrigerator.

Savoy Cabbage and Mushroom Packets

I consider Savoy the king of green cabbages. With its mild taste and lovely frilly leaves it is a wintertime favorite. Here the leaves are wrapped around mixed mushrooms, forming individual packets. You can combine your favorite mushrooms or use just one kind, but do choose strong-flavored varieties, such as porcini, shiitake, morel, portobello, chanterelle, or trumpet, to complement the flavors in this dish.

2 large heads Savoy cabbage	3 cloves garlic, peeled and chopped
10 scallions	3 sprigs fresh thyme, leaves picked
½ cup vegetable or olive oil	and chopped
2 pounds mixed mushrooms, sliced	Coarse salt and freshly ground black
2 shallots, peeled and chopped	pepper to taste

1. Bring a large pot of water to a boil over high heat. Cut the core from the cabbage and break off the larger outer leaves to use for packets; you should have about 20. Blanch the leaves in boiling water to wilt them, then remove them with a skimmer and shock in an ice bath to cool. Drain in a colander and pat dry with absorbent towels. Stack the leaves on a plate, cover with plastic wrap, and store in the refrigerator until ready to make the packets.

2. Cut off the root and half of the white part of the scallions. Cut each of the remaining green stem ends in half lengthwise so that you have 20 scallion "ties." Blanch in boiling water and cool as above. Set aside.

3. Pour the oil into a large skillet or wok and heat over high heat. Add the mushrooms and toss quickly to wilt. Add the shallots, garlic, thyme, salt, and pepper and cook about 3 minutes. Remove the mixture to a colander held over a bowl to catch the excess liquid. Reserve.

4. Preheat the oven to 300° F. To assemble, lay the cabbage leaves on a flat surface. Place a large spoonful of mushrooms in the center of each leaf and pull the outer edges inward to form a purse-style packet. Tie with scallion strips.

5. Set the packets in a baking dish, pour in the reserved mushroom liquid, and heat in the oven for 15 minutes.

Makes 20 packets.

PLANNING AHEAD: The packets can be assembled up to 8 hours ahead and kept in a baking dish (without the mushroom liquid) in the refrigerator. Close to serving time, add the heated liquid and heat the packets in the oven as above.

The dinner buffet arranged on the long pine sideboard in the dining room. FROM LEFT TO RIGHT: *Wilted broccoli rabe salad; Savoy cabbage and mushroom packets; tomato, pear, and cipollini relish; spiced rack of lamb; baked penne pasta and lobster.*

Wilted Broccoli Rabe Salad

When I plan menus I always like to have a contrast in tastes and textures. Here, I chose broccoli rabe as a salad because I love its crunchy texture and slightly bitter taste.

3 to 4 bunches broccoli rabe
2 cups extra-virgin olive oil
8 cloves garlic, peeled and thinly
   sliced

6 anchovy fillets, chopped
Zest and juice of 2 lemons
Coarse salt and freshly ground black
   pepper to taste

1. Break off any coarse stems and wilted bottom leaves from the broccoli rabe. Wash, drain in a colander, and shake off excess water.

2. In a large skillet or wok, heat 1 cup of the oil over high heat. When very hot, carefully add half of the broccoli rabe and cook quickly to wilt. Add half of the garlic, anchovies, and zest, sprinkle with salt and pepper, and cook approximately 1 minute, until the garlic is soft. Remove the contents of the pan to a bowl, then repeat the cooking process with the remaining ingredients, except the lemon juice.

3. Just before serving, toss with the lemon juice.

Serves 10, as part of buffet.

PLANNING AHEAD: This dish is fine at room temperature. If you make it more than 4 hours before serving, refrigerate it. Remember not to add the lemon juice until right before serving; lemon is a good flavor enhancer but it will fade the color of the broccoli.

Frozen Espresso Sabayon with Fresh Berries

Similar to a light and creamy ice cream, this dessert makes a stunning presentation in an antique or unusually shaped mold. It is also good served with chocolate sauce.

8 egg yolks
½ cup plus 2 tablespoons sugar
¼ cup Marsala
1 cup Espresso Syrup (recipe
    follows), cooled

2½ quarts heavy cream
Fresh mixed berries, for serving

1. Whisk the egg yolks and sugar together in a metal bowl or the top of a double boiler set over simmering water. Cook 1 minute, then add the Marsala and continue to whisk and cook 8 to 10 minutes, until the mixture is pale yellow and fluffy. Beat in the Espresso Syrup.

2. Whip the cream to full volume in a large chilled mixing bowl. In 3 additions, carefully and quickly fold the espresso sabayon mixture into the whipped cream until well incorporated. Place the mixture in a 6-quart mold or bowl and freeze at least 8 hours.

3. To unmold, place the mold or bowl in hot water for 1 minute, then reverse onto a serving dish. Serve with fresh mixed berries.

Serves 10 to 15.

NOTE: Do not attempt to make this dessert for a hot weather buffet; it will turn into soup!

VARIATION: You can use the basic sabayon recipe and whip in different flavored syrups to suit your taste.

PLANNING AHEAD: This dessert can be made up to 7 days in advance and kept in the mold in the freezer. Remove and unmold about 30 minutes before serving.

Dessert was a fabulous frozen espresso sabayon with fresh raspberries, accompanied by (on pedestal plates) hazelnut meringue drops and cocoa zinnsbar sables cut out in star shapes.

Espresso Syrup

2 cups espresso coffee   **1 cup granulated sugar**

Combine the coffee and sugar in a saucepan and bring to a boil. Turn the heat down and simmer until the mixture is reduced by half. Let cool. Store in a covered container in the refrigerator until ready to use.

Makes 1 cup.

Planning Ahead: This syrup can be stored for up to 2 months in the refrigerator.

Hazelnut Meringue Drops

The crunchy texture of these cookies makes them just the right foil for the creamy sabayon. These meringues are so easy to make—there are only three ingredients—I call them "in a pinch" cookies.

¾ pound roasted hazelnuts (about 2¼ cups)

¾ pound plus 2 ounces sugar (about 2¼ cups)
1⅓ cups egg whites (about 8)

1. Preheat the oven to 250° F. Line a baking sheet with parchment paper or lightly grease with butter.
2. In a food processor, grind together the nuts and ¾ pound of the sugar. Set aside.
3. Using the whisk attachment on an electric mixer, whip the egg whites until soft peaks form. With the machine running, add the remaining 2 ounces sugar and beat until the egg whites are stiff and shiny. In 3 additions, fold in the nut-sugar mixture until completely incorporated. Drop the batter by tablespoons onto the prepared baking sheet, leaving ½ inch between cookies. Bake for about 30 minutes, until the cookies are dry, light, and crisp, checking after 15 minutes to make sure they are not getting too brown (if so, turn the oven temperature down a little).

Makes 2 dozen cookies.

Planning Ahead: Meringues are more perishable than some other cookies, so don't make them more than 5 days ahead. Store in an airtight container.

Cocoa Zinnsbar Sables

Cocoa and cinnamon are a classic combination. You will love these versatile cookies, which are excellent with fresh fruit and sauces, or sandwiched with ice cream or mousse.

2 eggs

2 tablespoons milk

2 cups all-purpose flour

½ cup unsweetened cocoa powder, preferably imported Dutch

1 tablespoon ground cinnamon

½ teaspoon salt

9 ounces (2 sticks plus 1 ounce) unsalted butter

2 cups sugar

3 ounces blanched almonds, chopped

Optional: Flavored sugar (see Note)

1. In a small bowl, lightly beat the eggs and milk together. In a large bowl, sift together the flour, cocoa powder, cinnamon, and salt. In another large bowl, using an electric mixer, cream together the butter and sugar until smooth and light. Add the sifted ingredients, continuing to mix, then the egg mixture. Fold in the almonds. Remove the dough and use your hands to pat it into a flat circle. Chill in the refrigerator for at least 3 hours.

2. When ready to bake, preheat the oven to 375° F. Roll out the dough on a lightly floured surface to a thickness of about ⅛ inch and cut into shapes with a cookie cutter. Arrange on a baking sheet about ½ inch apart and sprinkle with flavored sugar if you like. Bake approximately 15 minutes, until the cookies are lightly browned around the edges.

Makes 2 dozen cookies.

NOTE: To make flavored sugar, place one vanilla bean, the peel of 2 lemons, and 4 sprigs of lavender (see Note, page 106) in a canister of sugar for at least a week.

PLANNING AHEAD: These cookies will keep for up to 3 weeks in a tightly covered container.

Index